PRODIGAL FATHER, PAGAN SON

Also by Kerrie Droban

Running with the Devil:
The True Story of the ATF's Infiltration
of the Hells Angels

Growing Up Inside

the Dangerous World

of the Pagans

Motorcycle Club

ⵏ ⵏ ⵏ ⵏ

PRODIGAL FATHER, PAGAN SON

～～～～～

ANTHONY "LT" MENGINIE

and Kerrie Droban

THOMAS DUNNE BOOKS

St. Martin's Griffin

New York

THOMAS DUNNE BOOKS.
An imprint of St. Martin's Press.

PRODIGAL FATHER, PAGAN SON. Copyright © 2011 by Anthony
"LT" Menginie and Kerrie Droban. All rights reserved. Printed
in the United States of America. For information, address St.
Martin's Press, 175 Fifth Avenue, New York, N.Y. 10010.

www.thomasdunnebooks.com
www.stmartins.com

Design by Kathryn Parise

THE LIBRARY OF CONGRESS HAS CATALOGED THE HARDCOVER EDITION AS FOLLOWS:

Menginie, Anthony.
    Prodigal father, pagan son : growing up inside the dangerous world of the Pagans
motorcycle club / Anthony "LT" Menginie and Kerrie Droban.—1st ed.
        p. cm.
    Includes bibliographical references and index.
    ISBN 978-0-312-57654-7
    1. Pagans (Motorcycle club)   2. Motorcycle gangs—Pennsylvania—Philadelphia.
3. Organized Crime—Pennsylvania—Philadelphia.   4. Gang members—Pennsylvania—
Philadelphia.   I. Droban, Kerrie.   II. Title.
    HV6439.U7P47 2011
    364.106'60974811—dc22

2010041292

ISBN 978-1-250-00732-2 (trade paperback)

10 9 8 7 6 5 4 3 2

For "Dead"

To the reader,

I am thirty-one years old. I was born the son of the Philadelphia Pagans' most notorious leader. I've been around some of the most hard-core Pagans: Mongo, Conan, S&S, Malicious, Cheese, Terrible Tony, and Dominic. The following events happened. This is not fiction. However, some of the names and locations have been changed. I was born into madness. This is my story.

—LT

CONTENTS

~ ~ ~ ~ ~

Part I:
Introduction
9

Part II
55

ACKNOWLEDGMENTS

NNNNN

A special thanks to my literary agent, Robert G. Diforio, and to my wonderful editor, Rob Kirkpatrick, for having faith in this project and in me. Thanks to my critique partners, Carol Webb, Kim Watters, and Linda Andrews, for your relentless and brutal edits. I treasure your friendships. Thanks to my dear friend Starr Cochran for your constant support and "secret" faith. Thanks to Sergei for giving me time to write, for educating me about motorcycles and shotguns, for promising me, one day, my own white space.

—KERRIE DROBAN

Where a man is doomed by no fatal flaw of character
but by the simple fact of being born.

—ALAFAIR BURKE

PRODIGAL
FATHER,
PAGAN SON

~~~~

PROLOGUE

∿∿∿∿∿

QUIETUS:
"Release from life. Death."

Johns Hospital in Delaware County was a good reason *not* to get ill if a person was an addict and poor. The walls resembled gray skin, lumpy with veins, blood-drained and thin. Staff shuffled through the halls, their chatter like that of rare species of birds. Smells of soiled sheets and general rot wafted through the air. Screams punctuated the bustle.

A doctor with a pocked face and pursed lips clicked his pen open and shut, open and shut, as he stalled for words. He looked as rumpled as the patients except that he wore a white coat and smelled of antiseptic. I paced the hallway outside intensive care, arms folded, shoulders squared, hoping my expression masked my fear.

"Menginie, right?" The doctor stumbled over my Italian name.

"LT." I shrugged as if it didn't matter anymore what people called me. *Little Tony. Kid.* I didn't even *have* a name until I was old enough to speak.

2 /~ **Anthony "LT" Menginie and Kerrie Droban**

"She has a thirty percent chance of survival."

I swallowed, glanced into the adjacent room. My mom curled like a fetus on the cot and rocked. She tossed off the thin sheet and it pooled on the floor. Thin wisps of blond hair were matted to her cheeks. She hadn't bathed in weeks and she smelled of vomit. My ears throbbed and I shivered, partly from cold but mostly from a growing sense of dread. *This is my mom. I can't lose her. She is my only family, my only witness.* My body numbed with resignation. I saw myself at thirteen again, sucking my thumb, unable to cry. At some point reaction replaced emotion, uncensored and raw. Pretty fucking pathetic considering I was twenty-eight years old and the son of the Pagan Motorcycle Club's most notorious power broker.

"Help me," my mom whimpered. "Make it dark."

"What's wrong with her?" I asked. *She sleeps and pukes, sleeps and pukes.*

"She's an alcoholic." The doctor tucked his pen into his pocket. "She has the d.t.'s. Hers is worse than a heroin withdrawal. At this point she'll get sick if she *doesn't* drink."

Gallon of vodka daily, and alternating between Grand-Dad and Jack Daniel's. Yeah, I guess so.

"Her pancreas is inflamed to sixteen thousand. Normal is two hundred and under," the doctor continued, but I was barely listening.

"She's going to die, isn't she?" I started to shake.

"I've been dead a long time," my mom hollered.

"She cuts herself, you know, with razor blades?" I hovered over the nurse, who shone a light into my mom's eyes, as if searching for her youth blowing at the back of a cave. The room smelled rank like urine. And this was only day two of what promised to be weeks of hospital visits for me. So far my mom wasn't improving. She was self-destructing.

Intensive care meant no one ever really left. That thought nagged at my conscience. Death had defined my childhood—thirteen funerals before the age of twelve. After the first couple of ceremonies, mourners funneled through the motions of what they thought they should feel but couldn't really justify. Mostly the bikers who attended clustered at the entrance of a stifling funeral parlor, stoic expressions masking their worst fear—their own deaths barreling toward them, full speed, sudden as double-aught (00) buckshot.

"She's fifty-two?" The pretty, starched nurse arched a brow at me as if I were making it up.

Going on eighty. Going on ten. Going.

"Do you know who you are?" the woman shouted at my mom, who, only moments before, believed George Washington was still the president.

My mom squinted at her and said, "I am an accessory after the fact." Her lips webbed with spit and her milky eyes swelled. She was so thin, she resembled a deformed child. Terrible pale hands fluttered to her throat and she jabbered something about bikers and the Pagan Club's code—bike, club, dog, women, kids. In that order.

"Help me," she screamed at me.

Help *me*. The television above her cot blared. My mom twined a skeletal arm through the chrome bedrail and reached toward me.

"There's something you should know about your father," she wheezed. The nurse slipped out of the room. *Here it comes.* I didn't care about Maingy. I'd lost touch with my old man. But a newspaper article described him as a turtle, cowering in an all-black neighborhood in Philadelphia, peeking out of his shell, king of his own dark world protected by the very citizens he once vowed to destroy.

"Mom, don't talk."

"Maingy and I met at a bar called the Accident. That should have been a sign. He never officially proposed. He just ordered me one day to become his old lady." She adjusted her pillow and her hands shook. "I wasn't a good one."

"I'm sure you were fine." But I knew she was right.

She shook her head. "I had the nerve to get pregnant, twice."

Now, *that* was news.

"I aborted the first one because a kid didn't fit with the biker life-style." She coughed. "But the second one"—she cocked her head side-ways and smiled at me—"I told Maingy *he* could fucking die."

"Thanks, Mom."

We sat in silence for several moments. I pointed the remote control to shut off the television, and the beautiful people with bold white teeth disappeared.

"He's watching me again." My mom's hands fluttered to her throat. Day three. Her whole body shook. She looked thinner, a bulbous head on a hanger. She was held together with white cords. A box beeped her vitals. On the monitor at least, she looked alive. Green peaks and val-leys recorded her pulse. A plastic bag bounced on her hip.

"Who?" I shrugged out of my red trench coat and draped it over the back of a chair.

"Your father. He's at the window."

"Mom, we're on the fourth floor." But I looked anyway. A blue sheen covered the street below. Headlights glowed. Snow fell. My head throbbed and I craved a hit of weed. I wasn't an addict or anything, at least not anymore, but marijuana calmed my nerves.

"He's come to give us money," my mom's voice interrupted. She had left her bed.

"No." I turned, cupped my mom's elbow, and led her to the edge of the cot.

"I'm so cold," she said, her voice small and childlike.

I lowered my mom into the sheets, streaked brown with fecal matter.

"Nurse," I called, as a cold draft explored my skin. A fan whirred overhead, casting bladed shadows on the ceiling. Johns Hospital, for certain kinds of people, was a kind of grave. The poor never really recovered. They were just *returned* to loved ones, pieced together as spare parts, hoping no one would notice the difference. The hall echoed with screams, muffled groans, and curses.

"What's wrong with all of you? Help her." I darted into the hall, frantic.

Nurses stared at me with dull, numb expressions. Papers blew around them. One, with a pencil wedged behind her ear, mouthed to her colleague, "Enabler."

Fuck you. Fuck all of you.

With shaking hands, I returned to my mom's room, dampened a washcloth in the sink, and gently dabbed at the sores on my mom's leg, carefully rinsing out the cloth, wetting it again, smoothing down my mom's arms, her face. Chilly tears slid down her cheeks.

"You're a good kid, such a good kid."

Mom. I shook her but she crumbled in my hands, a dry husk, teeming with maggots. I startled awake, my body sore from being folded so long in the chair. My legs tingled. My mom wheezed. She slept with her feet tucked into cat slippers with overstuffed heads. A doctor hovered in the doorway, his expression grim.

"She can't drink anymore," he said wearily as he pressed my mom's chart to his chest. The monitor bleeped a flat green line.

"Is she dead?" My voice shook.

"If she has another drink, she'll die."

The green line on the monitor peaked slightly. My mom was still with me but barely.

I squeezed her hand and the flesh was loose, like a sack of rocks. "You can't drink anymore, do you understand?" A lump formed in my throat.

My mom's lashes moistened and she said softly, "I promise." Then, after a pause, she asked, "What about pills?"

"There's a little girl in my room." My mom's clawlike fingers gripped the bedrail. Her sunken eyes were wider than they should have been.

"There's no one here, Mom." I stretched at the window and caught my reflection in the glass. My eyes dulled as if a light had gone out of them. I chewed the soft flesh inside my cheek. Monotony mixed with tension. At least funerals promised closure and celebration; illness, particularly dementia, just guaranteed heightened awareness of my *own* life. I wasn't sure I was ready for that kind of realization.

"She's right there," my mom insisted, jabbing the air with her claw. She tossed the sheets to the floor and moved her legs over the side. "Get her out of here. She'll die."

"Mom, what are you doing?" I protested. "It's my coat, see?" I pulled my trench from the hook and held it in front of me, waving the empty sleeves at her.

My mom's expression soured, she furrowed her brows, snaked her tongue around her upper lip. "Motherfucker," she screamed, and threw the remote at my head. She struggled to her feet, fell, and exposed a wet, brown stain on her hospital gown.

"Nurse," I choked. "Somebody fucking help her."

I lifted my mom off the filthy floor. I fell back with her on the cot, and her breath reeked of paste. My arms were streaked with excrement. She had diarrhea and the commode overflowed. I scrubbed my skin under the faucet, the force of the spray reminding me of the morning I interrupted one of my mom's suicide attempts. I was four years old the first time. She had locked the bathroom door again. It was dark, easily four in the morning. The sound of water woke me. A pot clanged in the kitchen.

I heard the familiar crinkle of plastic wrap as my mom ripped open the package of razor blades. I pounded on the door. No answer.

"Go away."

More pounding.

Plates shattered against the wall below me. Muffled laughter filtered up the stairs.

I heard a click and my mom slid back the dead bolt. The door creaked open and I found her naked, straddling the sides of the tub, one leg dangled in the water, the other with a blade plunged deep into the main artery.

"She'll be released tomorrow," the doctor said, hugging my mom's chart to his chest. "Does she have a place to go?"

I stood in my mom's kitchen, hands on my hips, heaviness in my chest. I didn't turn on the lights. Better to work in the dark and pretend I could actually clean the place. My mom's latest companion, Chuck, sat in a chair in a corner. He was hunched over, blind, shivering. Neither of us uttered a word. I felt displaced, like a fixture from another house that didn't quite work. Memory had a smell, like a sweetly rotten intimacy. Relief washed over me. I'll admit as a child I had worried that my life would leave no imprint. That all the violence and anger would just dissipate through wall vents like a potent drug. In its place would be another empty space for unsuspecting tenants to fill, to start over as if pain were just a glossy finish. No scars. No witness. Just odor.

I poured bleach onto a rag and inhaled. Dirty dishes filled the sink. The garbage bag overflowed with empty bottles of vodka, Jack Daniel's, and cans of SPAM. Water dripped from the faucet and slicked the counter. The refrigerator door cracked open. The bulb inside flickered. Flies buzzed on a half-eaten hamburger. Spilled milk sloshed over the shelves, the carton tipped on its side missing a lid. A child's smiling black-and-white photo was creased on its edges. Rows and rows of beer were stacked on the shelves. Cleaning became ritual, a cathartic exercise. A space evolved into the life of its inhabitants. Nothing was static. The filth would return. Still, it felt good to clean. To wipe away surface junk. Even if none of it mattered.

I opened a window and a cold breeze hit me full in the face. It was early and overcast. I promised to collect my mom later that afternoon. I dropped to my knees and moved the bleach rag back and forth over the linoleum until dull brown turned to ivory. Sweat dripped from my temple and stung my eyes. I scrubbed until my hands chafed. I moved to the counter, poured more bleach onto my rag. The light in the sky darkened with the threat of snow. I emptied another garbage bag. I had been at it for hours and my body ached with the strain. But the pain felt good, made me feel alive. That was something, to feel alive.

"Smells good," Chuck said, finally lifting his head.

"Do you think she'll like it?" I hedged.

"She won't even notice."

PART I

INTRODUCTION

1

∿∿∿∿∿

Blood Sport

In the beginning there is always blood . . .
and then there are bodies.

Rain pelted the streets outside my Upper Darby home, one block south of Linden Avenue in a working-class neighborhood once commandeered by the Pagan Motorcycle Club. The media trumpeted the group's close association with La Cosa Nostra and described the Pagans as the "fiercest of the outlaw biker gangs with 900 members in 44 chapters between New York and Florida." Founded in 1959, the Pagans, with all the other "outlaw clubs," according to the American Motorcycle Association (AMA), supposedly comprised the 1 percent of American motorcyclists who purportedly committed 99 percent of all bikers' crimes. But true outlaws were not criminals at all. They were conformists, a club of misfits who followed their own code of ethics, dress, and rules.

Typical Pagans "cuts" so frayed and filthy it practically shreds; depicts the 1 percent diamond patch and the club's mascot, Dark Zurt. *Courtesy of the Saint's collection*

Pagan vest (aka cuts) with grommets. *Courtesy of the Saint's collection*

It was the summer of 1985. I was eight years old and carried my few possessions in a plastic grocery bag—my collection of stolen baseball caps, a dented brass Liberty Bell from a school field trip, and a newspaper clipping of my mom on the front page of *The Philadelphia Inquirer*. The headline warned, "The New Pagans: The Power of Fear." In the photo, my mom straddled the back of the club's newest president, Egyptian. I kept the clipping not because it made me proud, but because it shamed me. The day before the photo was snapped, I had pointed a cap gun at my mom's face and pulled the trigger. Her eye swelled purple. The image seemed a fitting tribute.

I had just been evicted. I shifted uncomfortably on the sidewalk and caught the titters of my neighbor, a Philadelphia cop, who warned his young son to "stay away from that Pagan child." My father, Maingy, the former Pagan Club president, was incarcerated on drug charges. Money dwindled and what little the club offered my mom as support turned out to be counterfeit. My mom sold everything we owned, motorcycle parts, furniture, furs, drugs. But we still had nothing. I stared at my mom. She stood in a puddle in the street looking like a wet doll and my stomach lurched. She was all I had and I wasn't sure she would be enough.

Water washed over my own bare feet. Wooden planks boarded the windows of my home. An eviction notice flapped in the wind. The sour taste of fear filled my mouth. Rain smacked me full force in the face. A train whistled in the distance. I wished I were on that train.

The 1980s was the era of Pagan kidnappings and fish wraps and victims dumped naked in alley Dumpsters. Philadelphia mob boss Nicky Scarfo, who succeeded Angelo Bruno, my father's business associate, left behind a blood trail with every tax collection. He had a judge killed once for double-crossing him. Violence hummed in the streets like the purr of an engine. Egyptian, my father's protégé and temporary successor in power, became the youngest Pagan Club president at just twenty-one. Because he fully expected to be dead in four years, Egyptian occupied a crazy bold present. He was brash and irreverent and the mob disliked him. They considered him foul, and any business relationship Maingy had established with the mob quickly soured.

But more than that, the mob vowed to teach Egyptian some manners. One quiet night, mobsters, cruising in their black Lincoln Continental, rammed Egyptian from behind as he idled at a traffic light on his motorcycle. Egyptian flew to the pavement, bloodied and injured. But he informed police it was "an accident" and declined to press charges. He did, however, request the address of the driver who hit him for "insurance purposes." The police, convinced of Egyptian's purpose, provided him with the address listed on the offender's driver's license. The house belonged to the mobster's mother. The next day someone unloaded a volley of bullets through her front windows. As luck would have it, the mother survived and the Pagans remarked to reporters later that the incident was "unfortunate" and "probably just a coincidence." And so the games began between the mob and the Pagans.

Every game of cat and mouse revealed a rat. All it took was one. One who testified against another, who bargained with the police for a better deal, who agreed to snitch off a fellow Pagan and his drug exploits because the rat wanted an easy exit. I considered it survival, choice with payback. The rats I knew were hanged with wires, doused with gasoline, torched, or simply executed. Without consequences the cycle simply repeated.

Jimmy D for instance was once a righteous Pagan and a close associate of my old man's. Rumors swirled that Jimmy D, despite his strong denial, murdered a young couple on his birthday to keep them from testifying against a fellow Pagan in an assault case. According to notes of FBI interviews with Pagans, Jimmy D was ordered "to get rid of them." Criminal justice sources disclosed that Jimmy D drove the couple to Hunters Mill, a deserted, pitted dirt road surrounded by tall pine trees. He tricked the couple into believing they were driving to purchase drugs. Jimmy D shot the first victim execution style, put a .357 Magnum to her temple and pulled the trigger. He fired a second bullet into her eye. No witnesses. Jimmy D fired a third shot into the husband's head and later burned the husband's blood-soaked clothing in a fifty-five-gallon drum and tossed the evidence over the bridge between Longport and Somers Point.

After his arrest, Jimmy D brokered a deal with the police. He was an opportunist, like my father. He was a rat. But before the details of his contract could be solidified, Jimmy D was caught with methamphetamine in jail. He needed a better deal. First, he bribed the Black Muslim prison gang to keep him alive and thwart contract hits by the Pagans. Next, he agreed to conspire with the DEA and FBI, wear a wire for thirty days, and rat out his own. His efforts resulted in the indictments of twenty-two Pagans on RICO* violations, my old man among them. As far as I was concerned, Jimmy D was responsible for my eviction. Payback would be a bitch.

---

*Racketeer Influenced and Corrupt Organizations Act.

2

~~~~~

School Haze

She wasn't a bad mom, just a high mom.

But revenge would have to wait. I was eight years old and homeless. Puddles pooled at my feet. I had no umbrella, no possessions, just the same jeans I'd worn the day before, and the day before that. My stomach growled. My last meal had been a Pop-Tarts, sometime yesterday. I lived in the moment, and the moment was about survival.

"You know I'd keep you if I could, but we just don't have room." My mom blinked at me matter-of-factly as she pawned me off to my fraternal grandparents, Mom Mom and Pop Pop, who lived in a two-story brick house in Upper Darby. My mom's eyes pleaded for my understanding as she and her new boyfriend, Karl, disappeared into his beat-up Delta 88. Her hands on my shoulders were like a slow burn.

Apparently I occupied too much space. I was shuttled between houses like furniture, an odd corner piece that didn't quite fit with anyone's décor. My new quarters with my Italian grandparents smelled of old people and pressed garlic. They lived in a three-bedroom row house on a dead-end street. Their property bordered trolley tracks. Black puffs of smoke swirled in the sky. The muted colors in their home, browns and golds, reminded me of dead leaves. I sat propped on a yellow phone book at a cluttered table littered with piles of paper and eyeglass pieces, scattered envelopes and bills. I ate hot meals without conversation. My room was a box I'd just opened after years of attic storage. I had a bed with plastic sheets and I could shower daily. But I was miserable and acutely aware that I didn't belong.

My grandparents' home was close to Gallagher Elementary, my third school in three years. The administration labeled me Special Education. They might as well have called me retarded. "Special" kids were relegated to trailers, sweltering tin sheds attached to the main campus like afterthoughts. I had dyslexia and, unofficially, ADHD, although back in the day professionals called it "hyper behavior" and blamed the condition on "bad parenting." Without an official diagnosis, there was no medication, just a recommendation for "tough love." School made me feel like a reject, a "bad kid" and a "crazy/wild" "Pagan child." Exactly what my life had made me.

Part of me enjoyed watching the principal's face contort as if she were constipated because it was a reaction I could control. It was easier for me to become the label than to try to explain what had happened to me. And that's about the best the school could do, describe my behavior as if I were a virus the school had contracted but could not contain. No remedial measures were available.

"Anthony seems a bit hyper, agitated, and sometimes . . . his personality turns dark." The school nurse reported to my mom after my teacher sent me to see the nurse for uncontrollable screaming. "We're concerned. Has he ever talked to you about imaginary friends?"

"He's no rocket scientist," my mom remarked once as if that explained everything.

"Do you know why you're here?" The principal loomed above me one overcast afternoon as I disappeared into the soft leather of her couch. Her desk was a large oak door floating in the middle of the room, and I felt adrift like island debris. The principal was puffy with large teeth and thick sausage fingers that turned slightly blue at the tips. Tiny balls of paper littered the wood.

"Show-and-tell?"

She arched a brow at me and pinched a piece of paper between her polished nails. "What do you call this?"

"The world's smallest piece of paper?"

"Are you being smart with me?" She unrolled one of the balls and read the label aloud. "'Zig-Zag rolling wraps'?"

There was a pause. I heard the principal's breath rasp, short, quick bursts, until finally there was no breath. Just pause. Rain spit against the window. I caught my reflection, long and shapeless as if my face were melting. My eyes shifted to the lawn and my mom, stumbling toward me, her white hair matted to her head like a hood, her arms wrapped in gauze bandages. I leaped from my chair, darted outside in the drizzle to help her. She reeked of alcohol and her wide, bloodshot eyes brimmed with tears.

"You fucking made me walk here," she snarled.

"It's okay, Mom." I put my arm around her shoulder, leaned into her petite frame, and held her as we shuffled home to her roofer boyfriend. I was sorry the school had called her. Maybe they should have called my grandparents. But the administration was likely confused about my living arrangements. I too struggled with the concept of space, how I occupied too much of it, how my mother had no room for me.

"Does your mom often drink?" The principal removed her glasses the next day, wiped them on her sweater. I was in her office again, this time for something "obscene." I shifted uncomfortably in the leather seat. I studied her thoughtfully as if she were part of my wasp collection, a curiosity that inhabited a world behind glass. I was safe as long as I remained outside looking in. More important, my mom was safe. In my mind's eye I envisioned her propped at the corner of my bed, drinking the last of the beer in the refrigerator, pausing between gulps to take long puffs on her cigarette. She tilted her head, stroked my hair, and said with a half smile, "I should have swallowed you."

Although she repeated the phrase often in jest, the words stung and her eyes brimmed with familiar violence. Some mornings I'd look at my reflection in the mirror and shiver. I saw coldness there, a scrambled look like the inside of a bomb. I clenched and unclenched my fists, punched at the air, talked to myself, and felt temporarily

LT's mom, Kim Menginie, and her brother, "Uncle Kirk," celebrating Kim's twenty-sixth birthday. *Courtesy of Anthony "LT" Menginie's collection*

insane. Like the times I watched my mother sleep. Light slanted into the room. A fan blew the covers. I listened for air to exhale from her lungs. I thought she was dead and I found a corner in my living room, tucked my face into a pillow, and cried.

Later, I lied to my teachers, told them something bit me and made my face puffy and swollen. I ducked into dark closets, hid beneath the hanging coats that looked like headless children. I didn't know how to be vulnerable so I became tough. I dragged little girls into those coat closets and had sex with them before I was ten years old. I hurt them because I hurt and that hurt turned me ugly. Suddenly I lived inside out without clarity, with just base human emotions such as need and want. I didn't think anymore. I didn't feel. I didn't regret. I didn't evolve.

Sometimes I fantasized about a different mom, one who worked a menial job that had a title I could pronounce, who helped me with my homework, who collected me after school like the other doll-women who wore matching clothes, had puffy lips, and swung large shopping bags. They smelled like flowers. Mine complained the sun was too brassy and the light hurt her eyes.

"We can help you," the principal interrupted my thoughts. *Help me?* "Tell me about your home life."

I thought of the morning I woke up excited. My class had planned a field trip to visit the Liberty Bell in Philadelphia. I had never traveled outside Delaware County. Sharp sun beat into the living room. Icicles formed like crystals on my windowsill. Angel dust scattered on the coffee table. White haze filtered over sleeping bodies. I stepped on my mom's tangled hair. She stirred, moaned, and slapped away my rubber boot.

"I'm going to see the Liberty Bell," I gushed. She put a pillow over her head. I shivered, already cold. Cheese, my mom's Pagan friend, who sprawled half-naked on the couch beside her, adjusted his thick glasses and reached into his pants pocket. He tossed me a few dollars.

The bills fluttered to the floor. I stuffed the cash in my coat. Cheese reminded me of Santa Claus. His old lady, Crackers, winked at me, but before I could thank Cheese for his kindness, he had dozed off. I waded through the broken furniture, the crusted food on the counter-top, and the half-spilled bottles of beer. I shook out a glass of vodka and poured myself some curdled milk. I walked into the frigid street, shut the door behind me, and thought about heroes. They didn't wear capes. They didn't fly. They didn't put on gold masks. Sometimes they had thick red hair like a horse's tail and wore dirty denim and smelled.

The whole time I waited on line to catch a glimpse of the cracked copper bell with its forty-four-pound clapper, I thought about the dollars jammed into my pocket. I thought about freedom, about wanting to share some small part of it with my mom. It was bitter cold. Crows cawed around me. The dew on the dead grass soaked through my shoes. I wore gloves with half fingers and my fingertips turned blue. I purchased a miniature brass bell from the gift shop. The clapper stuck. It clunked when it chimed. Up close it looked weathered, beaten, cracked down the middle, but I thought it was beautiful. I couldn't wait to burst into my living room with my tiny bell replica.

At two o'clock in the afternoon, I walked home into a cave. Dim lights cast strange shadows along the wall. Half-naked women buried their heads between strange men's knees. My mom wailed like a siren. Curtains blocked the sunshine. Strange chemical smells assaulted me. Someone I didn't recognize cooked at the stove. He wore a troll's face, pale, rotten skin full of sores. A barbed-wire tattoo formed a noose around his neck. He barely glanced at me when I walked in.

"Look what I bought you." I shook the bell in my mom's face. She turned on me like a rabid animal. She spewed profanities and spit, grabbed the brass souvenir from my hand, and hurled it into the nearest lamp.

"Waste," she raged at me with white-hot fury. "You wasted money like that." I blocked out her voice. Inside I shook. This wasn't my mom. This was my mom on drugs. Glass shattered around me. I dropped to my knees and clumsily picked through the shards to retrieve my Liberty Bell. I didn't cry. I didn't feel anything but an unbearable sadness. Cheese emerged from the smoky haze and cupped my hand in his.

"You know she doesn't mean it." He blinked at me through his large glasses. "She's not herself today."

I didn't look at him. I fixated on the pile of glass. My mom's anger blew around me like a funnel.

"She's doing the best she can, kid." Cheese sighed.

Yeah. I knew that.

"We can help you," the principal droned on, but I had stopped listening. Instead, I fixated on the woman's neck, gray and wrinkled like turkey flesh.

"We have social services . . ." *Blah, blah, blah.*

I just want to be a tractor-trailer driver.

Later that morning my mom mom collected me at school, her eyes welled with tears.

"Expelled? He's only eight years old," she pleaded with the principal.

I'm not a normal eight-year-old. I struggled to my feet. Relief washed over me. I was going home. I could leave. My mother was safe. The child-protective people wouldn't take me away. I had heard stories of kids being snatched from mothers because of neglect or abuse. Part of me behaved if for no other reason than to preserve some kind of normal. My mom, after all, wasn't a bad mom. She was just a high one. Her multiple failed suicide attempts were some kind of apology. But I didn't understand forgiveness then. I'm not sure I understand it now. She probably thought simply disappearing would stop the hurt and destruction. She didn't realize addicts left a lifelong scar on the victims who loved them. People thought they could rescue me, but that implied I wanted to be saved. I wanted to be normal. Maybe they were the same thing?

"He mooned the entire playground, including his teacher," the principal explained calmly. She cleared her throat. Worry dimpled my grandmother's forehead. She looked at me, looked away, looked at me again as if trying to reconcile my small size with my terrible act. Maybe she hoped I would simply disappear if she stared at me long enough?

"Why do you do this to us after all we've done for you?" Her voice hitched.

I had no idea how to live any other kind of life. I was dying in front of her, every day, fading away like the negative of a photograph that never quite develops.

"You want something to cry about, I'll give you something to cry about. Pull down your pants." My mom mom bent me awkwardly over her knees in her compressed kitchen with the mountain of paper and broken eyeglasses. With each smack of her hand across my bare butt, I laughed until the tears streamed.

"I'm giving him back to you." My mom mom thrust me into my mom's arms the next morning, indignant. "I can't control him."

Fortunately, my mom had just landed an apartment in Sharon Hill, with Karl. I now had a crawl space to sleep in—trading places, one hell for another.

3

∿∿∿∿∿

Rites of Passage

Karl occupied one of four attic apartments in a government-subsidized housing project. My mom and he shared the cramped space with other nomadic drug families: Chrissy and her daughter, Marcy, Maria and her two sons. The space was uncomfortably crowded. Each family came with its own possessions, furniture with carved faces, old crafted chairs, and miles of stained mattresses they couldn't identify but insisted they needed and probably stole. Marcy was slightly older than me but a willing participant in sexual experimentation. That made it all right at least that I had to share my place with multiple people.

Each family had designated shelves for canned meat and potatoes and shared a common refrigerator. Food stamps were a hot commodity; they were actually used to buy *food* rather than drugs or alcohol. I tore pieces from a fluorescent block of cheese. The hard chunks crumbled in my mouth and formed a thick paste on my tongue. The taste reminded me of stability, of my mom and dad cooking noodles together in the kitchen of our old Upper Darby place. Their faces shadowed, billowed in steam from the large vat, almost phantomlike, reminded me of family. The routine signaled relief. Whatever other dysfunction happened during the day, at least we ate dinner together. It didn't matter that sometimes meals happened at four in the morning or that my mom cooked barefoot, dressed in oversize flannel shirttails as if she were trying to hide a much bigger pain and sadness. Beauty didn't survive in the biker world without sacrifice. Pretty things wilted and were reduced to mere property. The only way my mom made sense of her life was to destroy it.

Marcy stood in the doorway and watched me eat. Her dress was frayed at the edges. She resembled bones draped with skin. Wide, sunken eyes penetrated mine. Wispy hair tickled her cheeks. A muscle in her jaw ticked. Red smeared her lips like a bloody stain. The room had no television, no lamp, and no windows. Darkness smothered us. Smoky air filtered through the vents in the wall—the perfume smell of PCP—and my eyes smarted. An empty SPAM can rolled across the floor and hit the door.

"Don't be stealing my food," I snarled, and sat upright. Fear gnawed at my insides. My gaze followed the clumps of meat strewn along the floor like turds. I could endure being alone, being expelled, expunged, expired, or x'd-out entirely, but hunger was a cruelty that racked my very core. Desperation was weakness, and I decided that if I was ever to die, I didn't want to know about it.

Grunts vibrated through the walls. Furniture scraped in the living room. I heard the familiar sound of a fist smack against bone and a woman's howl. I heard rocking, frenzied movement that knocked faster and faster. I struggled to stand and tiptoed to the door. Marcy padded after me. She was taller than me by a foot, but her physical size belied her control. She put a sticky hand in mine, a hand greasy with SPAM. I cracked the door wide and immediately wished I could shut out the view. Marcy's breath hitched at the sight of her mother, naked on the kitchen tiles, her blond head wedged between a strange man's legs. The man snickered, took a long pull on his beer, and yanked Chrissy's hair. He spit into her shotgun face and shoved her backward. He dribbled his beer between her thighs and licked it off.

"Anyone else want a turn?"

Fluorescent lights buzzed on the ceiling. A man at the stove shook his head, stirred a large pot with a wooden spoon. His long pony-braid hung down his back like a dead snake. He wore jeans, a black T-shirt, and denim cuts. His boots rested in a corner near the overflowing garbage can. My gaze shifted to my mom, who slumped in a chair in the living room, her jaw slack, her eyes filmed over as if she were in a deep trance, not caring if the world ended or not. Karl sat next to her, equally still. A helmet of smoke was suspended over their heads. Minutes ticked by and I stood transfixed, my body crumbling inside. Marcy's hand trembled in mine. She whispered something in the shell of my ear. Her breath reeked of SPAM. Chrissy struggled to her feet, balanced awkwardly against the counter. The man at the stove smacked her bare ass, held the spoon to her lips, and smiled.

"*Now* you've earned a taste."

Even then I sensed darkness in people, human rot, like a prickle on the back of my neck. Pressure pushed against my chest. Pipes, smoke, vomit, blood. I was too close to it all; glazed addict eyes looked right through me. Instinct told me to run. But the rain and cold of the Outside shut me in. I did the only thing I understood for an eight-year-old kid.

I led Marcy to my mattress. She tripped over a can. Flies buzzed around the jagged lid. Rain dripped through a hole in the ceiling and plopped on my head. Wordlessly, Marcy pulled her shirt over her head. Curls fell across her flat chest. I unzipped my pants, reached across for a sandwich baggie, and secured it around my penis with a rubber band.

Marcy crawled on top of me, a child version of her mom. I saw her future behind her luminous eyes. I moved awkwardly beneath her. She cocked her head sideways and a slow grin spread across her face. *She'd done this before.*

"Did you feel anything?" I asked after a minute.

Marcy shook her head.

"Maybe I did it right then?"

I had already learned that sex was a purely selfish act. Emotion left scars. I didn't want Marcy to have any scars.

4

~ ~ ~ ~ ~ ~

Drifter

Cheese and Crackers lived in a dilapidated row house in South Philly, full of dopers and prostitutes and diseased stray animals. Broken bottles littered the sidewalks, shattered windows left gaping holes in the brick. Paint chipped on the shingles. The place had a shrunken look as if each time it rained the house warped. Cheese had no neighbors. Warehouses and gutted factory shells surrounded him.

"Would you mind?" My mom gently pushed me toward my baby-sitters.

Cheese ruffled my head. He stood in the doorway shirtless, dressed in a pair of boxer briefs in the middle of the afternoon. Blazing sun reflected off his Coke-bottle glasses. Crackers, his wife, towered behind him in the doorway, her raging red hair plastered to her face. She balanced a beer in one hand and a cigarette in the other.

"We'll have some fun." She winked at me.

"Just for a couple of days," my mom insisted. Although few words were exchanged, my mom and Cheese had an understanding. She needed time, a break from her dual role as mom and dope dealer. Typically my mom took me with her, left me alone in a locked car in the projects while I strained to see inside the crack house, to see the large black man sweat over plumes of smoke, to see my mom pace and pick at her skin while two Pagans pointed pistols at the cook's temples.

My mom would later leave me in strange parks, the only white child in a sea of black faces. As I swung on a broken swing, sharp wind biting through my T-shirt, a metal chain clicked against the rusty beams of the jungle gym. At dusk my mom returned. Her car smelled of sweet orange, bitter almonds, and some kind of home. Relief coursed through me. She had remembered to collect me. She had found me. Not that she'd ever forgotten, but drug dealing had its distractions. Others had left me in dark alleys near Dumpsters while bad things happened. I never considered it cruel, just precaution.

Cheese popped in a video, *Clash of the Titans,* a movie about fighting demons and saving damsels in distress. The demons I understood. But no one was ever really saved. I settled into the couch. Empty pizza boxes, half-eaten crusts, and a green chicken wing littered the floor. Chips were smashed into the carpet. Sounds filled the darkness, rhythmic, spasmodic retching. Crackers in the bathroom. With shaking hands, Cheese rolled a blunt and squinted at the television. He inched closer to the screen. Crackers emerged; her small bullet eyes shot right to Cheese. She marched over to him, grabbed his face in her hands, and kissed him full on the mouth, with such fierceness she may as well have branded him.

"You know I hate you," she said playfully.

"I hate you too."

Light cast a gray film through the apartment as if everything inside were mostly dead. Curtains blocked the outside. Bloody images flickered across the television screen. Cheese lowered the volume. He winked at me, shrugged, and took a puff on his cigarette. Crackers settled into

Cheese's lap. She held his hand. Smoke billowed around her face. Her eyes watered. I slid off the couch. Cushions toppled to the floor. Cheese and Crackers never flinched. I opened the front door and a cube of bright light framed the two like a photograph. I slipped into the alley between the row houses and found a stick and a couple of rocks. A dog loped into the street, thin and sickly. What fur it had left was mangy and covered patches of pink skin. The dog's legs were bumpy and oozed with puss. The animal stared at me, its blue, knowing eyes absorbed me. I shuddered. I was looking at my own reflection.

I tossed the stick near a row of Dumpsters. Garbage spilled into the street—spoiled fruit, half-eaten burgers, cans and cans empty of beer. The dog followed the stick with his eyes but didn't move. A siren shrieked through the stillness. I moved to retrieve the stick and my body was in slow motion. Out of the corner of my eye, the animal lunged at me, charged me with such force that it knocked me over. My head slammed into the concrete. White blotches clouded my vision. A loud roar resounded in my ears and sharp pain stabbed my right temple. Blood trickled into my eye and burned.

I felt the dog on top of me, its paws raking my cheek, its sweaty, mealy breath panting near my ear. And then an odd sound, chewing. I must have screamed because Cheese and Crackers were suddenly outside in the alley, straddled on top of me, their mouths moving in their stricken faces but no words coming out. My hands, as they pulled away from my head, were warm and sticky. Blood. Crackers wrestled the dog off me and threw the animal against the Dumpster. Stunned but still alive, it hobbled out of the alley. Crackers crawled on her hands and knees, frantically combing through debris and mounds of garbage, searching for something.

Cheese held me in his arms, his glasses slipped to the bridge of his nose, his grip so tight I thought he might faint.

"Find his earlobe, find his earlobe."

Cheese's face bloomed with apology and pity. It never crossed my mind that I might lose parts of me, that doctors might fail to fix me, and that I might live for the rest of my life in an unbearable silence. Nothing is more terrifying than registering fear in someone else's eyes. Cheese telegraphed to me that morning a potent reminder: that he couldn't protect me no matter how fierce his will, that no one could. That finally, there was just me and the dangerous ways people loved me.

5

~ ~ ~ ~ ~

Swallowed Whole

In the beginning I didn't choose. I drifted between two worlds, my Pagan family's and my citizen friends'. The two groups knew little of the other and I preferred it that way. The distance was closeness. By the age of twelve I was already a regular at Pagan pursuit of pleasure (POP) parties, raucous affairs that sometimes lasted for days at a dilapidated barn on five acres of farm hills outside Allentown. My job at those events was to scout for the cops who sometimes prowled the grass taking names and license-plate numbers and setting up roadblocks leading into the Pagans' special encampment area.

Mostly, the cops gathered intelligence on the Pagans hoping to catch them participating in bigger organized crimes. Not that the cops would miss an opportunity to arrest the bikers for drunk and disorderly conduct or possession of illegal drugs and paraphernalia. They would and did, but the Pagans were careful to cover their tracks even as they teased the cops by having pizza delivered to their patrol cars and spray-painting the freeway ramps with the invitation POP

THIS WAY. The Pagans used me as their scout, their scapegoat, their decoy.

The night beat percussion, filled with the rumble of Harleys, the howls of women, shattered glass, and cracked crates of beer. Wine spilled on the stage, staining the wood with dark red hues. Bonfires lit up the night sky, flames licking the tops of trees. The scene was dirty beards, greasy ponytails, sleeveless denim vests, and swastikas. PAGANS tattooed on the bikers' throttle arms. A makeshift stage splashed gold strobe against the dirt. The Rock Star and his band Classic pulsed over the loudspeakers so loud my eardrums throbbed.

Pagan prospects jammed cigarette butts into the cutout eyes of the club's mascot, the Dark Zurt fire god that loomed large on the cardboard sign. Beer, coke, marijuana, LSD, ecstasy, and Benzedrine flowed. Nameless women paraded past me wearing T-shirts emblazoned with PROPERTY OF MAINGY across their chest. It didn't matter that my father was still in prison. He had his mules, the more attractive the more useful and profitable.

On center stage a wiry blond honey writhed provocatively to the music and began to strip, tossing her clothing into a crowd of salivating wolves. Salt Lick Cherie. Rumor had it that she once boasted a personal best of fifty men in one evening. When she was completely naked even beyond her G-string, she dislodged a Maglite and shoved the handle between her legs. She crawled along splintered wood like an albino spider, legs splayed in front of her, the Maglite blinking at her fans like a flirty gold eye. Bikers swarmed around her, swilling beer, cheering, clapping with hands held high in the air. One shoved his face between her legs and removed the flashlight with his teeth. More cheers erupted.

I struggled to maintain my composure as men lined up, dropped their pants, and took turns mounting her, two or three at a time. She moaned and twitched, without protest, in a kind of drunken lust fest, a volunteer in her own exhibition. She ran her tongue across her lips; I had no blood left in my head.

Ironically, most of the women who partied with the Pagans worked respectable positions by day in banks, insurance companies, and law firms. They transformed at night into their alter egos, like some kind of monsters, shedding their conservative clothes for tight jeans and trashy blouses to experience the thrill of unbridled and desperate sex. The Pagans to them were just a curiosity, a carnival freak show, and after a while it was hard to tell who was using whom. But not all of the women led double lives. Some endured a different kind of prison. They escaped from fathers or uncles who raped them and mothers who became whores and addicts. The runaways stripped for money and drugs and laced their dope with chemicals, hoping to fog their childhood nightmares for a while until the real world intruded again. And when the girls started to shake, their freaky friends wordlessly took their scarred arms and injected them with heroin. The cycle repeated, each high bringing them lower and darker.

Some of the women talked to me. Maybe I amused them? Maybe they pitied me? They didn't choose this life. They surrendered to it, and maybe that was easier for them than mere survival? Maybe they believed they deserved the punishment? They weren't like the other women who left their pretty families and refined jobs for a night of sex only to return the next day unscathed and pregnant with stories. These women endured a life sentence.

I closed my eyes. My head tingled from weed. Sounds amplified. I heard laps and gulps. In my mind's eye, the bodies became flesh tangled together in one massive ball until Salt Lick Cherie was no longer a woman but some kind of freak circus monster. When I opened my eyes, those waiting to fuck Salt Lick Cherie passed each other hallucinogens like party favors—acid, mescaline, and PCP, a horse tranquil-

PRODIGAL FATHER, PAGAN SON   ~ 35

izer that actually caused muscle spasms and disturbing visions, as if
the idea of mounting Salt Lick Cherie wasn't grotesque enough. Bonfires raged high into the night sky.

I preferred to smoke weed, hoping to fall quietly awake. I rolled
down one of the grassy hills, my legs curled to my chest in a ball. The
Rock Star's music pounded in my head, loud and cacophonous like a
long scream. The singer's voice trailed into the trees. I felt nothing but
the rush of air and wet grass against my face. When I stopped at the
crease in the field, my body was completely relaxed, so light I could
not lift my arms or legs. I had a paralyzing headache. If no one found
me here for days, I would be okay, safe in my own darkness.

The next morning the fields resembled a battleground as unconscious denim-clad Pagans slept with their colors rolled and tucked
beneath their heads because Club protocol dictated that no outlaw
could sleep dressed in his vest. Smashed beer bottles and crushed cans
littered the hillside. The wail of a harmonica sounded in the distance.

I shivered. The dew from the grass dampened my jeans. The stages
were eerily quiet with no trace of the night's activities. Salt Lick Cherie was curled in a fetal position, naked on the wood, her blond hair a
shield across her face. The Rock Star snoozed with his guitar in his
lap. Sun blazed over the hillside. I heard the rev of motorcycles. Soon
the cops would arrive. It was time to move.

Later that morning, I mounted the back of the Harley of the club
president, Jerry Fox (whom some affectionately called Slow Poke),
and headed to the Atco Raceway. Speed transformed the world around
me into a shiver of color and shapes without definition. City lights
flickered like candles. Buildings flattened. Brass bells shook like gold
dust. The road was a black tongue filled with cracks and pits and

Pagans on a typical run. *Courtesy of Anthony "LT" Menginie's collection*

pedestrians. Cars blurred beside me, the people inside suffocated by glass. I thrust my hands into the wet wind, leaned into the turns, a light drizzle splashing my cheeks. The bike's tires slipped beneath me and I rocked side to side. Exhaust seared my shin. The smells of the street hit me full force, sewage like rotten eggs, bread rising from an Italian diner, road salt, tar, humid wind, burning rubber, the potent odor of tobacco flicked from an open trucker's window. Blasts of hot air mixed with cool pockets. Oil streaked the road behind me. Bugs smacked the windshield. Slow Poke's ponytail whipped my eyes. Wind rushed into my nostrils, made my eyes tear. I felt weightless, as if I were flying. I closed my eyes. Sirens sounded in the distance, deafening like the roar of a train. Like the first time I ever rode a motorcycle.

I was six. My father was already in jail. My mother needed money and so she sold motorcycle parts out of our garage. The Saint, who was all of twenty-one back then, roared up on his bike like some kind of movie star. He wore no helmet, Ray-Ban sunglasses, sleeveless denim cuts, and black jeans. He had long hair that blew around his face like a black mane. He dismounted, strutted through my garage, picked at the used parts, but seemed more interested in me, who crouched be-hind a battered checkered couch in the garage and whispered to my-self.

"Who's he talking to?" the Saint asked my mom. He pulled out a wad of cash and plunked it on the table. "For the light."

"His imaginary farm family." She turned the television louder. We had two propped one on top of the other. Neither worked well. One was black-and-white and the other had a giant hole in the center.

"Mind if I take him for a ride? He looks like he needs rescuing." The Saint punched on his leather gloves.

"Make sure he wears a helmet," my mom mumbled. She didn't look up. She was absorbed in *The Price Is Right*. A cigarette dangled from her mouth.

The Saint knelt close to me, patted me on the head. "Hey, kid, ever seen one of these?" He pointed to his motorcycle. Shiny chrome daz-zled against the bleak grays of the garage. I had seen plenty of bikes

The Saint on his motorcycle. *Courtesy of the Saint's collection*

disassembled in my living room, but none that anyone ever rode. I emerged from behind the couch, ran to climb onto the back of the seat. I fell off, scraped my hands on the concrete. My jeans tore. The Saint laughed.

He hoisted me back up. "Hold on to me, all right? Put your hands around my waist like this." He pressed my palms into his belt. My legs flared out. They hovered near the exhaust.

"Pull them up a bit," the Saint instructed. "You'll burn 'em."

I listened. I did everything the Saint told me to do. I watched his foot fire up the kick-starter to his Harley, and the boom of the throttle sent me screaming to my mom.

"Fucking pansy like your father," my mom remarked, hands on her hips, her mouth bent in disapproving commas.

The Saint came around more often after that. I enjoyed his company. He epitomized what I imagined a real father *should* be: honorable. The Pagans called it righteousness. Not every Pagan was righteous. There were degrees of honor. People listened to the Saint, dumped on him with their problems, and he magically solved them like some kind of wizard. He knew things, crazy private shit that no one else knew, about drug deals, potential rips and setups.

"I've just seen things," he'd say, and shrug nonchalantly when I asked him to explain how he got to be so wise, "the same things over and over again, and after a while I learned to shut up and listen." He'd teach me, describe scenarios, someone owed him a debt, someone owed him meth, someone disrespected his old lady.

"What would *you* do?" he'd test me. He played with the mirrors on his motorcycle, wiped them with a soft cloth, stopped to admire his reflection.

"Probably break his fucking balls," I'd reply in all sincerity.

"Then I'd have no use for you," the Saint dismissed me.

I frowned. The Saint sighed, tucked the chamois into his jeans, and explained, "There are three sides to every story: the truth, the wrong story, and the 'made-up' story. Picture carnival mirrors. Each one presents a different image of the same thing. The trick is to pick the *right* one."

"What if you choose wrong?"

"Then you get glass all over you."

"How do you pick the *right* one?"

"Listen," the Saint said simply. "If some guy tells you a story about another guy and he wants you to take care of business for him, call in the *other* guy, listen to *his* story. *Then* decide whose skull to crack." That made sense to me.

"It's the difference between animal instinct and human restraint," the Saint continued, though I had no idea what he meant. "Picture lions prowling in their cages. The zookeeper releases a goat into their den. What do you think the beasts are going to do?"

"Attack." I shrugged. At the time it seemed a ridiculously simple question. I spooned chunks of ice from the bottom of my frozen drink and chewed. Humidity soaked through my shirt. Rain threatened to pour.

"Exactly. It's their instinct. They don't care that in a minute a deer will dart in front of them. They go for the easier prey. We can't afford to do that. The deer might be the better meal. Do you follow?"

"I think so." I frowned and tossed my empty cup into the trash.

The Saint took me for a ride the next night to demonstrate his point. I slid into the backseat of his Lincoln Continental and clutched a McDonald's Happy Meal. My face hurt from smiling.

"You excited?" The Saint grinned through the rearview mirror.

I nodded and licked ketchup from my fingers. Of course I was excited. I was ten.

"Your first mission." He tossed me a napkin. "Wipe your face, kid." My heart raced. This was going to be huge.

We picked up Dagger. He wore a bulletproof vest over his bare skin. He slipped into the passenger seat looking like James Dean with his short-cropped blond hair, clean, ink-free flesh, and wide bodybuilder physique. He was the mob's "taxman." All business owners were expected to pay the mob or the Pagans a street tax for the privilege of doing business in their designated territory. Dagger worked as a mob enforcer, a kind of IRS agent with muscle.

"Hey, kid." He nodded at me. No one seemed to mind that I tagged along.

We drove for what seemed like miles through twisted residential streets with smoky lamp globes until we arrived at a dive bar in a part of town I didn't recognize. It was well after closing. The place was dark except for a bowl of light that framed the inside counter. The Saint double-parked and stepped out. Iron bars laced the windows. The front door was heavy brass. Dagger invited me inside, pointed to a back table, and told me to hush. The bar was empty. Music played softly on the jukebox.

Stale beer piqued my nostrils. I hopped onto a spinning stool. My legs didn't touch the floor. Smoke burned my eyes. The ashtray on the table still plumed with cigarettes. It formed the shape of a gorilla's hand. Wine spilled from a tall-stemmed glass with a lipstick smudge. Shadows played along the walls. My hands stuck to the bottom of the table. Old gum was mashed into the foam. I fixed my gaze on the owner, a grizzled Italian with a pinched, red face. He put down his dishcloth, replaced a stem glass to the ceiling, and asked the Saint and Dagger, "What can I help you gentlemen with?"

I noted a slight tremor in the Italian's voice. His hand shook. The glass tinkled slightly. Electricity zipped through the room. My heart raced. The Italian man visibly paled. Tiny veins in his cheeks brightened. No one told me what to expect. I just knew. Fear pricked my neck.

"We're here to collect some taxes," Dagger said simply. He cracked his knuckles, pushed his vest to the side to reveal his gun. He cleared his throat. The man swallowed. His Adam's apple bobbed. The Pagans worked for the mob, extorting money from bar owners, small-time crooks, and drug gangs. They were the "big tough guys." Mobster Ralph Natale said, "When [the Pagans] walked into a club, even the other criminals [were] intimidated. . . . The Pagans are all over the East Coast—they r[an] hookers, porno rings, drugs, and extortion rackets. And they ha[d] no problem with murder when they ha[d] to use it."

"I'm paid up." The owner shrugged. A muscle in his face twitched. Tension rippled around me.

"Says who?" the Saint asked. His stare was cold, icy, and I knew instantly something was wrong.

"Giovanni," the owner said.

"What do you think?" the Saint hollered at me. "Should we ask Giovanni?"

"It couldn't hurt," I said, thinking the Italian was the goat.

Dagger shrugged. "We're going to ask Giovanni." He swallowed his beer in one gulp and burped. I had no idea who Giovanni was, although I suspected he was the mobster who had hired Dagger in the first place to collect the taxes owed. I didn't understand then why the Italian had so easily and so foolishly lied; in retrospect I understood completely. He was buying time. He was a dead man already. He hadn't paid his taxes and he didn't have the money. He had no fast excuse; he had a detour. He must have known Giovanni would not corroborate his position. Dagger must have known it too, but he played along. It was about the Story and choosing the right mirror—the truth, the wrong story, and the lie.

A bead of sweat moistened the owner's lip. No one spoke for what seemed several minutes. The owner smiled weakly, spread his hands on the counter, and waited.

We slipped back into the car. Dagger placed his revolver in the dash. "In case we get pulled over," he said, and winked at me. He made sure I knew where he'd stashed the weapon. I felt important. We were off to Giovanni's place.

The Saint pounded on Giovanni's door. It was three o'clock in the morning. It was obvious we had got him out of bed. He stood in his blue boxers, long dark socks, and slippers. His hair looked mussed. The conversation lasted maybe three minutes. I waited in the car. I saw wild hand gestures, shaking heads, an indignant Giovanni. The Saint and Dagger returned to the car. They slipped inside.

"*He* says he hasn't received shit," the Saint volunteered. He glanced at me in the backseat. "Which mirror do you think is the right one?"

"I don't know." I frowned. "I still don't know the whole story."

"Good." The Saint smiled. "You're learning." I yawned, tired of the game already. I just wanted to sleep. I laid my head against the window and closed my eyes. I didn't understand any of what we were doing, but I was happy. I was safe. I was riding in a car with the Saint.

A few nights later, we returned to the bar owner. It was late, after closing. The Italian frowned when he saw us. His face blanched. He busied himself wiping the counter. He glanced nervously into the next room. I wondered if he had company. I resumed my spot at the tall table. Dagger sat at the bar and poured himself a beer. He blew the excess foam from the glass into the Italian's face and traced a picture in the condensation. It looked like a hangman. The Saint sat at a table across from me. No one said anything for several minutes. The Italian stopped wiping. He started to cry, deep, heavy sighs as if he had lost his breath. He dabbed his tears with his apron. He swallowed, shook his head. He shot me a hard stare. Maybe he thought I was his decoy, that somehow my presence would lessen his punishment.

"You lied to us." Dagger sipped his beer. He traced the edge with his thumb. His voice remained calm as if he were discussing the weather.

"No," the Italian sniveled. He averted his gaze.

"Do we look stupid to you?" Dagger raised his voice. He wiped his mouth with the back of his hand, drummed his fingers on the counter.

"No," the Italian stuttered. He untied his apron and folded the cloth into tiny squares. His chin shook. My heart raced. Dagger's eyes narrowed to slits. His face flushed. I wanted to shrink into a back room. Suddenly this wasn't fun anymore.

"What do you think?" Dagger asked me. "Do we look stupid?"

The Italian cried harder. My hands tingled. The Saint scraped back his chair. He produced his pickax. The handle glittered in the dim light. My mind drifted away from the scene, as in an out-of-body experience. None of this was really happening in front of me. I wasn't really a witness. I floated above the bodies and watched Dagger reach across the counter and slam the Italian's head into the bar. The Saint clubbed the man over and over again until the counter pooled with the owner's blood. It reminded me of smashing pumpkins on Halloween. The Italian mewled, slumped to the floor. The Saint wiped off the handle of his pickax with his vest. Dagger pointed his revolver at the safe and fired. The lock blew apart and the door flew open.

"Nothing here." Dagger shook his head.

The Saint shrugged. "Maybe the old man was telling the truth after all."

Dagger competed at the Atco Raceway alongside "civilized" professionals. Shirtless except for his denim cuts, he roared over the dirt moguls, looking more like a demon than a rider. A light drizzle dampened the crowd of mostly Pagan and citizen spectators. The air vibrated with tension and thunder. Pagans formed a human wall around the bleachers, standing shoulder to shoulder enjoying the revulsion and shock they sparked in the citizen spectators. Children recoiled. Women pulled away. The bikers thought it was funny. They flexed their tattoos, shoved into people just because, and started fights for no reason.

I swallowed my fourth hot dog of the hour and stood in line at the concession stand for another. The grease made me salivate. I hadn't eaten so much in days. I couldn't care less about the races or the competition. The motorcyclists revved their engines, the competitors a blur of color in sleek metallic jackets, matching helmets, and plastic numbers. Sponsor banners flapped in the wind—IT'S ALL ABOUT SPEED. Loudspeakers blared. Excitement buzzed around me. Cheese, who stood behind me, nudged me. He opened his trench coat and displayed his arsenal of deodorant cans. He winked and said, "Watch this."

"Something stinks around here." He pinched his nose. To the left of me a member of the Breed squared off. The Pagans and the Breed hated one another. Their club had once murdered a Pagan.

"After Storm Cloud died," Cheese explained, "the Pagans kidnapped a Breed member, rolled him up in carpet, and doused him with gasoline. Then we took the Breed's colors."

Nothing was solved but nothing mattered. No one exchanged words, just grunts, and they said the same thing over and over in their universal gibberish and somehow they felt better about themselves afterward. Cheese sprayed his deodorant weapon, pressed so hard on the nozzle that his fingers burned raw. Rain fell harder. I started to shake. The chemical haze stung my eyes. The Breed member's hands flew to his face. He howled in pain and knocked into me. I smelled his sweat and confusion. Cheese cackled behind me. He thought the whole episode was hilarious. I didn't laugh. I didn't understand the point. But then I was sober. *Payback for Storm Cloud's murder?* Cops' strobes flashed like angry red eyes on the hillside. But by the time they arrived to bust up the fight, none of the bikers remembered the details.

The smell of charred meat seared the air as barbecue pits flamed. Blankets littered the ground. Old ladies and their children shared chicken picnics. Some Pagans, grabbing blocks of shade, snoozed underneath parked cars. I scurried around as the Pagans' errand boy, sloshing water to the track, watching the Saint instruct on the virtues of the ax handle, acts that kept me useful, kept me safe. Meanwhile, my legs strained with fatigue. I lacked the same stamina for partying as the Pagans. At twelve, I struggled to focus through the hazy aftereffects of alcohol and weed. My head throbbed; water roared down my throat a little too loud. I might have been a kid but the Pagans didn't notice. Maybe I wanted them to.

"Kid, get over here." Redneck motioned toward me. He was a large, muscular Pagan with no neck, a ruddy complexion, and sandrust hair that clumped together in a greasy ponytail. He resembled an inflated balloon stuffed into a pair of jeans. Redneck stood guard outside a white van, his chrome, steel-toed boots clicked together, pickax and chain hanging from his belt. He was sleeved like most of the Pagans, meaning every patch of his flesh along his arms was inked. I obeyed because that's what was expected. I was there to be used. Whatever the Pagans needed, I obliged.

The doors to the white van swung open. I climbed inside the dark interior and the door lock clicked behind me. Painted fingernails groped my crotch as my eyes adjusted to the cramped space. A mold green carpet hugged the center floor. Spectator benches replaced cushioned van seats, and three grinning faces held me transfixed.

A woman unzipped my jeans, the same pants I had worn for seven consecutive days. She feathered the inside of my thighs with her hair. She pushed me to the floor, pinned me down with her hands. I heard a familiar chuckle. Cheese. *What is he doing here?* Teeth flashed at me. Cheese's goggles caught my reflection, my large eyes shone like a deer's, cornered in a dark wood waiting for the bullet to penetrate. Cheese wasn't there to rescue me, he was there to cheer me on, to participate. Smells assaulted my senses: wet socks, piss, and sweat. Fleas crawled in my hair. The woman pressed her mouth to my penis and pulled gently, then harder, harder, until skin slapped against skin and white ache exploded on my belly. Jeers erupted. My brain itched with hollow applause. I felt dizzy as my eyes adjusted to the dark. Others waited with no pants on for their turn. Pounding on the door. I heard my mom's whimper.

"You did real good, kid." I recognized her. Salt Lick Cherie. The woman licked her finger, winked at me, and whispered, "Sucking and fucking, that's what it's all about."

Later, in the quiet dark of my bedroom, I shook. No tears, just steely resolve. Rape, like death, was something that happened to *other* people, not twelve-year-olds, not boys, and not by a whore with my mom standing helplessly outside. But my chest hurt and pain throbbed near my temple. I needed release, something to make me forget, to make me pretend, to make the ugliness disappear. *Because I can't fucking stand this anymore.* It was too hard and I couldn't hold on. I was a good kid. A good kid. A *kid*. I locked my door. I got high, and when I emerged days later, groggy and hungry, the only thing on my mind was vengeance.

6

~ ~ ~ ~ ~ ~

No Easy Exit

You live like that and suddenly you're an outlaw. They call you an outlaw. But let me tell you something: they make us outlaws.

—FAST TANK, SPEAKING TO A REPORTER

The Pagans' clubhouse in North Philly, the former Tabor Athletic Association, contained a two-lane bowling alley and pool hall. The dilapidated building flaked with paint chips and cracked brick. My home away from home. Certain memories start with mood, a hint of rain, brisk night air, a strange sense of foreboding and disturbing quiet. The night it happened, I propped open a window and, with pool stick in hand, watched Fast Tank's approach. A light mist coated the Pagan's ponytail. He dismounted his bike, strutted to the entrance, his large belly peeking below his denim vest. He resembled a dark sultan. The Saint racked the balls forcefully, telegraphing his irritation, and I knew then the night would not end well. The Saint straightened, moved to the clubhouse door, and blocked the entrance. Tension rippled through the room. Rope scars and blood sores mottled Fast Tank's skin. The biker folded his arms across his chest and his fingers barely touched.

"You're kicking me out?" Spit flew from Fast Tank's mouth and settled in his beard. His question was a statement. A bald porch light cast him in a white glow. Bugs sizzled. Fast Tank's eyes watered. A dull silence fell over the scene.

"Look at you." The Saint folded his arms; a mixture of disgust and disappointment clouded his expression as if Fast Tank were a family pet who had just messed the carpet and disobeyed house rules.

"I'm a little messed up." He shrugged.

"You're wasted."

Junkies posed a control problem, weakness that threatened to topple the whole rank-and-file structure of the club. Selling dope was profitable; ingesting it compromised organized crime. The Pagans had a drug policy that resembled that of most moblike organizations: those who indulged had to control the drug. Narcotics trafficking brought unwelcome public scrutiny and lengthy prison sentences.

Fast Tank visibly stiffened at the Saint's accusation. I knew what was coming. Fast Tank had made his choice—drugs. Curious, I moved closer to the window and caught the whiff of rotted denim. The dirty patches of heat, soiled and frayed from years of wear, barely fit Fast Tank anymore, but no one traded in his colors for a larger size. The club's comic mascot, Dark Zurt, should have squatted in the middle of Fast Tank's back, but instead the demonic guardian of Muspell, with horns like a bull's and feet like a chicken's, sat in an arch of fire closer to Fast Tank's neck. The image had faded over time, emphasizing once again that the club should have implemented leather.

"It's retarded," the Saint remarked once to me when he thought I wasn't listening. "I get that denim is traditional. But look at this." He showed me the club's former top rocker with the embroidered letters PAGAN'S. "There's a fucking apostrophe before the *s*. It's just grammatically incorrect." But worse than that, denim faded over time. After a while, no one could even *see* the insignia on the back of the vest, and in time the Pagans had no identity at all. Fast Tank's cuts had no apostrophe.

The biker struggled out of his vest and handed his colors to the Saint. No apologies, no excuses. Just like that, Fast Tank was out. But I felt the jolt, the undercurrent of impending violence. There was a beat, a lull in conversation, a deafening pause, a tableau of pool sticks suspended in midair, pool balls snug in their pockets, bowling alleys shiny and quiet, the white pins stacked like soldiers poised for battle. No one moved.

Terrible Tony with his arm around an unknown Pagan. *Courtesy of Anthony "LT" Menginie's collection*

The Saint tucked the coat under his armpit, shut the door quietly, and slid back the dead bolt. He glanced at me and headed upstairs to discuss Fast Tank's exit. He held an emergency church meeting. Other members lumbered after him, their footsteps heavy on the stairs. The door closed behind them with a thud. Muffled voices filtered into the hall, argument, chairs scraping against concrete. My heart pounded in my chest. Terrible Tony sat quietly in a corner like a wall fixture. Brain-damaged from a stray bullet to his temple, Terrible's blond eyes flickered with knowing. His thin hands curled around the knob of the skull cane he'd crafted. Inside the shaft he concealed a rifle. Terrible gestured with his head toward the window.

I bent the vinyl slat. The white glare from the porch bulb flashed over the bikes parked one against the other like a chrome cavalry. The license plates faced away from the street to frustrate the cops, who made it their mission to collect intelligence on the Pagans by running their registrations. Fast Tank walked toward the bikes, his gait slow but deliberate. He moved methodically, slashing bike tires with the calm, stoic resolve of a hit man. No recrimination. Slice. Slice. Slice. He was a butcher carving deep grooves into rubber with a knife that still boasted a price tag. As the bikes flattened, Fast Tank moved on to the cars in the parking lot.

Fast Tank turned and moved swiftly toward the clubhouse, sheathed his knife, and slammed his fist through the frosted-glass portal in the door. He reached inside and unbolted the lock. I heard the whistle of air leaving the tires like a loud wail. I took the stairs two at a time and pounded on the church door, feeling my hands smart against the wood. *Open up. Open up.* Dizzy, breathless, tension pounding in my head. Fast Tank blew into the room like a funnel.

"He's slashed all the tires," I blurted, and heard commotion behind the door, curses, guns racked. The door whooshed open. The Saint's face flushed. He pushed me aside and practically flew down the stairs. I watched from the top landing, my heart racing, unaware that I had just rolled a strike and that Fast Tank's fate had just turned because of me. I didn't think about consequences. Purposeful brutality made *sense*. The club had rules and a code and no exceptions. Mistakes didn't happen. Fast Tank's conduct required *re*action, and while the Pagan didn't need to die, he needed to lose his dignity, a consequence *worse* than death.

Fast Tank stood near Terrible, hands on his hips, a wide grin on his face. The Saint grabbed Fast Tank by the throat and howled, "Motherfucker."

"I did it and I liked it." Killer words.

The Saint released his grip around Fast Tank's neck, grabbed his ponytail, and dragged him to the basement. I scrambled behind, propelled by the promise of action. I crouched at the top of the stairs, not daring to go to the bottom. Instinctively I knew I should leave. But time moved fluidly here and I had nowhere to go. The violence at the clubhouse was somehow less immediate than it was at home, and I felt safe on the landing, quietly watching, removed, like the time I was four and crouched at the top of the stairs. I watched bodies in my living room flop on top of each other like slabs of raw meat. I didn't understand the movements, but I understood the mood and the strange sensation in my legs that told me to run even as I remained transfixed.

In the dark underground, the Saint shoved Fast Tank into a corner and pummeled him with balled fists. Other members joined in and beat the Pagan with wooden sticks and kicks to the head and chest. I heard the sound of bones cracking. Blood spotted the concrete floor. The Saint chained Fast Tank's wrists to the radiator. After a while, I saw only lumps. My eyes adjusted to the dark haze, to the blur of movement. I heard barks to prospects and the dull slap of skin against skin as they all took turns punching Fast Tank in the head.

Boots knocked the air from the Pagan's lungs. Fast Tank's moans filled my head like the caw of crows. Knees pressed into Fast Tank's throat, flattening his flesh like dough. The Pagan vomited. Damaging bikes was as bad, if not worse, than killing a loved one who had done nothing wrong. Fast Tank was as good as dead.

The beatings continued through the night and into the dawn. Bright sun beamed through the blinds upstairs. I shifted, my legs numb from inactivity. *How much longer?* When the blood got to be too much, the Saint ordered prospects to hose Fast Tank down. The Pagan was raw and torn like a meat carcass. As Fast Tank slumped next to the radiator, his face unrecognizable, his nose cracked, his eye split and black, members took breaks, played pool, rolled a few balls down the bowling alley, discussed their options and what to do about the problem of repayment.

I stayed hidden, unsure about protocol, this being my first torture and all. Should I stay, leave, dare fall asleep by the jukebox upstairs? Would the Saint be angry if he knew I had watched? I justified the scene in my head—it wasn't *criminal* what was happening to Fast Tank. It was *necessary*. Pagans didn't commit crimes, they exacted revenge. Fast Tank had to pay for the tires he'd destroyed. Righteous violence was okay, even necessary.

It was a good theory and helped me process what was happening. But after days of torture, even the members were perplexed about the ending. Fast Tank wasn't dying, and it wasn't clear to me that the members really *wanted* the Pagan to expire. They wanted to teach him a lesson, and somehow mere discussion didn't seem appropriate. Clearly there would be no grand finale, nobody in the basement, no clear-cut retribution, just damage control and messy cleanup. Blood soaked through Fast Tank's clothes. Rank and wet, his jeans clung to him like a second skin. Eventually, the Saint peeled them off Fast Tank, and the fat Pagan sulked naked in a corner like a swollen Buddha. After a while, the Saint tossed a wool blanket over his friend's shoulders, and in that

Left to right: Angus with pals Kaz and the Saint. *Courtesy of the Saint's collection*

moment I realized the Saint *wasn't* a sociopath after all; he was kind to animals.

I stood, my hands resting on the railing, unable to tear away from the scene, transfixed by the darkness, the practical brutality that was so much a part of my world. I felt suddenly calm, peaceful. There was no exit. There was no negotiation. There was just action and reaction.

Angus stepped from the shadows, his massive frame as intimidating as his intellect. He was the club's enforcer and a close associate of the Saint's. I wasn't afraid of him. I respected him. There was a difference. Angus came from affluence but he knew what he was, they all did—misfits running from their own ugliness. They blended because they had to survive. He was an outlaw. He was supposed to *act* like one. Within minutes, Angus busted out Fast Tank's teeth.

"That ain't right," Fast Tank wailed. He slumped forward and spit bloody dicelike chips onto the floor. I held my breath. More than any other body part, loss of teeth symbolized powerlessness, an inside that slowly rotted no matter how tough a biker presented on the outside. I ran my tongue across my own teeth, still intact, still white. No one had fed Fast Tank for hours. My own stomach growled. Angus tossed Fast Tank a stale powdered jelly doughnut. Sugar to open wounds was like battery acid.

"Gorilla has his bike," the Saint said matter-of-factly. His hands were bloody mitts. Sweat matted his curly hair to his temple. He leaned against the wall for support. Angus nodded, seemingly unfazed by having just dislodged Fast Tank's teeth, and switched on the basement lights. Harsh fluorescent beams lit up the scene. Blood pools, dark stains, a lumpy body chained to the radiator, two assailants with glazed looks.

"Should we just take it?" Angus smeared blood on his vest, like a badge. The Saint shrugged. It was a simple solution to the problem of payback. Why they hadn't thought of it hours earlier was beside the point. They had to teach Fast Tank a lesson. Then they had to take his bike.

"Yeah, for starters. Then we'll sell it and buy ten new sets of tires." Fast Tank moaned his protest. Losing his bike was one of the worst humiliations he could have faced, worse than the torture he just endured.

"If we have any money left over"—the Saint patted Fast Tank's head for good measure—"we'll consider it a donation."

PART II

7

∿ ∿ ∿ ∿ ∿

In Memoriam

It was early evening by the time I finally ventured home from the clubhouse to Karl's apartment. I had been away nearly two days, not that my mom even noticed. Pagan children weren't missed the way other kids were; they were just *elsewhere*. They would appear when necessary, or they would simply drift lost.

Shadows lengthened the walls inside Karl's apartment. Candles flickered in the hallway. The electric bill went unpaid again. Muffled laughter filtered downstairs, tinny in my ears. I heard the sound of running water. Wearily, I gripped the splintered railing, dread in my footsteps. I wasn't in the mood to play adult. I climbed to the bathroom and stood in the doorway. Steam billowed from the faucet. My eyes adjusted to the cloudy figures of my mom and Karl, bent over, fully clothed, washing the reptiles I'd collected as pets. I felt the blood drain from my face. The animals were mine. I'd taken care of them, rescued them from the rain gutter and from polluted neighborhood creeks.

My mom splashed in the spray like a child, her damp hair clumped around her face like cords. Her hysterical laughter burned in my ears. I swallowed the lump in my throat. I smelled the alcohol on my mom's breath. Karl slipped in the shower. With shaking hands, I reached into the scalding water to retrieve the goldfish that flopped near the open drain. The fish squished out of my hands. Karl's boot crushed one. Air whooshed from my lungs. I stood in the spray. Water pounded my head and the burn felt good. I was inches from Karl's face, inches from his glass reptilian-like eye. My mom held a shard of the shattered aquarium to her face and blinked at me.

My garden snakes slithered across the tile; one plopped into the toilet. The snapping turtle in my mom's hand retracted its legs and head. Karl dropped to his knees, hot water blasting from the faucet, and boiled my hermit crabs. My chameleon retreated under a pile of towels, its tail and torso turned a mottled shade of brown. Cold-blooded creatures thrived in harsh environments.

I understood blind rage. I couldn't see Karl, just whiteness. Pain shot into my head, throbbing, as if a hammer had crashed down on my skull. Son-of-a-bitch Karl washed my pets, creatures I loved. I learned not to grow attached to things I loved. I learned they could easily and suddenly and often die.

My mom stood under the shower spray and said softly, "Terrible's dead."

At first, I didn't believe her. Terrible Tony had a habit of dying. He was more than my mother's closest friend; he was a permanent fixture in our home, like a dark presence. Once a hard-core Pagan, Terrible had withered in recent years to a mere shell of a man. He'd "died" before when I was ten, convulsing in my living room from heart failure, and while he was slumped unconscious, I had emptied Terrible's wallet. Two hundred dollars could buy a lot of food. And it wasn't as if Terrible would miss the money. Who knew he would recover? After his close call, Terrible decided to be more prepared. He packed a duffel bag full of burial items—his colors rolled in a rubber band, his club rings, skull cane, and, most important, his wallet containing the Pagans' phone numbers. *Just in case.* Terrible gave the bag to my mom with strict instructions to store it in a safe place. He was to be cremated in jeans and a T-shirt printed with the Pagans' insignia.

"Crackers found him. She went over to his place to check on him. He had a seizure, fell into his glass table, and bled to death," my mom volunteered matter-of-factly as if she were discussing a party she'd attended. Terrible was forty-one. News of his death rippled through the Pagan community like a dark current.

Before the services, I visited my uncle Russell's grave. His Pagan moniker was Dead, which, in retrospect, seemed fitting. My uncle's cemetery glistened with dew. Headless azaleas littered the ground. I tossed dimes and quarters on Dead's headstone, a tribute to the days my uncle begged for change at tollbooths. Thoughts of Dead evoked memories of my father, who spent a total of three hours with me my whole life and mostly because he wanted something. We didn't have a *relationship,* we had exchanges, moments that defined Maingy, not us. When I think of him now, I think of possessions: furs, expensive black soles, polished leather couches, and crystal bowls of PCP coated with oil, his locked bedroom filled with modified weapons and altered serial numbers.

Maingy moved a pound of methamphetamine a week and controlled one of the largest organized drug cartels on the East Coast, but to me he was just another son-of-a-bitch drug dealer whose family lived in the margins, like scribbled afterthoughts. His network encompassed Pennsylvania, New York, New Jersey, Delaware, Maryland, Virginia, West Virginia, and North Carolina. At the time the Pagans ranked in size behind the Outlaws, Hells Angels, and Bandidos. But I wasn't impressed.

"He was a fake," the Saint revealed to me later during Maingy's RICO trial. "The asshole testified that he *bought* his membership into the Mother Club for ten thousand dollars. And then he bought his way out of prison."

The fucker did twelve years; he should have received a life sentence. But it wasn't the *amount* of time Maingy actually served that bothered me. It was his attitude. Maingy could just as easily have brokered furniture deals as drugs with his sociopathic charm. I envisioned him in prison programs designed to upgrade his education, taking courses in psychology, sociology, criminology, just so he could learn the proper verbiage to convince his gullible counselors that he had been "rehabilitated" or "born again." That he deserved a second chance. He never bloodied his hands, never put in work for the club, not in the way the Saint did or Terrible or any of my other mentors. Maingy might have trick-bagged the justice system, but to me he would always be guilty, guilty, guilty. *You do time or time does you.* The Saint's words never held so much truth.

"There are gangsters and then there are potato-chip gangsters," the Saint explained to me one night as he ate dinner at the Melrose Diner. "Maingy was a piece-of-shit potato chip, a wannabe who hung around mobsters without ever really being one. He didn't understand gangsters, didn't know the first thing about *real* thugs who lived with their mothers because they couldn't afford to pay rent, or stole motorcycle parts because they needed drugs, or sent honeys out to turn tricks for them. Maingy never met a *rich* thug. *Racketeers* made the real money. Racketeers were smart about it. They hired the thugs to make the money *for* them."

Terrible was no potato-chip gangster. He earned his moniker because he *was* terrible. Back in his day he stabbed and shot people point-blank, then, when he couldn't walk anymore or ride his bike, he fashioned a skull cane whittled out of a pickax.

"No one ever saw him coming," the Saint remarked.

It was true. The Saint's tattoo shop had been the target of random gunfire. Terrible sat in a chair, hands on his cane, while bullets whizzed by him, some lodging in the wall above his head. He never flinched. The Saint never repainted the holes. The bullets were tributes to Terrible's crazy courage.

Apart from my uncle Russell, it was the first time I truly missed someone and missed what that person represented—Christmas. The holiday was never about presents because there were none. It was about being the center of attention for one glorious day, about witness, connecting with people even for two minutes, just to let that person know that someone in the world cared about him. I can still see Terrible, seated at his kitchen table, his face ablaze in the gold glow of candlelight. A twenty-dollar bill crumpled in his hand. The phone cradled against his ear. His fingers shook as he dialed each member's number.

"Hey, man, merry Christmas." Click.

Hours passed like that. A strange kind of reverence filled the room as Terrible made his connections and confirmed his friends had survived another year. No one had been stabbed, shot, overdosed, imprisoned, or defeated by diabetes. *That* called for celebration. As Terrible completed his ritual, I played the card game War with my mom. We sat propped on a pile of pillows while snow fell outside and I plotted to steal the neighbor kids' toys, hide them from my mom, look at them, and pretend I was just as good as those kids.

"Hey, man, sorry for your loss," Terrible's voice droned in the background like radio crackle.

∿

After Terrible's cremation, members honored his death by drinking beer and smoking angel dust at a clubhouse in the city that corralled chickens and a goat. Skinny dogs wandered the grounds. I hunkered outside where I could breathe, where I hoped no one noticed me. Fights sparked around me for no particular reason, drug-induced hallucinations that caused people to see things that weren't there, shadow people, ghosts, even Terrible himself rocking in a corner with half his head blown off. No one spoke of him. Sincere regret came in raw bursts. Evil Ed sat cross-legged in the middle of the corral on a mound of hay and hollered at the moon, "Teerrible." He seemed lost for words. Instead he shook his beer and sprayed it over his head.

"Teerrrible."

"Shut the fuck up."

Evil Ed snapped his attention toward the Bull, an ex-Pagan and roofer with a face like raw meat. The Bull, who had once been married to Maria, beat me regularly as a kid, chased me around the cold basement with a bat and chain, until one morning I put my hands on his sawed-off shotgun.

"You should have blown him away," my friend insisted later.

"Probably." I shrugged, although at the time it seemed impossible.

"What could they have done to you?" My friend frowned.

"True. I was already in prison."

"*I* would have killed him for you," Terrible's voice rang in my ear like a demon's.

"This one's for you, kid." Evil Ed struggled to his feet and smashed his beer bottle on a rock and fashioned his own glass blade. The scene reminded me of a western, two old cowboys finally squaring off on a dusty road in the middle of nowhere. The Bull's greasy hair flapped around his cheeks like a tattered headdress. His sleeved arms hung loose at his sides. He screamed and the veins in his neck bulged. He looked the way he did when I was eight, like a red storm. No words, just noise. And the walls shot up the way they did when I was a kid. Evil Ed charged the Bull, slashed wildly at his face. He didn't mean to kill him, just scar him the way he had scarred me so that every time the Bull looked at himself in the mirror he would remember. *I would have killed him.* Terrible's voice again.

Deep cuts split the flesh below the Bull's eyes. Blood spilled like tears. I stood paralyzed by the scene as other bikers joined in, pounced on the Bull's back, cracked his head with the butt of their pistols, kicked him hard in the jaw, and shoved his face into the dirt until he struggled to breathe. Evil Ed pulled the Bull's hair, wagged his head in my direction. "This one's for you, kid," Evil Ed repeated. The Bull, covered in dirt, sputtered for air. "Kill him, kill him," a chant hummed throughout the corral and reached a feverish pitch. Evil Ed grinned at me and, in one last dramatic slice, cut off the Bull's ear.

The Bull howled, clasped his head with his hands. Blood seeped between his fingers. The other bikers quickly turned away from Evil Ed and dispersed into clouds of angel dust. Evil Ed struggled to his feet, wiped the dirt from his jeans, and tossed the bottle into the garbage. Calmly he retrieved the Bull's ear, bloody and coated in dirt. He squatted to the Bull's level, leaned in close, and said, "Maybe now my screaming won't bother you so much."

I thought I might throw up. I didn't move from the wall. I couldn't shake the image from my head, of the Bull, curled in a fetal ball, locked in his own silent scream.

It was late, after midnight, and time to leave. Karl and my mom stumbled to the car high on angel dust.

"Let me drive." I slapped the keys from Karl's hands. Like hell was I going to die in a car accident because of *him*.

"Get in the car." Karl shoved me.

"Give me the fucking keys." I scrambled to retrieve them.

"You're thirteen. It's our only ride home." My mom stared at me with bloodshot eyes.

I hesitated, debating my choices—I could walk, stay at the funeral, or ride home with someone equally high. I slid into the backseat. The road dipped and curved and my stomach lurched. Roosevelt Boulevard was a four-lane highway. White fog lights pricked the dark night. Taillights licked the road like red snakes. Cars swerved to miss us as we weaved in and out of traffic. My pulse quickened at the thought of bashing Karl's head into the steering wheel. Quiet rage simmered inside me as I glanced at my mom, caught the shine of fresh purple on her cheek, her cracked lips dark and crusted with blood. The pickax on the dash glinted at me and I fantasized about plunging it into Karl's spine, twisting it upward, and gutting him like a fish.

The urge to kill coursed through me like an electric current, and I suddenly lunged at Karl, swung my hands at the man's head—hands that, at thirteen, knew how to squeeze a man's throat, how to press a knife blade into flesh until it drew a blood bead. I pummeled Karl's glass eye, over and over, until my knuckles cracked raw. The car bucked and skidded along the highway as Karl at once gunned the engine and then slammed the brake. The car did a burnout as smoke and exhaust plumed into the air. I jolted forward, crashed over the front seat and into the steering wheel. My mom mewled in the darkness.

I wanted to kill Karl, to feel the raw power of control, of hurting another human being the way I hurt. Murder was a perfect tribute to Terrible, who would have finished Karl in one bullet to his head, execution-style. I reached for the ax. It never occurred to me that I could lose. I could slice off Karl's ears and make him survive in a helmet of silence. The ax slipped off the dashboard. The car careened through several lanes of traffic. Tires screeched. Horns honked.

Karl's glass eye dislodged, revealing only white glaze.

"You're going to kill him," my mom hollered. She fell to her knees on the floorboard searching for the eye that I had watched Karl remove each night, clean, and wrap in a paper towel to dry in a soap dish.

Karl blinked at me, spit teeth into my face, and waited for me to strike again. I knew that if I released him, removed my knee from his chest, I was as good as dead. Karl would toss me into the road and grin as my head split open like spoiled fruit.

"You're making it worse for me." My mom again. She managed to put her foot on the brake. The car bucked, nearly missed a pickup truck in the next lane.

Snap his neck. Terrible's voice drifted into my head as if he were *there* in the car with me, as if he *saw* what was going on. I never believed in angels. I never thought of Terrible as mine. But something overtook me that night, something powerful and almost supernatural and it made *me* powerful.

"What are you staring at?" Karl's gaze caught me full in the face like a punch. It stopped me cold, returned me to the night Karl, chewing quietly on a meatball, swallowed and punctuated his sentence by slamming my mom's head into the table without warning. My mom cupped her hands to her nose. Blood squirted through her fingers. Shaking, she stood, staggered to the kitchen sink, splashed cold water on her face, and without saying a word grabbed the pile of dirty dishes. Turning, she flung them one by one at Karl, like Frisbees. The plates zinged by my head, shattered on the table, clipped Karl's shoulder, splintered at his feet. Shards lodged in Karl's ponytail, in my noodles, and soon the kitchen was a white blur.

"Get out." I kicked open the driver's door with my foot. Sharp wind bit into my face. The Delta careened dangerously close to a pair of red taillights. Cars swerved to miss us. A siren blared in the distance. Still pinning Karl with my fist, I pushed my mom out with my foot and dove into the street after her. Sharp pain pricked my chest as asphalt sliced into my skin. Karl weaved down the highway, smashing into cars, and walls, doing doughnuts in the middle of the road.

I grabbed my mom by the elbow, stumbled with her across four lanes of highway. Horns blared in our faces. Karl's car spun into a U-turn and bucked toward us. My mom crawled into the gore. Tires screeched around us. The smell of burning rubber filled the air. Karl's car was getting closer. I heard the roar of the engine in my ears. *Now.* I grabbed my mom and dragged her toward the shoulder where a small rock wall jutted from the curb.

"He's going to kill us," my mom screamed, her body shaking. Karl crashed into the barrier, the force sending debris and wind into my face. Karl crushed his radiator. Steam billowed around us. Karl's windshield shattered. His eyes locked with me. *Kill me. I dare you, motherfucker.* I wanted him to. I wanted him to spend the rest of his life in prison. I wanted him to stop hurting us.

Karl smirked, put his car in reverse, and squealed his tires.

"You're not worth it," he barked as his car fishtailed into the darkness.

8

Stray

When one Pagan swings, all Pagans swing.
—PHILADELPHIA CHAPTER PAGAN'S RULE

Most weekends I stayed at the clubhouse. The environment was peaceful and Karl couldn't try to kill me. It was early afternoon and Mongo stirred from one of the twelve soiled mattresses on the floor. He belonged in the dirt and filth. Tipping the scales at 350, people smelled him before they saw him. They deferred to his brute force and brash irreverence.

Every club needed a bull, a righteous member who, unlike an enforcer or sergeant at arms, had a führer mentality. He was willing to kill for the club, or *be* killed to preserve the club's mission—one for all, all for one. Mongo had the courage to be real. He was what the Pagans called "good people," someone who was willing to catch a case or go to jail for another Pagan rather than be a snitch. Mongo had no regard for personal risk.

"He once devoured a half-eaten pizza from the garbage," the Saint remarked one afternoon. We sat on the steps outside the clubhouse. I tossed rocks into the street. "And he didn't do it because he was hungry, mind you. He did it because the food was leftover, because it was *there,* because no one else dared."

"Foul motherfucker." A Chinese preacher lived next door to the Pagan's clubhouse in a Chinese church bordered by a smelly power plant. He spoke broken English and punctuated each sentence with spit. The Pagans could easily have finished him off for his disrespect, but he amused the club and so they tolerated him. Car husks lined the wet streets. Barbed wire separated the clubhouse from his church with no practical effect.

"Maybe today your friend shower," Chinese Man clucked, wagging a bony finger at the cloud-laden sky. He puffed on a cigarette, flicked ash near the curb as tension crackled in the air. A rock struck the building across the street. I paused, turned to catch the Saint's reaction. I imagined the preacher's crisp white shirt, short-cropped hair, and pinched nose drenched in blood.

Before the Saint could respond, Mongo cut the tension. He filled the doorway, stretched, rubbed his large belly, and nodded, saying, "Good morning," to the preacher. Food stained his vest. Sweat formed dark circles beneath his armpits. Dirt clumped on his jeans and patches of his thin brown hair fanned around his face like a clown's.

"It's five o'clock." Chinese Man scowled, inhaled on his cigarette, and clicked his teeth.

Mongo grinned, loped into the alley, and snatched up a stray cat by its neck. He shook the animal at Chinese Man. "Hungry?" He laughed as Chinese Man spit at him and rattled off a string of what sounded like Chinese profanities. The cat hissed.

"He likes you," Mongo said.

"Motherfucker." Chinese Man dropped his cigarette onto the ground and smashed it into the gravel with his shoe.

"Your pet looks kind of sick." The Saint recoiled as Mongo waved it at him. The damp white cat made choking sounds. His large blue eyes had burst blood vessels and his mouth bloomed with foam.

Mongo studied his cat, stroked the underside of its chin with his thumb, and shrugged. "It's feral."

"It's spewing spit," I added, not that I knew much about cats.

The cat suddenly lunged at Mongo and sank its teeth into his large,

Mongo straddling his motorcycle just before he is bitten by a cat. *Courtesy of the Saint's collection*

pudgy hand. Startled, Mongo shook the animal from his grip and it fell hard to the ground. Blood bubbled in the cat's teeth imprints.

"Son of a bitch." Mongo threw a rock at the cat. It hissed and jerked into the alley. Mongo sucked at his open wound. "You see that shit? That's a devil cat."

I thought of the dog that bit my ear. When my old man heard about the attack, his reaction had been to hunt down the animal and shoot off its head. As if killing the beast would somehow remove *my* pain, replace my ear. But Maingy wasn't about comfort, he was about instinct, violent, aggressive outbursts that masked as a front for survival. He couldn't help himself. Emotion would have been a telltale sign of weakness.

"You should probably go to the hospital," the Saint interjected matter-of-factly, pulling his keys from his pocket to take him.

Mongo's eyes grew wide. He shook his head in protest. "No hospitals. I have no insurance."

"Okay, but you might lose your mind." The Saint shrugged.

Five days later Mongo's hand swelled to the size of his thigh and he relented. He flopped into the backseat of the Saint's Lincoln. Folds of skin spilled onto the vinyl cushions. He positioned his sausage legs sideways so that they wouldn't jut into his chin. Sweat beaded his temple. Puffy welts had formed near the bite marks. Mongo's lower lip trembled. His blue eyes flickered with apprehension. No one was immune to death. Not even a Pagan. Not Mongo. Not a bull. Any of them could be killed in a moment, in a drive-by shooting by a rival gang, by a knife plunged twenty-seven times into the chest just because of who they were, what they represented, and where they happened to stop for the night. And then there were the strange, unexpected accidents like the cat.

"How're you feeling?" The Saint nodded to Mongo through his rearview mirror.

"Like a cat bit me. Crazy fucking shit. How about you?"

"I dreamed of losing my teeth." The Saint peeled away from the curb. "They say that's a sign of powerlessness."

"Or that someone close to you is about to die."

"You're not going to die," the Saint said, but his voice wavered.

There were no guarantees. Not in this life. There were no accidents. There were choices and cause and effect. There were exits. I thought of Jessie James, the Pagan who tried to leave the club back when the Saint prospected, but he mysteriously crashed his motorcycle, veered off the road when metal poles replaced the road signs. James's doctor prescribed him Percocet for his pain. He became an addict and returned to the club. Malicious, another hard-core Pagan who prospected with the Saint, also left the club. But he later burned his hand in a freak roofing accident and crunched pills for his pain. The Saint lured him back with the promise of control and power; Malicious was shot in a Baltimore

S&S before he was fatally stabbed. *Courtesy of the Saint's collection*

bar on his way to nowhere. *You ride hard and sometimes you don't make it. And sometimes roads become switchbacks, brakes fail, engines stall, high rates of speed result in amputated limbs.* Death was an expected perk.

"It was a fucking cat," Mongo insisted.

"The point is, you picked it up. You thought you could control it until it bit you. If you're *lucky,* you'll last three years in this club and then you're done. Drugs, murder, or prison"—the Saint counted on his fingers—"the three easy exits." His speech was for my edification just in case I had any interest in joining.

Mongo moaned in the backseat. "That must make you a fucking god to have lasted this long."

"No, just lucky." The Saint grinned and recounted again the story about Machine Gun McGurk, the "crazy motherfucker who flapped his jaws too much about the Pagans." The Saint bragged how he needed to take care of business. He carried an ax handle strapped to the front of his motorcycle waiting for his opportunity to smash McGurk's windshield. When he finally did it, McGurk was still seated behind the wheel.

"He aimed his nine-millimeter right at my temple and pulled the trigger," the Saint said matter-of-factly. "I should have been a dead man."

The Saint attributed his fate to random luck. No one ever found the bullet. No one ever found McGurk either. The Saint stopped for a red light and shrugged at Mongo. "It might not be your time."

I turned my gaze to the rainy street, the degradation and filth, hitting the window like a dirty smear. A child squatted on the curb, his bare feet splashed in a puddle. He wore no shirt and his ribs dented his chest. He stacked rocks to the sky, building a tall tower, a refuge. I wiped condensation from the window. The child followed the car with his eyes but didn't wave. I wondered about *my* time and whether I would be so lucky?

Mongo's breathing was labored. When he finally spoke, his voice was small and tight and pitiful. "If I die, lads, don't tell anyone it was a cat."

Later, in the hospital, the doctor who wrapped Mongo's hand asked him matter-of-factly, "Do you still have the cat?"

The hospital smelled of antiseptic and bleach. Mongo lay on the adjustable bed fully clothed in his boots and vest. He struggled to sit up and said fiercely to the Saint, "Tell him I'm not dressing in that gown with the hole in the ass."

"I don't think he cares," the Saint remarked.

"We can probably find the cat," I offered. I shoved my hands in my coat, leaned against the wall.

"Good. You'll have to cut off its head."

By the time the Saint and I returned to the clubhouse, darkness had settled over the street. A light drizzle fell. The Saint recruited Angus, and the two of them gathered an arsenal of weapons—a TEC-9, a .22-gauge rifle, a pistol, and a pickax. They prowled the alley, flicked on flashlights and lighters and lit up Dumpsters, shells of cars, even puddles. I followed behind them intent on finding the cat. From his window, Chinese Man watched. Gauzy drapes blew across his face.

The Saint spotted the white cat stumbling as if drunk. It slammed its head into the wall. Bloody whiskers stained its fur. Angus raised his .22 and fired. He pulled the trigger over and over, thirteen times. I counted. With each shot Angus's hand shook. Blood spattered the walls around me. Drops hit my cheeks and hair. Angus didn't stop. He emptied his gun and after a while the cat twitched from pure reflex.

I lowered the beam of my flashlight and shivered. It wasn't cold. White film settled around me. Gunshot residue. The cat soaked in a bloody pool. Angus lowered his gun. No one spoke. Words seemed like overkill.

Angus knelt by the cat's limp body, retrieved his buck knife from his shin, and with a swift movement sliced off its head. A window above the alley slammed shut. I looked up. Chinese Man stood behind the curtains, his silhouette like a dark ghost. Angus lifted the cat's head and kicked the bloody body to the side. No triumph was in his gesture, only despair. Semblance of control was better than no control at all. Helplessness was not an emotion any of us relished. It ranked up there with loss of dignity. I thought of Maingy again and the dog he once wanted to shoot. But unlike Angus, Maingy didn't want to do it for me. He wanted to do it for *him*.

The rabies shots only prolonged the inevitable. Two months later, Mongo was back in the hospital.

"Lads, I'm finished," Mongo barely whispered to the gathering cluster of bikers near his bed. Some slouched on the arms of the green, oversize chair; others leaned against the wall, all toughness and hard edges leached out of them. Steely resolve replaced grief. Others paced the hall, their boots clicking on the hard linoleum, waiting for some kind of release, for someone to exhale and tell them it was going to be okay. *But it was never going to be okay.*

Mongo's skin was a dull yellow as if he were slowly rotting from the inside. The window in his room was cracked open, and hot, muggy wind fluttered the cardboard signs posted on the monitors and at the edge of his cot: SELF PAY the letters read in bold black Magic Marker. The hospital faced bankruptcy. I remember my mouth parched; it had been hours since my last drink but I didn't dare leave. A stillness like death draped over the room. Resignation swirled in my gut. Doctors and nurses scurried past the room, in a hurry to tend to patients who had money. Strays were forgotten, tossed into alleys, left to shiver in dark, damp spaces until they slowly faded from life altogether. It was too late to give them attention; they were already damaged.

Death smelled of age and humility.

"What's wrong with him?" the Saint hollered down the hall at anyone who would listen.

"Meningitis." A nurse hesitated at the entrance. She was slight and young and smelled very clean, like chemicals, like disinfectant. I remember feeling somewhat relieved by the diagnosis, that at least the cat hadn't claimed Mongo. Some other "respectable" disease had got him. I never asked whether the two were related. I liked to think they weren't. The nurse shivered, maybe because it was cold, or maybe she had poor circulation? Her name tag read JANE. She *looked* like a Jane, no frills, blanched, all about business, her pocket in her coat bursting with pens. She hesitated, glanced at the room of bikers clad in vests and tattoos, and fear clouded her eyes. She flipped open Mongo's chart and clarified as if no one understood what Mongo had, "a brain infection." It sounded expensive. A hush fell over the room. There was no mercy in a life sentence. Eight days later Mongo lapsed into a coma. A certain unreality hit me as if I were awake in a dream state. No one said much. An easy exit.

"Does he have any family?" The nurse bit her lower lip, hesitated. I thought I detected genuine sadness in her voice.

"We're all here." The Saint gestured to the many Pagans who had spent nights asleep on the floor listening to Mongo breathe. My attention drifted momentarily to the man across the hallway. Nurses had wheeled him in during the night on a stretcher, the victim of a gun-shot wound to his thigh. He looked no more than nineteen. Blood oozed from his leg. Illness and injury were the great equalizers. He wasn't so tough in this place. Nurses whispered something about his family and remarked how he had had no visitors. Not even friends. Confined to his dark thoughts, his isolation, the man could simply disappear and no one would notice. At fourteen I thought about death often, about good places to die. Mentally I crossed off the hospital.

"We need someone to—," the nurse began, but the Saint cut her off. His hand trembled as he signed the release to let Mongo go quietly, in dignity and in grace. The nurse unplugged Mongo, ran her hand across his eyelids, across the words FUCK YOU. Even in death he wanted to shock, to be outcast.

Mongo's funeral was marked by a cavalry of bikes, three hundred or more, riding tight and in rank order. The rumble of engines re-sounded like thunder on the empty streets. Police cordoned off traffic. At the cremation ceremony, bikers and estranged relatives alike hugged one another, expressed condolences, openly wept in a strange confla-gration of sadness. Pagans made T-shirts commemorating Mongo's passing—PHILADELPHIA MADNESS the graphics read. As I stood over his ashes, a tremor coursed through me and I thought of one thing: strays.

9

∾∾∾∾∾

Killer Instincts

Private Eyes Too, the strip club where Dagger worked as a bartender, was unusually quiet for a Thursday night. Car husks and engine parts mounted in a pile of metal rubble in the back of the building. Snow dusted the road. Inside, heavy percussion pounded the walls. The place catered to Warlocks and Pagans mostly, but there were occasional strays, regulars who stumbled in and propped at the bar like fixtures. A wooden stage protruded from the center like a dry tongue. Most nights bare-breasted women jiggled down the splintered plank. Scurvy, the bouncer, managed crowd control at the entrance. His pocked face resembled a slab of bullet holes; he twitched with each crisp bill. The place had an undercurrent of violence, a distinct hum that sharpened the air, made me edgy and excited all at once.

I was underage, just thirteen, and relegated to the dark kitchen, which smelled of boiled chicken parts and stale tobacco. It beat home and so I tolerated the cramped quarters, the chilly air that whistled through cracks in the drywall and made my fingers itch. I was all right as long as I could see the entrance. No outlaw ever put his back to the street.

A wedge of light cast shapely shadows on the linoleum, women undressing, bitched from the start. I caught the flash of a young girl in the room, a slight bump to her belly. She hummed something in a minor key, haunting and lonely. Silver bangles lined her arms but didn't mask her track marks. Pierced eyebrows and trowel-thick makeup hid what must have once passed for a pretty face. I thought I recognized her, on her knees outside near a corner before a homeless man, head bowed as if she were giving him a blow job, until I saw the man's hand crash down on her skull. At the time I hadn't even flinched.

She caught me looking at her; she wasn't much older than sixteen.

"It beats the Centerfold." She rolled panty hose up her leg.

I nodded, envisioning her working there in a couple of months. It was the one bar that allowed pregnant women to strip for bills.

"Come on, just the top."

I jerked my head toward the familiar Greek accent coming from the bar. It was the Painter again. He had harassed the Saint's old lady the night before, mistaken her for a common stripper. The Saint had left him with a warning: a purple eye and a chipped front tooth. Short, middle-aged, and dressed in ivory overalls with splotches of crimson on his chest, the little troll's peppered hair glistened with fresh snow. I cracked the kitchen door wider. The Painter carried a buck knife on his tool belt. The exposed blade swung low near his groin.

Terry, the pretty bartender, smirked at the Painter as she emptied a beer stein into the sink.

"I'll give you a hundred bucks."

"She's not for sale," Dagger interjected as the man's tone sharpened. Dagger took a sip from the half-open Jack Daniel's bottle in front of him. His face was flushed. He'd been sober for four years, and the alcohol was making him sweat. My curiosity was piqued. Why did

Dagger care what happened to Terry? Sure, she was classier than the others, untainted. Maybe he thought he could save her?

"Everyone's for sale." The Painter laughed.

"I'm not a stripper," Terry said as if the very word left a foul taste in her mouth. She was young, no more than twenty. She chewed her upper lip, twisted the ends of her hair. *What is the big deal?* Three minutes of humiliation for a hundred bucks. Nothing wrong with a fair trade. Women did it all the time; I'd seen some barter ink for blow jobs. It was just business. Not that *I'd* ever pay for sex or cheap sexual thrills. I didn't need to. Being around the Pagans was a bit like being in the company of rock stars. Female groupies were plentiful and indiscriminate.

The Painter flashed a roll of bills at Terry. "Easy money." He punctuated his sentence with a sip from Dagger's Jack Daniel's as if the two shared a common goal.

Dagger flinched at the Painter's gesture. There were boundaries. The Painter had just crossed the invisible line.

Terry rinsed the beer stein, slowly wiped the inside, and returned it to the shelf. She lay the dish towel down on the counter and, with shaking hands, curled up the edges of her T-shirt. The Painter sat quietly, his gaze unwavering as he caught the first glimpses of flesh. I ducked into the shadows by the kitchen doorway; tension zipped up my spine. Minutes ticked by. Terry pulled the T-shirt over her head and unhooked her bra. She stood naked in front of the Painter, her body quivering, her full breasts mottled with shadows under the rose pin lights. A small crowd gathered around her like wolves salivating over a wounded doe.

"That's enough," Dagger said, breaking the tension. He snapped his fingers at the Painter. "Pay up."

The Painter grinned, pocketed the cash, and said, "Just kidding. I enjoyed the show."

Terry's eyes smarted with tears. It was over for the Painter; it was the natural order of things and not because he had insulted a woman but because he had broken a code of ethics, an expectation. Terry stripped; the Painter needed to deliver the cash.

"Get out." Dagger moved from behind the bar. The Painter laughed and raised his hands in mock surrender. Scurvy stopped counting cash. He stood like a column at the open door, a panel of snow falling behind him. The Painter brushed past Scurvy, muttered something in Greek, and left the bar.

Cold bit into my cheeks as I moved from my post in the kitchen. The crowd hung behind me like a heavy fog. Dagger downed the last of his Jack Daniel's. The Painter stalled on the sidewalk, his hands hidden. In a flash Dagger joined the Painter outside, his leather duster draped over his shoulders. Red light from the bar slashed the sidewalk. Empty cars, buried in snow, bordered the street.

The Painter lunged at Dagger. The shadow of a blade sliced across brick. After a flash of gunfire, the Painter's body crumpled to the ground. The snow bled scarlet. Dagger fled. A hush fell over the scene. No one moved.

Scurvy nudged the body with his foot. The Painter had no face.

"Reliable sources" later reported that the Saint, who never smoked, lit one cigarette after another, jammed the butts into a plate of pizza crusts, and raged about discretion. "I told the fucker not to keep a bullet in the chamber." The Saint shrugged out of his vest, turned it inside out, and hid Dagger in a cabin in the woods. On his way, he nearly killed a buck, swerving to miss the animal and sliding into an embankment. Tires spun in the snow, headlights flashed into the bare trees. Gold eyes glittered at him. The buck stumbled as if drunk and prepared to charge again. In rut season the deer's nature was to attack until it put its head through the windshield.

I thought about Dagger's nature; how likely was it that the club's enforcer would cower for long in a dilapidated cabin in snow-packed woods with only his bulletproof vest for warmth? No clock, no sounds except occasional shifts of snow on the roof, and the wail of a wolf, the yip of a wounded doe. Fear was a precursor to madness. Survival depended on hallucination. I created fantasies when I could no longer stand my circumstances. The night Dagger murdered the Painter, I imagined myself on a bike, a fierce wind blowing me over the graves of Pagans who had died, into a gold field where I was the hero riding out of a storm.

"Two channels on the television worked. And I bought him some groceries," the Saint relayed to me later almost as self-assurance. He implemented a code with Dagger, a way the two could communicate without detection; two rings on the telephone and the Saint knew to call Dagger back. But sometimes the phone rang twice, three times, six times, once. Several weeks later, Dagger announced he was tired of "living like a fucking mole."

Surrender signaled relief, closure, and an odd freedom. As a fugitive, Dagger lived practically invisible. He must have sensed his own end. A killer never returns to the club, never regains independence. Nevertheless certain protocol still applied—Dagger's murder was not club business. The club, therefore, could not absorb his heat. There had to be finesse; Dagger's exit had to be heroic: brutality with *purpose*. A private investigator later suggested that Dagger shot in self-defense. It didn't help. Dagger became a lifer in the New Jersey state penitentiary.

The Saint drove me home after the Painter's murder. It was nearly dawn when he pulled into my driveway, idled the engine, and lit a cigarette. Snow fell on the windshield. I glanced at my house; it was unusually dark and a chill coursed through me. I spotted Karl's car in front of ours and exhaustion numbed my legs. I opened the door, my sneakers soaked and cold. My legs moved independently of my body. A headless carnation spiked from a potted plant on the sill. Dread filled my head. Every addict can recount his worst moment, the point at which he hits rock bottom and knows he needs help but lacks the courage to ask. Instead he hides his pain, makes regrettable choices, and leaves a path of destruction so twisted it's impossible to ever really recover. My mom's moment happened the night of the Painter's murder.

As I opened the door, I caught the sharp whiff of ammonia. The kitchen was dark. Only the glow from the Saint's headlights shone over the counter littered with broken glass, hardened noodles, and PCP. Movement near the corner drew my attention. Thin puppet arms waved me over, pale, shaking, wedged between the sink and the oven. My heart was a riot of wings. I fumbled for the light switch.

"Mom?" A sob escaped my lips.

She was a tangle of limbs, slumped at the waist, dressed in thin cotton, barefoot, her blond hair streaked with blood. I crouched to her level, my fingers encircled her biceps. Her flesh was a mass of scabs, infected sores. I brushed a wisp of hair from her cheek and nearly vomited. The middle of her forehead was tar black. One eye was squeezed shut in a swollen mass of burst vessels. Her breath was shallow, quick.

"He broke my eye socket," she whispered. Her sticky fingers trailed my cheek. She sat in her own blood. Rage simmered inside me. Dizzy and nauseous, I pulled my hand away and stumbled backward, clipping my shoulder on the oven door.

"Please," she pleaded, "no doctors."

The room suddenly shrank, framed my mother's frail skeletal form in sharp edges. I opened my mouth but no sound came out. I struggled to stand, balanced myself against the counter, and steadied my breathing. This wasn't happening. She needed a hospital, but if anyone saw the bowls of PCP in the refrigerator . . . my mom would see nothing but the inside of a cell for years. I grabbed the first thing my hands touched, a rock planter on the sill, and headed for the front door. The Saint was still outside, waiting as he always did to make sure I was safe. I aimed for Karl's car. Shattered glass fell on the street. Neighbors switched on their lights. No one called the police. Karl loomed behind me, his monstrous form swallowing me.

The Saint exited the car, slammed the door shut. I turned, balled my fists. I wanted to hurt the son of a bitch. Maybe even kill him. At that moment I didn't care about consequences. I cared about revenge. Action.

"Don't," the Saint warned, reminding me how easily things turned. How easily they could be construed as self-defense.

"It's either me or him, Mom," I screamed, my hands stilled in midair. "Me or him."

"*Him,*" my mother's weak voice carried through the open window.

10

~ ~ ~ ~ ~ ~

Happy Spot

Later that night I huddled in the cold on a packed snow mound near the train tracks in Collingdale. Winter whistled through the bare trees. *Him.* The word sloshed in my head like potent liquor. Dawn was sharp as a knife's edge on the horizon. I hugged my knees to my chest, the tips of my fingers fringed with blue, my torn jeans, several sizes too short, barely covered my ankles. I shivered. The train whistled. A branch cracked behind me and I turned. My friend Chal appeared, a tuft of blond hair, a face like carved stone, a black peacoat with a wide wool collar framing pale rat eyes. A ghost of a smile lifted Chal's lips as he pulled a worn cloth from his pocket, unfolded the edges, and offered me a mushroom chunk.

"This will help."

With shivering hands, I accepted the token and slipped the fungus onto my tongue. Within minutes the snow bubbled bloodred and spilled onto the tracks like a river. The color tasted metallic and was soft velvet to my touch. The cold burned my skin. My heart ticked louder than it should have and I put my hands over my ears.

It hurts, it hurts. And I deserve it.

I flapped my arms, wanted to fly over the awful brightness. Gold winked at me from the trees, eyes watched me in the woods.

A voice near me howled, "Remember when we robbed trains?"

I squeezed my eyes shut. Memory was such sickness. Laughter rippled my toes.

Little hoodlums, the echo in my head had a sharp bloody taste. *We stole rubber blocks, paper wheels, newsprints, anything from the cargo loads . . . even tampons. We derailed a fucking train . . .*

Chal loomed above me, a large black bird with a tail made of light.

We should have gone to prison . . . do they lock up children?

I'm so tired. Make it stop.

Wind clawed my eyelids. Open. Open. Open.

I looked up. I wanted to see my own eyes. I wanted to look beneath the surface of the pale blue film and *see* what was inside me. But the closer I approached, the more I was afraid. There are some places from which you cannot return. Some damage can be irreparable. There, in the cool dark, my mom stumbled toward me, her mouth startled open like a doll's. *I should have swallowed you,* her words floated into the wind. She fell. Whiteness buried her. I forced my legs to move and watched as my feet cracked the snow, the beautiful diamond patterns rippled.

"Where're you going?" Chal asked in slow motion as if his batteries had drained.

Nowhere.

I was close enough now to the shape of my mother.

"What are you doing with that log?"

I raked the snow with my fingers and left streaks of blood in the whiteness. Her body reeked of Jack Daniel's, and when I turned her over, the alcohol sloshed over her sides. I knelt, cradled my mother in my arms, lifted her tiny body, and carried her into the woods. But when I tried to prop her against some snowy bark, she collapsed into a pile of bones.

"You all right, man?" Chal's voice made my skin pebble.

I'm fine. I'm powerful. I am in complete control.

"We're happy now, right? This is the absolute best it gets."

This is my happy spot.

"HWA, Honkies with Attitude." Chal saluted as he invoked our earlier days as members of the gang HWA.

"Here, this will take the edge off." Chal pressed a blunt between my fingers. I was on the mound again, shivering. I looked at my hand. *When did it grow so huge? Fat, swollen, like a fucking pig's. Do pigs have hands? How did I get here?* I inhaled, sweet marijuana clouding my thoughts.

"It's cold out here."

Yes. It's cold in here.

Sun slashed across the train tracks. I would have to leave soon.

"You going to school?"

I could sleep in school. And it was warm. No one bothered me there. I was invisible.

"If you go, ditch at lunch. I need your help with something."

Chal patted me on the back and his touch sent a chill up my spine. I watched my friend clap his gloves together. White powder sprayed into the wind.

"You'll be okay," he said, avoiding my gaze.

I would never be okay.

A few hours later, I crashed at Ashland Middle School, my head on the desk bursting with brilliant flashes of blue, gold, and mauve. Sounds around me were amplified, the scrape of a chair, a pencil scratching across paper, a book thudding shut. I yawned and thought my jaw might disconnect from my body. *I'm so tired.* The words skittered across my eyelids. But sleep eluded me. I smelled like sweet vomit. An alarm resounded in my ears. I awoke in my own drool. Recess. Chal. I was late. My legs were numb and heavy as I stood. I found my bike outside, my front tire bald, and unlocked the chain. My fingers tingled as I gripped the handlebars and pedaled furiously the few blocks to the cemetery. The old graveyard bordered a black township.

In my bike mirror my school disappeared, the wide barbed gates shutting me out. The day was overcast. Fat clouds hung in the sky and threatened to snow again. I knew where to find my friend, staying warm inside a corner Wawa, stuffing his face with Little Debbie chocolate éclairs.

"Where the hell have you been?" Chal was indignant, white cream stuck to his chin.

I felt nauseous and dizzy still from the night before and thought I might throw up.

"Pooh Bear's coming. He's a real gangster. I need your help with this one, you know, in case he . . ." Chal balled the foil wrapper between his hands and tossed it at my face.

"Yeah, all right," I said, glancing across the street to the graves. A broken beer bottle littered one of the headstones.

Pooh Bear emerged from the cemetery on his bike. He was large for a fourteen-year-old. His winter coat barely covered his middle and flapped open as he waddled. I caught the glint of chrome in his waistband and dread filled my thoughts.

He's a real gangster.

I straddled my bike, cold nipping at my exposed ankles. Pooh Bear grunted and shoved a .38 Special between my ribs. I had become indifferent to violence; it was expected, as much a part of my life as hunger. Still, I had ringing in my ears and a sense that the scene was surreal, not really happening to me. And if Pooh Bear freaked and pulled the trigger, maybe it wouldn't be so bad? Exhaustion rattled my legs; a dull ache throbbed in my stomach. I imagined a different place, one that wasn't filled with graves and whiteness and cold.

"It's cool, it's cool." Chal threw his hands up in surrender and handed him the cash for the pound of weed. Pooh Bear slipped the gun into his pocket and waved us on.

Chal grinned, flashed the pot at me. "Happy spot? Tonight?"

Why not? I was no longer living, I decided, I was surviving. My friendship with Chal had been instant, one of those inexplicable bondings that defy analysis. Maybe that's why I didn't want to ac-knowledge Chal's darkness. *You're my brother from another mother, my citizen friend.* We had drugs in common and getting high. Chal was my release. I didn't have to be anybody with Chal.

I didn't have to be at all.

Night fell, and the lights from the bar on MacDade Boulevard cast funky shadows in the street. I squatted by a parked car, rubbed my bare hands together to stay warm, and watched the homeless loiter near the entrance. Chal swatted me playfully on the shoulder and pointed to a skittish old drunk wrapped in dirty rags, slumped against a wall with a bottle of booze in his lap. "That one." My friend popped a handful of Percocets into his mouth and crunched. Something feral twisted inside me as if a part of me identified with the lonely men who shuffled past me. Disposable shadow people no one missed. Hunger ravaged my insides.

Chal lunged at the drunk, hit him in the head, and stole his bottle.

It wasn't so bad. He had something we needed. It wasn't criminal. It was survival. It was . . .

"Good fun, isn't it?" Chal grinned.

But it *wasn't* fun. And beating up drunks at Cookies 'n Cathy's only left me hollow and anxious. Committing assault didn't make me a badass, it just made me an ass. Prison didn't look like a place that caged heroes. I'd visited my old man in prison for regular yard picnics before the facility transferred him to Texarkana and the distance was too far to travel. The monthly exchanges played like an old movie clip. The same scene flashed over and over, but with a slightly different backdrop. Maingy shuffled over to me in his oversize rubber sandals. Flies buzzed around him. His skin glistened from hot sun and he looked as if he were leaking. He squinted at me, registered my connection to him, then motioned to the guards who stood like painted stones around the perimeter. Other inmates played the extras. They milled around us like bulls; their web tattoos and bald heads formed a blur of mottled pattern. Children scaled the barbed-wire fence and climbed the wooden picnic-table legs. We each had fifteen minutes and it was too much time.

Still, I continued to make the effort. I thought it was important for my old man to clock the moment I completely disappeared. I didn't visit out of obligation. I didn't care. I visited out of anger. I wanted him to know that he left me on the outside bothering the margins of a life I didn't understand or want or even deserve. I wanted him to hurt. I wanted him to *care* about something besides himself. I wanted too much. When the prison transferred him, my old man called my grandparents once a month at a set date and time. He had made it easier than ever for me to visit him.

But he never specifically asked for me. I waited anyway in the awkward silence at Mom Mom and Pop Pop's kitchen table for my turn to take the phone. When I finally did, I heard mostly static. My old man worried that the phone lines were tapped. Sometimes he just hung up. Sometimes I spoke to a dial tone. Eventually I stopped talking altogether. His calls interfered with my work schedule and it became too hard to take the multiple buses to get to my grandparents' kitchen just to listen to silence.

I stood outside Karl's apartment, my home too, and scanned the windows for glimpses of figures. Sweat dripped from my temple despite the cold. I twisted the aluminum baseball bat in my hands, the bat I had stolen as a kid from a business in town just because I could, just because it made me feel important. Frost burned the tips of my fingers. I tucked the bat beneath my armpit and ventured inside. My mom and Karl slept in a drug-induced stupor full of dark visions and crackle. As a kid my living room was filled with bodies like that, lumps prone on the floor, tangled in each other, stinking in their own piss. No chance of movement. I stood at the entrance to their cramped bedroom and waited for my eyes to adjust to the blackness.

Spilled moonlight illuminated two shapes sprawled between the sheets, my mom creased against Karl. I crept to the side of the bed and stood there for several minutes, my breath shallow and quick. The room reeked of filth and rot. Dirty clothes littered the floor. Stained sheets wrapped around my mom's ankles. Her flannel shirt flapped open to reveal a scar tattoo on her thigh. Shallow lines and loops had been carved into her ashy skin with a razor blade. I studied Karl's features the way I imagined a potter might consider the shape his lump of clay should form. I nudged my mom to the floor. Karl snored.

My hands shook around the neck of the bat, and before I lost my nerve, I swung wildly at Karl's head, as if it were a Halloween pumpkin. Blood spatter pocked the walls, my hands and face. The sheets darkened. I swung again. Karl flopped on the bed like a puppet, too weak to deflect blows, too stunned to mewl.

"Stop!"

My mom's wail echoed in my ears but I *couldn't* stop. My hands moved independently of my body. Rage surged through me like a toxin. Sirens whined and sawed along my nerves. I reviewed various arrest scenarios in my mind, *aggravated assault, murder*–convicting me would be redundant. I swung again. Blood bubbled from Karl's head.

"You're going to kill him." My mother again.

I might.

I wanted to leave my mom with no choice. *It's either me or him, Mom, me or him.* But if I killed Karl, who would take care of my mom if I went to prison? *Like hell can I let that happen, Karl isn't worth it.* My hand stilled in midair. I panted, wet from blood and sweat. I wiped the bat with a corner of sheet and spit at Karl. Without another word I slipped out the door. I should have been arrested, should have gone to prison for aggravated assault or attempted murder. But Karl never called the cops. He couldn't, wouldn't. He had too much dope on him. The beating was our secret. He knew I would do it again if provoked.

I retreated to the snow mound near the train tracks and smoked a blunt. It was late. The weed calmed my nerves. Fatigue gnawed at my insides. I could sleep for a hundred years and still feel restless. A dull ache enveloped me, mind-numbing and calming, the way I imagined the few moments before death. I inhaled deeply, letting the drug fog my thoughts, my ravaging hunger. In the morning, the bakery on the corner cooled its rolls on the docks. I could steal a few and no one would notice.

The snow crystals in my hands reminded me of afternoons when I was a child and my babysitter, Ruthie, taught me to build snowmen. We shaped fresh clumps of powder into fat heads and bellies, fitted snapped twigs into armholes, and traced the blank-palette faces with sly upturned smiles. Night wind blew away their frozen heads. But Ruthie didn't just expose me to white-glazed landscapes.

"Come on." She pulled me into the woods. Her red scarf flapped in my face. She had bold, penetrating eyes like a wolf's. "Ever been to a keg party?"

I was five. I had no idea what Ruthie meant, but I loved Ruthie, loved the way light raked through her dark hair like a jewel. She forgot my coat. My fingers frosted blue. My whole body itched with cold. But I didn't care. Ruthie was the most beautiful woman I had ever seen. When we arrived at the clearing in the woods, tall, bare trees formed a circle around a fire pit. She patted a cold shelf of snow.

"Sit here." She smiled. I felt special, important, like a forest king.

Ruthie lit a cigarette, stomped in the snow with her fur-lined boots. She buttoned her coat to the collar, looking more like a wolf than before.

"You'll be okay for a while." Her face was the color of burnt cinnamon.

After a while strange men joined her around a raging fire pit. They smelled of bark and had thick skin and beards like tails. They frightened me. They reminded me of my old man. The men and Ruthie spoke in hushed voices. She looked like melted gold against the flames. She swallowed little blue pills. She drank yellow liquid from round wooden crates propped in the snow. She knelt near the fire. Men gathered her long hair in their hands. They shoved her face between their legs. Ruthie's eyes were white globes. I knew she could still breathe because her head bobbed up and down. I shivered. My heart raced. The woods grew darker. Rows and rows of trees clawed the night sky. I counted snow prints, wondered if they led home. Wolves were in the forest. *Wolves are beside me.* I hopped off the shelf, curled closer to the fire; my head rested near a large revolver. My hands looked like frozen pork chops. I closed my eyes. No one noticed me. Ruthie nudged me just as dawn filtered through the branches. The men had left. The fire pit smoldered. Smoke snaked into the air.

"Time to go," Ruthie whispered. Her chapped lips were frosted over. She lit a cigarette. And another and another. She looked nervous as if maybe she'd forgotten I'd been with her all night. She wrapped her red scarf around my throat. "You think you can find your way home?"

Home was where my uncle Russell killed himself. I never saw Ruthie again. As I trudged into the woods, I saw flashes of memory—a skinny hallway, fire bursts, instant stillness, a child wandering the street dressed in only a diaper. Dead's death was some kind of sacrifice.

"He *had* to die," my mom explained to me later as if it were obvious. "He broke club rules. He blew off another Pagan's hands without permission." Ruthie had broken the rules too.

A train thundered in the distance and I imagined Dead roaring through the darkness in his classic 1977 Sportster, spitting oil in the street, until he dumped his bike in my driveway.

"Your father was asleep upstairs," my mother recalled as if my uncle's death were a bedtime story she had told me over and over. She looked tired. She crossed her legs, tightened her lips around her cigarette. "Dead stormed into the house." She flicked ash onto my sheets. "He aimed the muzzle of his gun at Maingy's chest." She acted out that part, squinted her eyes and formed her fingers into the shape of a gun.

"Why did Dead shoot *him*?" I asked.

"Maingy gave the club the orders to kill your uncle." She paused. "The thing was, Dead never killed that Pagan, he only *thought* he did."

"Where was I?"

"You were too young to remember," she said dismissively. "Your father blocked the blast with his hands." She paused and her voice grew tight. "After that, everything changed."

I remembered color and sounds, red on white sheets, chunky gray spittle on the walls and lampshade, voices like snapping dogs. Cops burst in, some in uniform, some in plainclothes, some as disheveled as the bikers because they worked surveillance or undercover. They shoved guns in people's faces.

"I ran into the basement because I thought it was the Breed coming to kidnap me," my mom recalled. "I saw what they did to people, the slow torture and buckets of raw shrimp. The cops found me in the basement squeezed between flanks of raw meat in the walk-in freezer, a machete tucked between my thighs ready to cut off their fucking heads."

I recalled my mom's plea and she sounded like Ruthie: "I need to do something about the kid." The room filled with white dust; all our expensive leather, furs, widescreen TVs, crystal bowls—shattered, shred, and gutted. Chunks of foam blew into the corners of the room. That night I waited for my mom, acutely aware that if I moved even a fraction, she might not find me again. Police tape fluttered outside. Night wind banged my front door open. I looked beyond the door, into the night sky full of stars and tiny explosions. I focused on the darkness.

After my mom chose Karl, I stayed for a while at another citizen friend's place. His house boasted a fully stocked refrigerator, a swimming pool, and ordinary family pets such as a dog and large, colorful birds. Nothing complicated. No attachments. No frills. I could be anyone I wanted. No pressure. No accountability. I could drift as any drifter between worlds. That was okay with me. It was better than okay, to pass the hours high in an unbearable quiet. My friend's mom had an ordinary job. Petite and refined, she worked as an artist and designed graphics for government pamphlets. She parlayed her inspiring talent into making fake IDs, birth certificates, and even high school diplomas. Instantly, I had my GED and a new enterprise. If I could make fake documents and sell them to the Pagans, I could dispense with risky street deals, the pounding in my chest and encroaching darkness laced with gunfire. I could forget about romantic ideals of what it meant to be a Pagan, to ride in vans with them loaded with crank and PCP, to be left to toss rocks in alleyways while members conducted church, to be asked to wash bikes because it was honorable and not profitable.

As I sat cross-legged on my friend's roof with the full moon overhead, I inhaled a bowl of angel dust. My mind fogged and the pool below rippled and swelled and turned from an acid blue to a bloodred foam. I felt empowered and in complete control. I now had endless possibilities, fake money, fake death certificates, and fake licenses. I now had credentials. I no longer had to *achieve* anything or pretend to be useful. I *was* useful and I could be anything I wanted.

11

〜〜〜〜〜

Safe

Home was really more about people than shelter. Mine once consisted of tangled limbs, naked women on their knees, blank pellet eyes, skin gouged by rivers of scars. Still, as bad as it was, the alternative was worse. Unwittingly, I had become a drifter, a shadow person whom no one missed or noticed. I wanted to be noticed, and not in the way wolves notice prey just before they attack. I knew what happened to homeless people. Desperation compelled them to do things, vandalize cars, steal clothes, and deflate tires with cinder-block spiked nails. I saw the payback; some were doused with battery acid, others clubbed with pickaxes.

At fourteen, I stayed on and off in an efficiency apartment above the Saint's tattoo business. Other Pagans shared the space with me, sometimes crashing at three o'clock in the morning. I was expected to let them in. I cracked the door and slipped the chain back. I recognized Deuce, a hefty Pagan from the New York chapter. He stared at me through his oversize glasses and with arms the size of tires, motioned for me to produce the keys to the Saint's shop.

Soon after, Evil Ed arrived, dismounted his bike, and stowed it in the alley. He waddled up the street, his arms pumping at his sides, chunky legs like a toad's dropped from his formidable belly. As he emerged from the shadows, he acknowledged me with a nod and ducked into the shop. The lights dimmed inside and Evil Ed lowered the blinds. I stood at the entrance, a kind of sentinel. It would have been inappropriate to leave, disrespectful, yet my role was finished. I had provided access. But no one ordered me home. Gorilla's arrival signaled serious business. As he loped toward the shop door, he grunted at me, his goatee quivering on his flat face. Gorilla's powerfully muscled arms were sleeved with a web of prison tattoos from his days in the Allentown penitentiary.

A car squealed its tires on the curb and my attention diverted to the street. A man dressed in a bloodred skirt, heels, and lipstick stumbled out. His dark, curly wig tipped slightly to the left of his face. He babbled something unintelligible to his passenger and popped open his trunk. The squatty male partner opened the passenger door and stepped out. The two unloaded groceries and glanced at me standing in the shadows of the tattoo shop. Mistake number one.

"Are you lost?" Red Lips sneered, balancing a bag of brightly colored fruit on his hip.

"Fuck you." I flipped him off and watched as the two transvestites tittered and descended the spiral stairs to the basement apartment they rented beneath the Saint's tattoo shop. Through the glass portal, the only window that allowed light into the apartment, I watched their shadows shift. The trunk of their car was still open. More groceries were inside. I waited for Red Lips to emerge, wondering if he'd challenge me.

Part of being safe involved knowing *when* to fight. Skill had nothing to do with it. I was no martial artist or boxer, but I knew how to throw a punch. Red Lips ignored me, brushed past me as if I were invisible or, worse, nonthreatening.

"Is there a problem, kid?" Deuce poked his head outside. Tension had a smell.

Red Lips swished to his car, his heels clicking in the road.

"He's just messing with me," I said, not realizing that my complaint sealed the man's fate. I hadn't asked for Deuce's help, but that was the point: I didn't need to ask.

Deuce grunted and, without a word, marched up to the transvestite, pulled out his buck knife, and plunged the blade between the man's ribs. Shock slid behind the man's eyes. Air whooshed from Red Lips' lungs. His groceries spilled into the street. An apple rolled toward the metal grate. Silence, like expectation, filled the air. The man slumped against Deuce. Blood stained the man's red skirt and spurted onto Deuce's arm. A few drops spattered his vest. The man gurgled, convulsed in Deuce's arms. Deuce calmly removed the blade from the man's ribs, and the transvestite slumped to the pavement.

I stood transfixed near the tattoo shop, paralyzed with fear, stricken with guilt. I had never meant for the man to get stabbed. His had been a foolish exchange with me, a verbal duel; for the first time I realized the power of the Pagans' company. If someone disrespected me, he disrespected the *club*, with terrible consequences. Faces peered in the neighboring windows. Lights clicked on. The moon shone unusually bright. Deuce was lit up as with a spotlight. His blade glinted with blood.

"Gil?" an errant voice called from the basement. Boots clunked on the stairs. Red Lips' partner emerged seconds later. His dark eyes widened at the sight of his friend crumpled in the road, pooled in his own blood. The partner hesitated, raised shaking hands in surrender. His screams tore through the night like bullet spray. He backed into the alley, a cornered animal. He tripped in a pothole and scrambled to his feet. With one last desperate glance, he locked eyes with me, and in that moment I felt sick, sucked into a strange road play where I was suddenly The Witness. My heart raced. Sirens wailed in the distance. Deuce instinctively pocketed the bloody knife and wiped his hands on his vest. Relief washed over me as I heard the transvestite gurgle. At least the man was still alive. My legs froze. Fear paralyzed me. The scene happened in slow motion. My breath filled my head like the roar of a train.

"What's going on out here?" Evil Ed's gaze traveled from Deuce to the body in the road and he frowned.

"Taking care of business." Deuce shrugged and fled into the shadows on foot.

Gorilla motioned to me. "We've got to get out of here."

As the sirens approached, Gorilla pounded on a stranger's apartment and startled the young woman who answered the door. I plastered myself against the wall and struggled for air, careful not to expose my shadow to the window. There were no rules for this kind of thing, just adrenaline. Deuce had defended me. My loyalties were with the club. At the time I lived in mad rationalizations. I didn't ask Deuce to stab the transvestite, but he did. I didn't ask for his help, but it didn't matter, he helped. It wasn't as if we ever discussed whether the punishment fit the crime. Disrespect necessitated reaction. Sometimes overkill. Sometimes just kill. Part of me felt grateful that the club would go to such lengths to prove a point for *me*. That's what members of a *family* did for one another, whether right or wrong. That was the power of the club, the allure of loyalty. Nowhere else had I evoked that kind of immediate and unconditional response, and it felt good. It felt great.

Suddenly it didn't matter anymore *what* happened on the street between Deuce and Red Lips, only that the club *cared* about what happened to me.

Without a word Gorilla muscled his way inside the tiny apartment and clamped a hand over the woman's mouth so she wouldn't scream. He slipped underneath the woman's bed with her and held the frightened lady to his chest just in case she squirmed. I crouched in her bathtub and barely remembered to breathe. I tossed the vinyl shower curtain over my head. Little cornflower-blue petals fluttered around my face. The room was coated in plastic.

"I'm a little claustrophobic," I heard her whisper.

"Shut up, bitch," Gorilla ordered.

I heard fire trucks roar down the street. Giant ladders clattered against the outer brick of the building. White lights flooded the woman's room, flashed over her bed and into the bathroom, where I pressed my back into the porcelain, willing my body to shrink. My fully loaded Ruger dug into my side, and I worried briefly that the gun might accidentally discharge and shoot me in the testicles. Moments ticked by. I heard sounds. The woman's pants, Gorilla's labored breath. I unclenched my fists as I realized the police had no reason to enter the woman's apartment. We were safe. Gorilla released his grip on the woman. She scrambled away from him.

"Please," she begged. Her eyes brimmed with tears.

I put a finger to my lips.

"I won't tell." She drooled. "I won't tell."

"Shut the fuck up," Gorilla said, and I thought he was ready to punch her again.

"I'm not a rat." Her lip trembled.

I peered outside the window. The streets teemed with people, curious onlookers, police crime-scene tape, cones, fire flares. Paramedics placed the body on a stretcher. The man's partner squeezed into the ambulance and pulled the double doors shut. My only thought: *He saw my face.* Gorilla and I slowly eased out of the woman's apartment. Our shadows elongated on the brick walls.

Evil Ed emerged from the basement apartment, poked his head out of the dark hole. He glanced behind him. All clear. But just as he prepared to bolt, I cried out to him, "Evil Ed, Evil Ed, Evil Ed, we're here."

Evil Ed turned toward me, his face sweaty and pale. Without a word, he slapped me hard in the face, knocked the wind from my lungs, and said tightly, "Never yell my name when we're on the run like this."

For several nights afterward, I saw the ghostly image of Red Lips waver in my room. The figure clutched his side. Blood seeped through his fingers. His mouth opened and words blew out like wind: "Payback's a bitch."

With shaking hands, I curled toward the wall and squeezed my eyes shut.

After a while people forgot about the transvestite and business resumed as usual. I performed menial labor in the Saint's shop, answered phones, monitored the customers, watched the street for cops. The primitive pulse of the machines, the flash on the wall, patches of skin pricked with dark curves, bloody edges and pink fringes, were a familiar comfort to me. The place never closed. Like moths to a lamp, strippers, addicts, and strays wandered in from the street after hours. If they had no money, they bartered, ink in exchange for drugs, sex, or something more sinister.

Jed, the Saint's pit bull, curled in a corner of the shop, his large, spiked collar circling his neck. The dog fixed me with penetrating black eyes. Flies buzzed around the animal's nose. He pawed his water bowl until it flipped over. Crows flew in through the open window, fluttered around Jed, their blue-black wings dipping into the puddle. In a flash, Jed lunged, gulped at the air, and swallowed them whole.

A lady stumbled in, a Bank Lady from New York. Dressed in stilettos and a tight black skirt, she announced she wanted to fuck. She needed a quick fix, like a street junkie looking to get high.

The Saint mumbled something about being busy. Jed yawned for effect.

"Why don't you try him?" At the time Jed had testicular cancer.

"I'm allergic to dogs," Bank Lady said, and then, as if it didn't really matter who or what she fucked, she shrugged, knelt, grabbed the animal's penis, and sucked it between her lips. Bank Lady epitomized what the Pagans were all about: no inhibition, no accountability, and no scrutiny. The difference was, Bank Lady had to pretend. She didn't *really* want to fuck a dog. She didn't *really* want to live in our world. She wanted to experience it and then walk away, return to her ordinary life and brag about her thrill or, worse, invent a rape scenario as some women did and implicate a faceless Pagan who kidnapped her at knifepoint and dragged her unwillingly into South Philly. Not to say that it never happened but . . . most women volunteered to be humiliated, to *feel* anything but numb.

At sixteen, more than the *experience* of being part of a group, I wanted to belong. I wanted my first tattoo. Ink, like club colors, branded a Pagan to a particular philosophy, committed him to a way of life that kept him loyal. Of course I was too young to tattoo Pagan Club insignia on my body, but I wanted to memorialize my life memories on a flesh canvas. I had seen members with the initials PMC (Pagan Motorcycle Club), LPDP (Live Pagan, Die Pagan), PFFP (Pagans Forever, Forever Pagans), GFPD (God Forgives, Pagans Don't), PAGANS on the throttle arm, or the

1% diamond. Certain numbers had meaning as well, #4, "live or die"; #5, the German SS motto; #7, "in memory of."

"Maingy should be here for this," the Saint suggested, his needle poised in midair. He worked on Bar Fly's neck, darkened the outline of a large eyeball tattoo, and fleetingly I wondered about its significance. Every tattoo told a story. Unlike conversation, markings made it permanent communicated pain with the telling. Something had happened to the man with the eyeball; he had a reason for putting it on his neck and not in the middle of his forehead, a displaced Third Eye, a sixth sense that betrayed him. I hadn't thought about the image I wanted on my body or the story I wanted to tell. The Saint took care with his customers, listened like a therapist. Sometimes he shared his personal struggles. Once I heard him discuss in vitro fertilization and

Jessie James's tattooed torso depicting typical Pagan insignia, the Zurt Fire God, the 1 percent diamond patch, and a memorial tribute to a fallen brother who was "Loved, Respected, Ride On." *Courtesy of the Saint's collection*

sperm travel with a renowned mobster—two tough guys discussing ways to produce babies and not destroy them. I supposed raising me wasn't the same as raising a *real* son. In the end I belonged to someone else.

"He's out on parole," the Saint added, almost as an afterthought.

I hadn't seen my old man since I was four, but I thought he at least owed me a warning, something to prepare me for his sudden reentry into the role of my father. Foolish of me to think prison could change a person for the *better*. As far as I knew, institutions *created* criminals, or at the very least reinforced an already developed criminal mind. Maingy was like a shark unleashed into a freshwater river. His unsuspecting victims swam uncomfortably in the dark current, unsure why they felt uneasy, why they crunched their knees to their chest, why their heart beat just a little faster in his presence. He could describe the most brutal events as casually as if he had just gutted a fish.

The Saint fulfilled the "father" role for me, a detail that bothered Maingy in theory given his penchant for powerful motorcycles and weak, compliant women and dogs, all possessions he could control. I fit in somewhere after dogs. I have "emotional flashbacks," memories of mewling in the kitchen, of Maingy snapping at my mom, "Can't you get it to shut up?" I purged as a kid, I didn't cry. I admired people who cried. It took real strength to sob, to admit *feeling* anything at all. People who cried evolved. I stayed the same. I didn't get better and I feared I would never get better. Maingy's return reinforced that hopelessness. He never cared about *me*. He cared about position and influence. As an original Mother Club member, Maingy always served as the Pagans' figurehead, the ghost in the room whom everyone feared but no one respected.

"You talked to him?" I tried to sound casual, as if I didn't care, as if Maingy were just a curiosity. But inside I imploded and worried that the tremor in my hands might telegraph my rage. Maingy never talked *to* people, he talked at them and mostly through them if he wanted something. Pressure pulsed at my temple. I wanted to smash things, put my fist through a wall, inhale so much dope that the burn scorched my throat.

"He wants his old job back." The Saint paused.

"The position's been filled," I said, but I knew what he meant. Slow Poke would have to go. It wasn't fair but it was righteous. I liked Slow Poke. He was harmless.

The Saint lifted his needle, dabbed at the blood beads on Bar Fly's neck.

"Can't we just make Maingy go away?" I wiped the pay phone with my chamois. It rang. Once. Twice, just as it did when Dagger was holed up in his cabin. At one time I didn't even want to *look* at a phone; rings

LT with former Pagan President "Jerry Fox." *Courtesy of the Saint's collection*

signaled tragedy, someone overdosed, took a bullet, died of natural causes.

The Saint paused, waited a beat, then pressed his needle into Bar Fly's skin. "It's not that simple."

The Saint invited my old man. But Maingy had a nonassociation clause as a condition of his parole, and he couldn't be seen in the company of other Pagans, other felons. I hoped that detail would be deterrent enough. But surprisingly he showed. Maybe curiosity compelled him? I expected him to wear some sort of disguise, a wig at least, or insist on being smuggled inside the tattoo shop rather than risk exposure. But that would have been a sign of weakness, deference even to the system Maingy had conned for his early release. Maingy had looked smaller than I remembered, stocky and sure as a pit bull. He had the same constipated expression he had when I visited him as a child for prison picnics. I didn't realize then that my visits signaled dope deliveries, that I served as some sort of decoy. My mom and I traveled the interstate in a hatchback hauling garbage bags full of weed. I squeezed into the window dome, my face plastered against the glass, and flipped off the highway patrol as they drove by.

"You motherfucker." My mom veered off the freeway onto the shoulder so she could smack me. Once at the prison, my mom and I dragged our garbage bags filled with dope out of the hatchback and propped them at the fence alongside identical others filled with cut grass. The guards never knew the difference. That's how my mom smuggled drugs in to my old man.

"We're family," she said simply. "Families do things for each other."

I remember sitting at an acre of picnic table trying to catch a glimpse of my old man. He grunted at my mom, forgot I existed, and laughed knowingly with the guards.

Entering the tattoo shop, Maingy said to the Saint, "I could use a retouch."

LT at age five in Maingy's arms visiting Maingy at Dalles Prison in eastern Pennsylvania; also pictured from left to right, Kim Menginie (LT's mom) and Aunt Joann (LT's aunt). *Courtesy of Anthony "LT" Menginie's collection*

My heart raced at the sight of him. I chewed on handfuls of Percocets and ecstasy hoping to the dull the pain of the needle. I invited my citizen friends. Chal shot me a canary grin: "This is it, man." He rubbed his hands together, flopped dramatically into the tattoo chair, and writhed in imaginary pain. I rarely allowed Chal a glimpse into my Pagan life. I worried if he knew too much, he might judge, accuse, or discard me. More than that, what frightened me the most was not what was *different* about our lives, but what was strikingly the same. In the end it didn't matter that my old man had abandoned me as a child,

LT at age five visiting his father, Anthony Menginie (aka "Maingy"), at the Dalles prison in eastern Pennsylvania for one of his "prison picnics." Maingy had to bribe the inmate who snapped the photograph with chocolate bars. *Courtesy of Anthony "LT" Menginie's collection*

served prison time, or led a violent motorcycle gang. That was just the explanation and excuse. I was fucked-up because I was fucked-up. My old man was just another son of a bitch whose acceptance I wanted.

"Do you even have enough flesh to put a needle *through*?" the Saint mocked me, and I don't think he meant to be cruel. I *was* birdlike, skinny from hunger, all color leached out of me. But I thought if I could just belong to something, have permanent markings, I might make progress at least.

I closed the vinyl blinds at the Saint's tattoo shop and bent a slat. I peered into the empty street. The Saint's business sign buzzed red on his roof. I clicked the dead bolt on the front door. Mr. Big stood like a giant muscle at the entrance. He was the perfect bouncer. He picked people up for no reason, slammed them into walls, crushed their faces with his fist, and wielded a heavy construction chain because he liked the way it sounded when it clattered to the floor. It didn't matter that he once killed a man, that he spent five years in prison for his crime. What really irked Mr. Big was that the court insisted he pay for his victim's funeral.

"Have you decided what you're going to get?" Chal asked me. An artist worked on Maingy's elbow web tattoo. I scanned the rows of stencils, the flash designs that covered the wall, and slipped into the large chair that resembled an ancient torture apparatus.

"Can you do it on my chest?" I asked the Saint.

He laughed quietly, pinched a clump of loose skin. A small crowd gathered around me. Oval eyes blinked at me; faces elongated and sounds amplified. I craned my neck to see past the bodies, to see my old man's reaction, but his chair was empty. I deflated, as if someone had stuck a pin in my side. My heart thundered in my chest. Probably a side effect of the drugs. As a child I had learned to detach myself from ugliness, transform whole scenes into blood-berried orchards or grass-

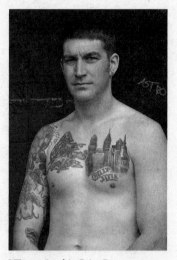

LT sporting his Grim Reaper tattoo." *Courtesy of Melissa Marsella*

lands littered with cattle and fresh-faced farm families who soothed with their eyes. But as I grew older, it became harder to find those pretty places. The orchards had all been stripped, and rotten fruit bruised patches of dirty heat. The farms had scarecrows and all the cattle had died. The people who once comforted me had morphed into beggars.

"Where's Maingy?" I managed, although I already knew the answer.

"He left," the Saint said quietly, wiping his tools. He didn't look at me, didn't want to see the hurt that had transformed to rage.

My head buzzed with white noise. I stared at the needle in the Saint's hand.

"What's it going to be?" he prompted.

"The Grim Reaper."

12

∿∿∿∿∿

Bitch-Slapped

Getting a tattoo didn't change much for me except that I felt branded, marked the way an animal is stamped as part of a herd. But I wasn't *officially* part of anything. At most I was the club's honorary prospect. I wasn't even sure I wanted *that* much responsibility. But I won't lie, I did like the perks. Pretty women smiled at me, impressed that I could mix with one-percenter bikers. Citizens stared at me admiringly, secretly wishing *they* too could wear badass. Being with the Pagans and getting my first tattoo had almost the same allure as wearing a uniform, like putting on an alter ego. In the bikers' company, I *became* the tough guy they imagined. I understood finally the power of the patch; when bikers put on their vests, they commanded instant respect, recognition, and prowess. They could stand in a crowded room and luxuriate in the attention. They never had to feel lonely or useless or dejected.

The Saint epitomized the biker image; he wore expensive leather dusters, the kind that strapped to his leg and made him look like a

Jessie James and the Saint. *Courtesy of the Saint's collection*

real cowboy when he straddled his motorcycle. He attracted people like moths—women, tough guys, me. He owned more than thirty-seven bikes at once, dressed his old lady in Gucci and Guess?—even dressed *me* in Guess? For hours at a time I pretended I was classy, rich, respected. It was all about respect. It didn't matter that sometimes I didn't shower for a week.

It didn't matter much who the girl was, only that I had a girl for the evening. I had become something of a sex addict, needing my fix each night like a heroin junkie. I made regular trips to Philadelphia twice a week, hung out in dive bars until closing, and charmed my prey. Girls twittered around me like squab, dazzled by my tattoos, positively glowing at my dangerous life. I fed them drugs, pills, and booze. My motto was Fuck, Chuck, Next.

But there was always a price for recklessness. At the time I still lived above the Saint's tattoo shop, an arrangement that brought obligations. I was never really free. I had planned my regular excursion to Philadelphia one night. It was approaching dusk. Under my bed I stashed my collection of high-top Nike sneakers, one in every style. I chose a bloodred pair, ran my thumb over the rough texture of the canvas, snaked the laces through the cool metal grommets. I owned the shoes, purchased them with earnings from my auto body job. No one could steal them off my feet. That was big. Apart from dope, I never possessed anything. Ownership led to power, collateral, and freedom.

I popped my head into the Saint's tattoo shop. "I'm going out for a while."

He flashed me a poster of the Big Four outlaw motorcycle gangs—the Hells Angels, the Outlaws, the Bandidos, and the Pagans. I knew he had stolen it from the police department. The Saint rolled the poster, tapped the sides, and slid a rubber band around the tube.

"I need twenty copies, laminated," he ordered, and tossed me the job. The nearest Kinko's was at least thirty blocks away, easily a forty-minute jaunt. Silence stretched between us. I tempered my irritation, thought fleetingly of my lost evening, and climbed into my car. I never refused the Saint and certainly not for anything as insignificant as a girl.

The afternoon faded and the skyline plumed purple. I rolled down my window and listened to the chorus of screeching cars. Washers rattled in the middle console and reminded me of the road game I had witnessed some Pagans play. For protection, or to deter possible surveillance, they tossed washers out the window, hoping to shatter the windshield of some unsuspecting motorist, to hear metal crunch and watch busted glass spray onto the highway. No one saw them. No one called the cops. Most probably thought an errant bird had flown into its own reflection.

The Kinko's sign flickered at me from the street. I parallel-parked, scraped the door of my car on the curb, tucked the poster in the crook of my armpit, and went inside. The place was crowded, full of suits and heels and people that didn't look like me. I approached the counter, feeling like a foul wind as customers recoiled and brushed past me.

A teenager took my order, and as I waited, I scanned the array of office supplies, paper, pens, folders, and accessories I would never need. Minutes ticked by. Soon it was dark outside. Kinko's emptied. Fluorescent lights blazed above my head, made me dizzy, agitated. I caught my reflection in the black window glass. Leather jacket, high-top sneakers, ripped jeans, short-cropped hair. I didn't *look* different from the other customers. But it didn't matter. The poster spoke volumes. Outlaws. The Big Four. "Terror Campaign." I was from the other side, the side that rebelled against the establishment, the side that *caused* America's problems.

"Here you go," the teenager said, practically shoving the posters at me.

It was close to nine o'clock by the time I drove back to the tattoo shop hoping to salvage my evening. I weaved through traffic, tailgating, signaling with my hands as if I were on a bike, and nearly collided with a couple in a Honda. I felt drunk with recklessness. A rush coursed through me at the couple's stricken faces, their white-knuckled driving, their poker stares straight ahead in the darkness as if I didn't exist.

Close your eyes. I'm not here. Fear was a powerful toxin. I had played that same game over and over as a child. I called it snow blindness—too bright to miss, too painful to stare. *If I close my eyes, maybe they won't see me.* I parked the car in the alley, slammed the door shut, and walked into the tattoo shop. The posters were now stiff, cumbersome, laminated. I balanced them on my hip. The place teemed with customers. The Saint huddled in conversation with another Pagan I knew only as the Gorilla. He dangled his short legs over the side of the desk, looked up, and registered me as if I were a fly that had buzzed in unexpectedly.

"What do you have there, lad?" The Gorilla nodded toward the posters.

I showed him.

"Can I have one?" He turned to the Saint.

"Make us five more copies." The Saint snapped his fingers at me.

"No fucking way," I protested, and immediately regretted my outburst.

The Saint's expression turned dark, his neck corded. He slapped me hard in the face with such force that I reeled from the blow, stumbled backward, and dropped the posters. They fell to the floor. I put up my hands to deflect another slap. My cheek throbbed. Pain shot up my left side. Gorilla fixed me with flat, black eyes. Oddly I felt inspired, not humiliated. The Saint had, unwittingly, just treated me like a prospect.

"Maybe you didn't hear me." The Saint leaned in close, his breath in my ear. I heard him. I heard him loud and clear. I had crossed some invisible line. Gorilla was someone important, someone the Saint needed to impress, someone I needed to respect. The language had suddenly changed. I was now part of a code. As I regained composure, dabbed at my bloody lip, I overheard Gorilla say to the Saint, "That kid's serious."

"I raised him," the Saint said with pride. "He's good people." He called after me, "Hey, try not to get arrested."

Suddenly I didn't mind climbing back into the car and shutting the door. *Try not to get arrested,* the Saint had warned. I didn't make a habit of going to jail. I was arrested once when I was ten for stealing a backhoe at a construction site, but otherwise I had led a pretty clean existence.

I sat for several minutes inside the car, listening to the silence, aware of the stillness. Relief washed over me. I felt . . . safe. It was after nine.

I paged Rebecca something or other to let her know I was going to be late and put the keys in the ignition. But I didn't return to Kinko's. Instead, I drove to New Jersey, idled in a dark alley two blocks from the party I was supposed to attend, and beeped my date. My car lit up with red strobe.

"Got any ID on you?" A local cop tapped on my window and shone his flashlight in my face.

"Did I do something wrong?" I shrugged, aware that I had a knife in my pocket. I had no reason to fear the cops; I'd always had a decent rapport with the locals. When I was a child, I fed them hoagies while they conducted surveillance on my house. I'd ride right up to their tinted windows, knock on the glass, shove wrapped sandwiches between the cracks. They'd laugh, amused, thank me for the gesture. I was just "that Pagan kid," the one they delivered home to my mom after they caught me riding the neighborhood on my dirt bike. Even then I liked riding in the dark, feeling the wind against my face, the rush of being alone.

"You're a nuisance." The cop tapped on my window with his baton and motioned for me to exit. Across the street I spotted a drunk asleep on the picnic table, and I thought I was staring at my own reflection. I opened my door, climbed out. The cop tapped my legs apart with his baton.

"Hands on the hood." More orders.

I couldn't help but think maybe on some level the cops appreciated what the Pagans did for them. Biker and cop understood each other and practiced the same code of silence when it was convenient. The Pagans never started trouble, they *reacted* to it. And they were polite about it when they got caught: "Sorry, Officer. I would help you if I could, but I can't identify anyone." It was a game—a blindman's buff. As long as everyone was professional, no one got hurt.

But cops had a darker side too, the side that took my father away, that shoved a gun to my mom's temple and left me alone in an empty house, snow falling outside, white space.

My pocket beeped.

"What's this?" The officer retrieved a knife from my side. The blade glinted in the darkness.

"Protection," I said simply.

"You won't need this where you're going."

My jail cell was a cage that smelled of wet stone and stale beer. I sat on the edge of a bare metal bench and stared into dark haze. Feet shuffled in a corner, a man moaned next to me. Someone spit on the wall. Depression sank in. I had never been arrested before for "real" charges, and some small part of me had hoped when I *was* finally cuffed the charges against me would be more glamorous, more important, more worthy. I had heard that some people subconsciously *wanted* to be caught, like murderers who couldn't help their habit, who craved killing the way others craved chocolate, once a day, once a month, whatever the addiction, and the only means of stopping that bloodlust was to be confined. Maybe they had the strange delusion that law enforcement could help them, that the structure of prison or jail could quiet the cruel voices in their head. But that wasn't my situation. I wasn't a criminal; I was just being ordered to act like one.

"What did they get you for?" a voice grunted.

"Being a nuisance."

"Shit, man, we all pests." The man laughed and shook his head. He had large gold teeth and thick hands that tapped his knees. *I'm not like you. I'm nothing remotely like you.* But the truth was I was *exactly* like him—guilty until proven innocent, thrown into a piss hole, confused, scared, and claustrophobic. Familiar panic clogged my throat. *I have to get out of here. I have to call someone to bond me out.* But that was just it, I didn't have anyone. Not really. I couldn't bother the Saint. He expected me to be making duplicates.

"No one belongs here."

A few hours later, my date, Rebecca something or other, pressed her face to the bars.

"You coming?" she sighed.

13

NNNNN

A Real Killer

After I bonded out of jail I needed to get my own place, something I didn't have to share with night visitors, a place where I was no one's witness, no one's bitch boy. I plopped my trash bag of clothes in the middle of the one-bedroom apartment I rented in a duplex in Marcus Hook, a low-income borough in Delaware County. The place was cheap, mostly vacant, and convenient, just five blocks from my job at the auto body shop. The slumlord squinted at me suspiciously and twirled his keys. Maybe he was incredulous that anyone would *want* such a dump, but I was desperate. A sixteen-year-old had few choices. As it was, the Saint agreed to cosign the lease for me. The stench of rotten eggs filtered through the cracked windows. Black soot coated the walls from the refinery nearby. The place was bare of furniture. But I had a small TV, and my trash bag could double as a blanket. I took the keys from Slumlord and shut the door in his face. I smoothed the trash bag out in the middle of the floor and breathed. My fingers left a spider imprint in the fine layer of dust.

The room filled with gray afternoon light. No lamps, no bald, suspended bulbs from the ceiling, just approaching darkness. It felt good. It felt great. I stood by the window, attracted to the street bustle, the strays that scuttled along the curb in their spiked heels, the dogs with bloody sores in their eyes. They had a little of me in them, a desperate edge that made them hard. I detached from the scene. I now carried a gun. Just in case I too acted on impulse. No one ever practiced killing, just rehearsed skill sets, on-the-spot training. Like the time a Pagan member, Sailor Eddy, visited the Saint's tattoo shop. A stocky Italian with a wide grin, he had clumpy hair and pudgy, oversize mitts.

"Right here, kid." He snapped his fingers at me, touched the jowls in his neck. "Press both thumbs into the soft, fleshy part." I leaned in, recoiled from the stench of Sailor Eddy's soiled vest, and jammed my thumbs into his neck. I found the pressure points.

"Like this?" I asked, eager to please.

Sailor Eddy's face turned ashen. His eyes rolled back in his head. He gurgled. His legs buckled. He slumped forward and his head banged into the metal cooler. *Shit*. I dropped to my knees, put my hand to the back of Sailor's head. No blood. I felt for a pulse.

"Tell me you didn't kill him?" The Saint looked up from his stenciling, needle poised midair, mild worry furrowing his brow. "Sailor *Amnesia* might need a hospital."

In the darkness of my apartment, I woke to the sound of clicking. My bag moved. My legs and arms tickled. Slowly, I peeled back the bag, waited for my eyes to adjust, and watched slick, lumpy shapes dart across my skin. My head tingled and a wisp of hair fell across my face. I stood shakily, and my bare feet crushed something soft and squishy. It popped like a fish eye.

I snapped on my flashlight. Roaches. Hundreds of them spewed from cracks in the walls and chased the smooth column of my leg. My heart raced. My first instinct was to blast them with bullets. *Reflexive action.* My hand stilled on the butt of my gun. If I was lucky, I might strike one or two. The rest would simply scatter like ripples in a pond, hide in the walls, and reemerge the next night. I lit a blunt, inhaled, and picked up my sneaker. I threw it against the wall. Score. I picked it up, aimed again. Score. A surge of power coursed through me. I decided which roach should die.

My hand stilled in midair and it occurred to me for the first time that *I* was a kind of killer, although there were certainly degrees of killers. Some killed out of a raw need, like sex, which explained why serial murderers were sometimes married with families, why there were time lapses in the body count, why some picked up strangers and drove around with them hoping to release tension. Some killed out of instinct. Others had motive. Some, perhaps the cruelest, killed indirectly. My old man may have inspired bloodletting but he was too much of a coward to actually *kill* anyone himself. Others were like Brutus, the massive Pagan who once hustled drugs for Maingy and used his own wife for target practice until she finally relented and swallowed Brutus's shotgun.

I was afraid to sleep. I had no cotton to stuff my ears. If a roach crawled inside . . . I might just lose it. The critters were incapable of reverse. They would get stuck in the cavity, flail their legs; scream in the hollow of my ear canal. I stared at my roach-stained walls and counted the casualties. I plugged up the drains in my bathroom, shoved my trash bag in the band of light under the door, watched as roaches dropped from the ceiling unharmed and skittered across the floor. I took a broom to them, a shoe. Roaches streamed from the cracks until it looked as if the whole room shimmered.

"I'll kill 'em for you," Bar Fly offered the next day at the Saint's shop.

"I need more than muscle," I said.

"How about a bomb?"

"That should do it."

Bar Fly solicited reinforcements, his buddy Joey Gaitor, a former painter who, after placing his ladder on railroad tracks, survived an electrocution. Gaitor's sister owned an exterminator company.

"Have you ever used this stuff?" I asked as we surveyed Gaitor's sister's shop at 1:00 a.m. and borrowed machines that resembled steam cleaners with giant hoses.

"This'll be our test run," Gaitor said.

"I can't pay you," I said. I had no money at the time.

"Can you manage a case of beer?"

We ascended the stairs to my apartment, opened the door, and blasted the inside. A chemical fog plumed in the room so thick no one could see his hand in front of his face. Bar Fly wore no protective mask, but he removed his shirt, wet it in the sink, and wrapped it around his face. In the dense white, roaches plopped from the walls, the ceiling, and cracks in the windows. Bar Fly and Gaitor blasted the vacant rooms next door, the downstairs apartment that housed a Chinese family with small children.

"You need to get out." It was two in the morning. The woman stared at me. We had never met. From her expression I guessed I must have looked like a crazed hoodlum with my wild mane of hair, bloodshot eyes, and two tattooed badasses in tow.

"I live here," she said in broken English. A slight woman, she had a face like porcelain. Thin hands trailed her throat, wrapped around her gold chain.

"We need to blast your apartment. The fumes will kill you," I warned.

"No." She tried to shut the door in my face.

I shoved my foot against the jamb. "You don't understand, lady. This isn't negotiable." If I didn't bomb each apartment, the roaches would simply disperse to the untreated ones and reemerge again when the chemicals wore off.

She looked at me, narrowed her eyes.

"Where you want me to go?" She took a defiant stance, hands on her hips.

"I don't give a fuck *where* you go. Just leave."

She blinked at me, considering my demand, nodded, and put up a hand. "You wait." She woke up her children. They emerged groggy, disheveled, unfazed by me and my roach gang. A pall of apprehension clouded the woman's face as she passed Bar Fly, toweled in his shirt, lugging a machine with a hose, Gaitor, sleeved to the wrists, and me, wheezing in her doorway. That the woman didn't call the police was a testament to the crime in the neighborhood and not, necessarily, to her implicit trust in me.

Bar Fly moved in, fogged up the one-bedroom apartment until it looked like a winter blizzard. Days afterward roaches streamed from my walls like an armored brigade. They died slowly in the chemical haze, littering the floor with soft brown shells.

Exhausted, I slept for two days in a car husk at the auto body shop. I had vivid dreams of stocked freezers, sliced pig parts, flanks of steak, food enough to sustain me for a month. No welfare checks. No blocks of yellow cheese. No Pop-Tarts and definitely no pizza.

"Jed's missing." The Saint paced his tattoo shop. His face was flushed. A muscle in his jaw ticked. He looked as if he might explode. I had never seen him so agitated. After working a ten-hour day detailing cars at the body shop, exhaustion pulsed through me. But sleep was a luxury I couldn't afford, and the thought of curling into my trash bag in my now fumigated apartment didn't appeal. I preferred the hum of action. The Saint put me to work wiping the flash on his wall.

"What do you mean *missing*?" I paused midswipe, but I knew the dog was gone.

"Someone took him." The Saint produced a notepad with a scribbled address. "The guy lives in the projects." We were going for a ride. I never asked how the Saint gathered his information. I just knew he had his sources. All it took was a simple phone call, a hushed conversation, coded words. It didn't matter *how* the Saint knew the identity of Jed's kidnapper, only what the Saint planned to do to him, and it usually involved violence. He called it "taking care of business."

I much preferred the club's swift justice to the drama of the courtroom. At least at the end of the day everybody *felt* better. Even if the dog never returned, at least the son of a bitch who swiped him would get what he deserved. Unlike in court, there really was only *one* story: Jed was missing. The whole innocent-until-proven-guilty thing really had no place in my world. My old man had a trial; he became a chef in prison, a perfect job for a drug dealer. He just changed his operation, smuggled the dope inside oranges, flour, meat. He probably liked prison. At least he could save money. No family to support. No mortgage to pay. No responsibilities. No worries that his own brothers would try to blow his head off. As a felon he had enormous freedom.

I hadn't been to the projects in years. As a general rule Pagans avoided the black townships. But for a time when I was a preteen, I thought I might want to *be* black, live a life I *chose* rather than a life I inherited. For a while I even joined a black street gang called the Double Light Posse. I think I mostly joined for the food, large seafood spreads in nightclubs. I was accepted in the ghetto even though I was the token white boy. It started with casual drug deals and hand-to-hand negotiations on the outskirts of the barbed-fenced community that resembled a prison more than a neighborhood. But then I met Rich, a member of the Atlantic City Skinheads, who preferred to date black women. I found that detail useful since it gave me instant credibility with the black drug dealers. Rich and I both raced BMX bikes, but Rich was considerably older than me, and judging from his arsenal of weapons, he had a darker agenda. I didn't realize at the time that Rich tolerated me because I helped him buy drugs.

The Saint climbed into his Lincoln, a pistol shoved into his waistband. I followed in my truck. Unease itched up my spine. Death hung in the air like expectation. It was dusk and the brick buildings in the Bartram projects shimmered with an eerie gold glow. Barbed wire barricaded the homes. Trash blew onto the sidewalks. The streets were deserted. The Saint drove to a corner row house I instantly recognized as Rich's. The son of a bitch probably had no idea whose dog he stole.

"I know this house," I shouted through my open window.

"You *know* this house?" The Saint screeched his tires, aimed at the broken windows, and emptied two rounds. Firepower sprayed the walls. Glass shattered. Curtains blew in the gaping holes. Lights snapped off. Bullets ricocheted off garbage cans and parked cars stacked like mere husks along the street. Screams resounded. A baby wailed. Then silence. Eerie silence. The Saint backed out of the projects slowly, like a shark carefully swimming down-current.

But that wasn't the end of it. The Saint still wanted his dog.

"The asshole used Jed as a bait animal," the Saint's brother reported. Pit bulls bred for fights whet their appetite for blood on small pets, like Jed, that had been stolen expressly for "practice." The fighting pit was no doubt unleashed to maul Jed for hours, perhaps even drifting to sleep with his jaws locked on Jed's throat. "We found him caged and anchored to a pole by a weighty construction chain."

"Motherfucker." The Saint cradled Jed and choked back tears. It was the first time I had ever seen the Saint show emotion. The dog was listless, cold to the touch, and bundled in a blanket. Blood crusted Jed's eyes and ears. He had a jagged scar on his hind leg, and one of his front canine teeth had been dislodged.

"We found him asleep with his jaw locked on another dog's throat." Stitches clamped Jed's upper lip.

"I hope I killed the fucker who took him."

It turned out, the Saint missed. Justice came unexpectedly years later while the Saint and I attended a tattoo convention at the Radisson Hotel in Essington, Pennsylvania. I spotted Rich sucking down a beer in the hotel bar as if he had been there for years just waiting for a purpose, an expiration date, like spoiled fruit on a grocery shelf. Rich looked the same, still shaved, still square-cut and still an asshole. He had a different stray with him. I had heard it rumored that his black girlfriend had committed suicide. But none of this mattered to the Saint. He reacted like a bull to the news that Rich was close enough to strangle. He stood in the hotel room and removed his jewelry. Gold chains dropped into the ashtray. He slipped off his knuckle ring, unclasped his chunky bracelet.

When the two finally confronted each other in the bar, Rich bolted. But the revolving hotel door acted like instant suction, trapping him between glass panels and making him a perfect target for the Saint. My job was to contain the Saint's old lady. She wriggled in my grip like a wet puppy, hollering and yelping for the Saint to stop punching Rich with his fists. As the blood splattered inside the revolving door, no one in the hotel called the police. The lobby bustled with people. The convention continued. Guests streamed through different doors.

We were a moment in their busy day, a blip of violence, much like a commercial on the television screen. They could tune us out, shake their heads, and pretend they didn't notice.

Maybe after a while I didn't notice either?

I sought comfort in women. Staci, a striking redhead with pale blue eyes and a fringe of freckles on the bridge of her nose, was elegant, otherworldly, and she spoke in full sentences. We were an unmatched pair. I was a work in progress; she had achieved perfection. She maneuvered easily in social settings and taught me manners without insulting my pride. She represented, for the first time, some kind of commitment. I *dated* her for several months; I didn't just fuck her. She was the first woman who looked past my unfashionable clothes, my awkward haircut, and my coarse Philadelphia accent.

"Maybe you should show her off to Maingy?" the Saint encouraged.

From left to right: Paulie, (an unknown pagan), Mr. Big, and LT at tattoo convention sporting Pagan T-Shirts: "Support 30 Years of Madness." *Courtesy of Anthony "LT" Menginie's collection*

"Why?" But I knew what the Saint meant. Whatever else Staci meant to me, she was a prize, a trophy I could display, a symbol I could use to convey the one message I wanted to spit at my father—*I did okay without you. Look who wants me, you motherfucker. Can you do better?*

"He owes you a meal." The Saint shrugged.

He owes me a lot of things. "He might devour her." I was pretty certain my old man never thought of women as human beings. Most in the club considered them property. The lookers had a harder time of it. Pretty just made them more desirable, more abused, lonelier. I never saw a pretty woman who didn't hate herself. My mom was a cutter. Staci hung with me. I dated a college girl once, a psychology major who plucked me from a park one day after I finished a job in the affluent neighborhood of Lower Marion. I did nice things for her. I bought her watery ice on hot days. She fucked me. I might have been her thesis? She studied me after sex as if I were a rare curiosity, a strange combination of innocence and pain. I'm sure I needed therapy. I turned to drugs instead. It wasn't that they were cheaper, just more accessible. It gave us something in common, and at least for a while we became each other's habit.

But I never stayed with women long enough for them to fix me. Part of me didn't believe I deserved it; the other part of me didn't want to relive the darkness.

"Give him a chance."

"Why?" I had a three-strikes rule. A person could be an asshole to me three times before I discarded him or her. Three seemed to be a good number. A lot of important events happened in threes: wishes; baseball; the Trinity; the life cycle: birth, life, death; past, present, future; mandatory prison sentences. I had even heard somewhere that the number three appeared 523 times in the Bible. My old man so far had only one strike. It never occurred to me then that the Saint had his own motive for encouraging the awkward reunion. The Saint wanted to show off *me*. I was some kind of prize pig going to market: the Saint had spent a lifetime feeding me, weaning me, *being* the farmer. Maingy now wanted a turn. But the hard work was done. All Maingy had to do was eat. And I wasn't sure I was up for that.

Staci and I drove in silence to Maingy's row house, a redbrick building in west Philadelphia. The place was eerily close to my childhood home, and the memories assaulted me. I parallel-parked, exited, and slammed the door shut. My skin pebbled. Something didn't fit. *How did the fucker get a house so soon? He's only been out a few weeks.* The thought nagged at my conscience. It took me a while to connect the dots. Later, I would learn that Maingy lived just three blocks from the Hells Angels' clubhouse.

Staci took my hand as we walked up the gravel path to the front door. Her short skirt hugged her ass. Wind fluttered the fringes of her clean, shiny hair. Fresh grass sprung from cracks in the pavement. Guilt consumed me. I knew I should turn around. I couldn't subject Staci to *him*. I wished I were stronger. But I spoke the only language I knew how to speak with my old man, the language of competition.

At the front door, I hesitated, knocked. My old man cracked it open, squinted at me as if I were an ingredient and Staci a main dish. He widened the opening, draped a dishrag over his shoulder, ran a hand through his greasy, unkempt hair, and smiled the way a hyena smiles even as it scavenges.

"Come in." He ushered us inside and his gaze lingered too long on Staci's chest.

The place was dark and smelled of mold. Cobwebs draped the ceiling fan. A fine layer of dust coated the overstuffed leather couches and easy chair. The carpet needed a vacuum. Some of the vinyl blinds were cracked. A bullet hole pierced one window.

"Tara, they're here," Maingy hollered to the thin, cronelike woman in the kitchen. Tara waved a large stirring spoon at us and grinned. She was wearing a khaki shirt with 69 stitched on the back. She was missing a front tooth and the rest of her mouth was rotten and pointy. She had short-cropped hair that looked razor-shaved. Hot water dripped onto her hand from the spoon and she swore. Tara's vacant expression told me she was just going through the motions. Even in poor lighting the skin on her cheeks mottled bluish yellow, and I knew prison hadn't changed Maingy; it had empowered him. Even if Tara *wanted* to leave Maingy, she couldn't. He had become the center of her small world, and the more he abused her, the more she believed she deserved it. Tara was one of many replacement women, and I knew she too, like my mom, would spiral into self-loathing, her need so great she would turn to pills, razors, sex, anything to dull the pain.

"Sit down." Maingy gestured to the kitchen table with no settings.

Staci hesitated, a fraction too long, before settling into her chair.

"How long have you had this place?" I hedged, my fingers tracing the vinyl tablecloth. Everything in the place looked covered up and preserved.

"A little while."

A little while? As in days? Years? Had the fucker had the place the whole time he was in prison? The whole time my mom and I struggled? Survived on welfare checks, lived in hovels unfit for even animals? Had someone paid the rent for twelve years on an empty house? Blood drained from my face. My throat parched. I felt like a long scream. I glanced at Staci. She stared at the floor, folded and unfolded her skirt. I should have left, but I was paralyzed, ravaged by hunger.

"His parents kept it up for him while he was in prison," Tara chattered. Her words hit me like a punch to the gut. Maingy pinched Tara's ass, completely unfazed by her revelation. He grinned at me but his eyes remained the same, and it occurred to me that no matter what Maingy's mood—anger, irritation, excitement—his eyes remained the same. His cold, penetrating stare riveted and unsettled with a malign intensity I found spooky.

"Who's hungry?" He clapped his hands together.

As the meatballs steamed on my plate, my mind filled with images of loss, my childhood, being left in the snow without shoes or a coat, pawned off to alcoholics or drug addicts, hungry, emotionally starved, wandering wet streets, eating canned potatoes, meat, and clumpy chunks I never imagined *could* be canned or meat. I didn't pick up my fork. A chill coursed through me. I found it difficult to look at my old man. His gaze confused me. I couldn't decipher his intentions or emotions. I'm not sure he had any.

I wanted to throw the hot plate into Maingy's face, burn him, scar him the way he had scarred me. Cruelty to children was just one characteristic of a psychopath. But for me it was the only one that mattered.

"What kind of father does that to his son?" I asked my friend later.

"A motherfucker," Chal remarked. "If it were *me,* I'd kill him."

14

1 Percent

*No one graduates from Harvard and decides to join the
Pagans. Although the club did have a graduate from Vanderbilt once, but education is not a requirement.*

—ANONYMOUS

But of course it was never that simple. I couldn't *really* kill my old
man. Preserving a smelly, rotten house for years was technically
only Maingy's first strike, although he had always generally been an
asshole. In prison my old man never called, never wrote, never apologized, and never acknowledged he *had* a son at all. Those should have
counted as strikes, but I had degrees of asshole just as the club had
degrees of nonconformity. Maingy qualified as the 1 percent of Pagans who considered the club's rules inconvenient, unreasonable, and
generally an impediment to his own advancement.

But even the club had standards; not everyone was invited to join.

"We didn't want 'fillers,'" the Saint explained, uncapping his beer bottle with his teeth and settling onto the steps of the clubhouse. "We wanted mentally tough prospects, people who could bench-press three hundred pounds but still form a sentence. Mice can't attract lions. Only lions attract lions.

"You don't get to be the vice president of this club without earning the rank. Mongo sponsored me into the club when I was only eighteen. At that time initiation took place at the Farm. I packed sneakers with me even though Mongo warned me to wear boots just in case I had to kick someone's head in.

"The Farm was muddy, hilly, and dotted with rusty tractor-trailer husks. Part of the hazing involved rolling down grassy mounds in crapped-out machinery and wooden barrels. You have to understand, I prospected during a time of paranoia. Jimmy D had just ratted out twenty-two of his own on federal racketeering charges, including your old man." Later I learned that the Saint prospected during the time of Nicky B., the Pagan who, according to the newspapers, cut off his prospect's finger *accidentally* with an ax and then killed him because he tired of the prospect's attitude. B. had at the time just completed a ten-year prison run. He would later become a federal informant and eventually serve thirty years for the second-degree murder of a pledge.

The judge dismissed B., deemed him to be a "danger to the community," and puzzled why "a person with a stable job and family would want to join the motorcycle gang" in the first place. Joining the club wasn't ever a conscious choice for me; I already lived the lifestyle. But even a person *born* into organized crime makes mad rationalizations and fashions a code of felonious ethics that somehow justifies degrees of unacceptable behavior. Like stealing bread from a business and not a person because you're hungry and not because you're mean. I already knew that. I didn't need a club to tell me that. But the idea of unconditional acceptance was pretty potent. I'd pass any test to have some of that.

"That asshole had me chopping wood, disassembling the barn, re-assembling the logs, fetching beer, a blunt. I was his bitch." The Saint sobered. "Until one day he up and shot me with his .357 Magnum before he bashed my head in. He didn't appreciate my attitude either. He kept me awake for four to five days at a stretch, made me ingest meth, starved me, and turned me into a predator so that by the end of that six-month run *I* wanted to kill." The Saint finished his beer.

"Did you?" I asked. It was a lazy Saturday afternoon and I had nothing better to do than listen to the Saint tell stories. "Kill anyone?"

"I killed a deer once. I felt badly about it," the Saint said matter-of-factly. "Don't *you* ever think about prospecting." That was the closest he ever came to advice. He never warned me off drugs or sex; he talked to me about the club, its energy and pull, its fire. He compared

Pagan "Malicious" hanging out with other Pagans before he is fatally gunned down in Baltimore by a rival gang called Fates Assembly. *Courtesy of the Saint's collection*

membership to heroin addiction—no one ever really recovered, he just went into remission.

"We did stupid hazing shit, like making me ride in the backseat with two trash bags filled with angel dust. Not even in the *trunk* mind you; exposed so that any fucking cop could peer inside. Fucking Nicky federal informant B. was so whacked at the time. He didn't even know my name because to him I was 'prospect.' No name. I rode with that asshole across state lines. I was his heavy while he sold drugs to dealers not Pagans. 'Prospect,' he'd order, 'just stand there and shut up and look like you'll kill someone if they make a move.' Crazy thing was, if we had gotten pulled over, that shit was mine. You know what I mean? I would take the fall for him. I showed him I wanted to be there. I wasn't lame. Pretty fucking stupid of me. Prospects were their folly. It was 'Get me dust,' do this, do that. I got my head cracked twice, lost some teeth, and eventually fought back."

"Was it worth it?" I asked. I could tell the Saint had to think about that one. He answered by recounting the story of the Rock Star, the wiry guitarist from the band Classic, who was desperate to become a Pagan. The guy owned a bike and wore denim, "and that's where the similarities stopped." The Saint laughed. "He was just a pussy."

"What did *he* think he was?"

"He thought he was a lion." The Saint laughed. "He offered me shelter."

At the time, the Saint lived in the Wood House, a steel barn on five acres of forest, surrounded by a landfill and twenty miles from the FBI building. It was quiet and perfect for target practice. The surrounding woods were riddled with bullets from AK-47s and TEC-9s. I spent summers there target practicing. Painted on the side of the house was a bloodred mural of a Nazi bomber plane. The only heat inside the cabin was emitted from a woodstove. One winter the pipes froze, swelled, and burst, and when the ice thawed, the place flooded with water.

"Stay with me." The Rock Star fawned over the Saint.

"The place was too clean," the Saint recalled. "White rugs, walls, countertops. I felt like I was in a fucking church. He thought white was the color of success. The Rock Star gave me the grand tour."

But nothing about the Rock Star's existence was successful. The white was a cover. No one could accuse him of beating his wife if his carpets sparkled.

"One night I woke to the sounds of glass shattering and a woman's wail. The Rock Star had accused his old lady of messing around." By the time the Saint pulled back his sheets, grabbed his pistol, and cracked open his door, he saw the Rock Star's hands encircle his girlfriend's throat.

"The worst part"—the Saint paused and took another pull on his beer. A muscle in his jaw ticked—"his little girl saw this." I pictured the scene, her eyes wide with terror, her whispery nightgown and pale face casting her in a ghostly glow as if she had just glimpsed her own future.

"The old lady dropped to her knees, her lips slate gray. She gripped the Rock Star's knuckles. He was dressed in a duster, bandanna tied around his head, a shotgun strapped to his shoulder. I told him to marry her or kill her," the Saint said. Part of me wondered, were they the same thing?

"He was going to kill her." The Saint described how he jammed the butt of his gun into the Rock Star's head. He put the beer bottle down and began the pantomime. I figured the Saint's "choice"—that the Rock Star either marry her or kill her—wasn't meant to be a choice at all.

The Saint clipped the Rock Star's eye and drew blood. Crimson stained the white carpet. Spatter sprayed across the popcorn ceiling. The old lady vanished with her daughter, barefoot into the flurries. The Saint pummeled the Rock Star with his fists. A punch to the jaw and the bone cracked. An uppercut to the nose and the bridge bent.

Adrenaline shot through the Saint. He was a reflexive machine digging his hooks into the Rock Star.

"He begged me to stop," the Saint recalled. "He had just shit himself."

The Saint's knuckles burned. He marched to the kitchen sink, ran cold water over his hands. He resembled a butcher, covered in blood.

"You call this brotherhood?" the Rock Star wailed. But it *was* brotherhood, certain codes of conduct prevailed: killing women or children was not sanctioned.

The Saint picked up the Rock Star by the shoulders and slammed his head into every cabinet in the apartment. Wood splintered. Glass shattered. Dishes tumbled to the floor. Blood streamed from Rock Star's mouth. His eyes swelled shut. After a while, the Rock Star's head had the recoil of a rubber ball; it bounced off the counter, popped back, and bounced off the cabinets. The Saint released him and the Rock Star slumped to the floor, unconscious. The Saint waited a beat, washed the blood from his body, and sat in the easy chair. Then he reached for the phone and called the cops. "I couldn't risk *the Rock Star* calling the police and telling them what *really* happened."

"Asshole, wake up." The Saint pulled back the Rock Star's head by his hair and slapped his cheeks.

"What happened?" he gurgled, still unable to open his eyes.

"You got beat up at the Wawa."

The Rock Star coughed and spit up blood. The Saint dressed. The cops arrived, knocked at the door. The Saint answered it politely; appropriate concern furrowed his brow.

"I don't know what happened. I just came home and found him like this." The Saint shrugged.

One cop frowned, walked over to the Rock Star, and kicked him gently with his boot. "What happened?"

The Rock Star squinted out of one bloody eye; he caught the Saint's gaze full force and said, "I got beat up at the Wawa."

The cop stared at the crimson walls, the streaks on the kitchen counter, the pool of blood on the carpet. He nodded knowingly at the Saint. An ambulance lifted the Rock Star onto a stretcher and carried him into the snow. The cop didn't seek charges. Apparently there were degrees of *acceptable* lawlessness.

The next day, the Saint awoke to the sound of rattling. Sunshine blazed through the apartment. The Saint suspected it was noon. He opened the door. The Rock Star stood outside, dressed in his hospital gown. The backside of him was exposed to the street. Traffic whizzed by. Three kids on bikes stopped to gawk.

"Get the fuck out," the Rock Star managed. He had broken ribs, a fractured jaw, and some missing teeth.

The Saint sucker punched him in the face. The Rock Star stumbled backward, fell into a mound of snow. He howled as the cold bit into his ass. Sirens resounded. The Saint picked the Rock Star up, threw him into the back of his van, parked in the street.

"What's going on here?" the cop asked as he exited his patrol car.

The Saint grinned, leaned against his van, arms folded. "I'm just here to see my girlfriend."

The kids on the bikes snickered. Their jaws dropped.

The cop squinted at the Saint; his eyes traveled from his shirtless chest to his bare feet. "Right." The cop nodded.

"But the Rock Star became a Pagan," I said.

"That's my point. Filler doesn't last. He became a crack addict and never played music again."

I decided I didn't want to be "filler." Drug dealing and stealing wasn't getting me far, and I thought it was time I earned a legitimate income.

I liked cars. Fancy, flashy ones such as Mercedeses, Ferraris, and BMWs. Specifically, I liked detailing them and landed my first real job in an auto body shop. I worked regular hours with regular pay, and I have to admit it felt pretty good to be a regular citizen. Cottman Mike gave me my first real break. He was the oldest of nine children and a descendant from my own white-trash neighborhood in Upper Darby. We had an instant connection; more important, he was the son of Arty Gibbons, an "active" drug addict and dealer who, though fueled by heroin, was still impressively functional. Arty owned a successful transmission business until he overdosed suddenly on the toilet. He made no apology for his habit, insisted he was sick, obsessed with a potent street heroin called Homicide.

"Arty was my friend," the Saint recalled. "He was good people."

Arty had been a club "hangaround," one rank lower than a prospect, not even officially a Pagan, but he was a *serious* hangaround and that qualified him to be considered "family." Cottman, who was unusually bright, talked real elegant, and even attended the prestigious Williamson Free School of Mechanical Trades in Philadelphia, approached me one day about a business opportunity. He said his old man's shop could use a detailer next door. He offered me half of his garage. The Saint loaned me capital, and I spent the first four months of my new, revised life painting, making flyers and business cards, and hustling for customers. It felt good to be responsible, to make the bills and to have an income that didn't constitute drug money or my next score.

But the more profit I earned, the more I wasted; Saturday night rolled around and it was time to treat everyone to booze and dope at my Happy Spot. Pretty soon I could no longer afford to pay my apartment rent *and* the shop's overhead, but I didn't want to disappoint Cottman, didn't want him to realize that I lacked the strength to reinvent myself. I slept in the shop. I shut off the heat to conserve energy and cost. I worked in dim lighting. I recycled tools. My gloves had no fingers. My belly rumbled with hunger.

Winter storms blew around me. I watched hopelessly as snowdrifts thickened on the streets. Parked cars were buried in fresh powder. Nothing but whiteness stretched for miles. Weeks passed with no work. No one wanted his car detailed. People just wanted help stabbing the ice sheets off their windshields. I spoke to no one for days at a time; the phone connection crackled, voices sounded far away and warm. I existed in dead space, completely isolated, alone as if I were in hibernation, until one night the Saint called.

"Pack up your shit," he barked over the phone.

I knew better than to ask questions. Later, I learned that the Saint had argued with Cottman's mom.

"She's a psychopath," he explained simply. "She threatened to kill my son."

"I guess that means I don't have a detail shop anymore, huh?"

That was pretty much how it went in those days. My loyalty was to the Saint. If he said walk away, I did. No questions asked. I figured he knew more than I did about situations. I could always get my job back. But sometimes it just seemed easier to be a criminal.

The split turned out to be pretty advantageous for Cottman. He opened up a successful recording studio and, later, Gibbons Automotive. I'll always remember him fondly. He had introduced me to Hammer, a guy twenty years my senior, big as a train with a pocked face that looked like target practice.

"I like your work, kid." Hammer scheduled weekly visits to have his car detailed.

"Your car needs *that* much help?" Cottman asked him one afternoon.

"The kid does little things, polishes my leather interior, waxes the tires, touches up the paint." Hammer had a smile like Christmas. I knew why he came so often. He *liked* me, wanted me to succeed. And I wanted to show him I was worth it. At night Hammer worked as a bouncer for the Champion Sports Bar on Market Street. Every so often he'd call me up: "Interested in earning some extra cash?" I never passed on an opportunity. I didn't want to disappoint Hammer. I probably weighed one hundred pounds wet, but if Hammer asked me to do something, I obliged. I assumed my post at the entrance of the bar and checked IDs. Hammer roamed the parking lot making sure whomever I kicked out stayed out. We made a good temporary crew, so much so that he asked me to substitute with him at other bars in the area.

"You're not afraid to fight," Hammer remarked once.

That is true. I had no particular style and I wasn't classically trained like the Saint as a kickboxer, martial artist, or street fighter. My method was improvisational. I figured I would swing and keep swinging until I was either stabbed or shot. One night I had a chance to showcase my style. It was near closing. The bar's twenty-two television sets blared inside. Stragglers idled at their tables, sipping the last of their beers, thrashing wildly at the teams on the screens. I worked the front entrance, checked IDs as usual, until one brazen bull poked my shoulder and shook his head.

"Not me, kid. You don't need to check my ID. I'm a regular here."

"Sorry, sir, but my orders are to check everyone." He smelled of tobacco.

"Not me." The man towered over me. His neck skimmed the top of my head.

Undeterred, I repeated my request for his ID. He punched me in the jaw with such force I stumbled backward and banged my head into the door. My eyes smarted. The room spun. I saw white flashes like strobes go off in the back of my eyelids. A shape barreled into me, knocked the wind from my lungs. Pain burned my ribs. I doubled over, gasped for breath, swung wildly at the air. My vision blurred. I couldn't see. Around this time I began to wonder what I was actually doing in the bar. I was no bouncer.

Hammer's voice droned in my head: "He's with me. He's with me."

Something hard cracked my skull. Glass sprayed into my mouth. I wiped my chin with my hand and couldn't feel my chin. I tasted blood and beer. *Son of a bitch,* I thought. *I'm tasting my blood.*

"Do something about this asshole." Hammer's voice again. I couldn't make out his features. I just saw shapes, two hulking figures looming in front of me.

"Go ahead and punch him," Hammer ordered me. "Go crazy, man, close your eyes."

I blinked. My jaw throbbed. Hammer had the guy in a headlock. I hesitated.

"He's all yours." The voices in slow motion again. I heard chairs scrape. People shoved into me, placed bets, slammed drinks on the tabletops. I was now the entertainment. I forgot what the fight was about. I knocked the guy's teeth into his bottom lip. I swung again and again until my arm throbbed and my knuckles bled. In that moment, I wished I were a Pagan. At least then I would have reinforcements, members who would have rallied around me and shoved a shotgun down the asshole's throat.

But more than belligerent drunks, I had to worry about angry mobsters. Occasionally bar owners borrowed money from the Greek Mafia, and sometimes they forgot to repay their debts. The mob never forgot. They came to collect. I started to dread closing time. I was at a bar called the Dive when I had my first encounter with loan sharks.

Hammer and I fell into a routine. As the bar emptied of patrons, we swept the floor, mopped, wiped down tables, and looked forward to quiet. But as I sprayed down the windows, the front door burst open and three wide Greeks entered, two enforcers built like tanks and their boss, the short, stumpy middle guy. I didn't bother asking them for their IDs. One of them with a wide chin, bold black eyes, and curly hair motioned for me to stop. I put down my cloth and spray bottle and moved toward the door. Not a chance he would let me leave, but maybe he would tape my eyes shut so he'd have no witness? He aimed his revolver at my head.

At that moment I really started to rethink the bouncer thing. I just needed money. The owner smiled weakly at me and tried to reassure me with his eyes that he had everything under control. I didn't move, didn't breathe, didn't believe him. Familiar panic returned. I felt sick. My worst childhood memories flashed in my head: Pooh Bear's gun in my side, tiny white pops from a black Lincoln, spider glass in my home. I remember staring at the mobster's tie. It looked hand-painted, expensive, and green-washed, the color of money. Minutes ticked by. Hammer shifted his weight. He smelled of fear. I was afraid to lift my head above the barrel of the gun. The slightest movement might trigger a reaction. The mobster didn't flinch. I stared at his shoes, clean and polished. I stared at *my* shoes, dirty and missing a sole. I smelled urine, my urine. My leg was wet.

"One moment," the owner repeated in his thick accent. "One moment."

The gun at my head clicked. I flinched waiting for the bullet, waiting for the darkness. My hands grew clammy. The gangster laughed, shrugged as if the misfire were an accident. The owner's voice wavered. *Shit. Please have the fucking money.* The owner swore in something that sounded Arabic. He gestured wildly with his hands. Sounds amplified. I never felt so helpless. I realized I was in big trouble and there was no way I was talking my way out of this. My mind raced. Hammer's breathing was labored and I hoped he wasn't about to be a hero for me. I didn't need a savior. That just implied hassle, more indebtedness. As I stood pinned against the wall, gun pointed at my temple, I actually felt *relieved,* as if it almost didn't matter anymore whether the mobster pulled the trigger. I wasn't afraid of dying. I was afraid of living incomplete.

He pulled the trigger again. Click. This time the mobster smacked me on the side of the head with the pistol butt. Relief turned to anger. I wanted to clock him. *Give him the fucking money.* I heard a shuffle at the table. The mobster tucked his gun into his pocket, slapped both of my cheeks, and apologized, "Sorry to have caused you trouble."

As I watched them exit, my knees felt like rubber. I thought I might pass out.

"You all right, man?" Hammer asked.

I could barely speak. "Fucking fine."

15

~ ~ ~ ~ ~

Strike Two

Two can play and lose.

The whole concept of a Mother Club was the brainchild of Satan, one of the Pagan's original founding members. Satan, who looked the part with his piercing blue eyes and black mane of hair, established rules and enforcement measures for the club. Before the uniforms, Satan created a "black T-shirt squad," whose sole purpose was to "take care of business." But after an entire chapter in Virginia disbanded due to the arrest of all of its members, Satan was forced to rethink the club's structure. The Mother Club created four or five subsidiary chapters, each with its own president, vice president, sergeant at arms, and treasurer. But the chapters still answered to the Mother Club, whose members, such as Maingy, were elected for life. Democracy didn't exist. There was no recourse against the power hungry. The structure was designed for failure, because if a Pagan rebelled, eventually that Pagan was beaten into submission, defeated until he became compliant, conforming, and lame.

I didn't have to report my actions or decisions to the Mother Club once a week after church. I didn't have to be Maingy's adviser or explain Maingy's decisions. I wasn't part of the rank-and-file structure. I didn't care about sergeants at arms or enforcers, or impressing prospects and drug dealers. I could be all of those roles or none of them.

"He's fucking up the club," I said, voicing what I knew the Saint felt.

Maingy, anxious to increase club membership since his release from prison, recruited "fillers," geriatric Pagans who wheezed and struggled to mount their bikes, reckless addicts who jittered and compromised club code, trolls who *dressed* the part but then disappeared when the scene turned violent.

The Saint was more diplomatic; he called the chaos "retraining" the new recruits to righteous ways. The lessons usually involved breaking someone's arm with an ax handle. Discretion didn't apply to the teacher. Order had to be restored quickly: "They had to learn that there were rules for displaying guns or pulling knives." There were *ways* to dispose of a body, to ensure beatings happened *off-camera*. Real Pagans knew to put their backs to photographers, smash cameras at parties, and avoid security screens. No witnesses. Drugs made the new recruits careless, interested in the label 1 percent and not the code. Disgruntled Pagans, reluctant to catch a case for something stupid, dropped out altogether, unable to follow the whole One-for-All, All-for-One motto. Most worried that the old salts such as the Saint might leave the Pagans in droves, giving Maingy free rein to create another empire in his own image. Exactly what Maingy hoped. As long as the old-timers stayed, the club had its own internal police.

"Why do you hang around with those clowns?" Maingy asked me one afternoon as I helped him repair motorcycles in his garage. It was one of the few activities we shared, out of necessity. I maintained a relationship with my old man because I respected the Saint, who still reported to Maingy, still followed his orders, still fell under his control. Maingy tossed me a wrench and it clattered to the floor. The sound rattled me more than it should have.

The day was overcast and smelled of rain. Wind blew debris and leaves into the open garage. Motorcycle parts littered the floor— pistons, gaskets, and wire harnesses. Maingy did benchwork, including star-hub wheels and transmission overhauls. He specialized in valve-seat restoration and had parts for vintage Indian and Harley-Davidson motorcycles. Grease coated Maingy's fingers and made them look rotten.

The garage served as a decent front for Maingy's *other* business, drug dealing. Although the club had "officially" banned the practice because the penalties were too stiff, "unofficially" the club was steeped in the dope trade. But I wasn't a fool. The only reason Maingy talked to *me* at all was because he feared the Saint's influence over me. The Saint had taught me everything I knew. Everything I knew about *Maingy*. For the first time, the roles reversed, *I* posed a threat to my old man. I knew of only two ways to handle a threat: either kill it or make it loyal. Noise from the torque punctuated the silence between us. Maingy stared intensely at me through his large safety goggles. Sparks flew around us. Someone had to make the first move.

"What do you want?" I managed, but I already knew his answer.

Maingy smiled as if his hands were already around my neck. "It's either me or him."

I could not be a slave to both. Rain rushed in with the wind. Maybe I just imagined the hint of desperation in my old man's voice. A low train whistle sounded in the distance. I stared at Maingy and felt nothing but numb. I looked around the garage, at all the parts scattered like tombstones in a graveyard, and then it hit me.

"Where's Dead's bike?"

The motorcycle was a classic 1977 Sportster with a Shovelhead engine. The bike represented the only tangible memory I had left of my uncle Russell. I had preserved it for so many years like a shrine. My old man removed his safety goggles, played with the rubber strap absentmindedly, and shrugged. "I sold it for a couple grand."

I felt the blood drain from my face. His mental abuse tore at me. He reminded me of a viper, coiled and puffed in the grass waiting for the right time to strike. His stare bore into me, made me stumble two steps backward until I banged my knee into a steel table. Maingy never flinched. He just followed me with his eyes, looked at me as if I were already dead. I hated him for that, hated that he had that kind of power over me. I wanted to smash his fucking face in, press my thumb into his neck just below his Adam's apple and watch him gag, choke, suffer the way I had suffered. But instead Maingy stood, hands in his pockets, rain spitting at his cheeks, and laughed.

"That motherfucker," the Saint exploded later. "After all I did for him. I took care of you so that he wouldn't have to." *Thanks.* I suppose I should have been grateful to have had a father at all. The title didn't mean much. The club always came first. I didn't like it but I couldn't change it. I was just an extension of the club, PROPERTY OF MAINGY. Still, I wondered exactly what all the Saint did for my old man besides buying him a guitar so that the fucker could learn to play music in prison.

The veins in the Saint's neck corded. He paced, cursed, building up to something huge.

"You tell that motherfucker I'm done."

Just like that, without protocol or fanfare or even announcement at the next church meeting, the Saint resigned his post before he was

tossed out because he refused to serve a zealot, because he would not
risk jail for lames, for outlaws who were fast becoming outcasts. At
one in the morning, in the middle of the week, the Saint drove to the
president's house to deliver his years of service, his folded colors inside a cardboard box.

It was so unexpected it took the president a week to react, and
when he arrived at the Saint's house in the middle of the night and
tapped on his door, he said simply, "I'm here to take your bike."

The president had a thin build and slow gait. "He shifted uncomfortably on my sidewalk, unsure what to do with his hands. He made
no eye contact. I whipped out my .38 and pressed it to his temple.
'Fucking come and get it then,' I said," the Saint recalled.

But of course the president never did. Like most presidents, the
club's at that time was more a figurehead than a leader. His real source
of power came from the Saint. They both knew that. The Saint's uncer-
emonious departure left the president exposed to Maingy, to the end of
a regime and to the beginning of a frightening dictatorship, something
neither of them could afford. The Saint loved the club too much to see
it dissolve.

"I left him a present," the Saint said. "I left him Gorilla."

It would be years before I understood exactly what the Saint meant
because when he left the club, I left the Pagans and the Saint left *me*.
It wasn't his fault. Drugs replaced him. Acid and weed transported
me to new levels of false hope like a spotlight in a dark room. I folded
into myself, blinded by what I couldn't see. When I was seventeen, my
friend Chal handed me white blotter paper and winked. "Try some,"
he said, and mischief glittered in his eyes. I licked the thin square and
tasted nothing.

"It's defective." I shook my head and knocked back a beer. I sank into his puffy black couch and it was like sinking into a hole. I rubbed my palms against my tattered jeans. Dishes clattered above us and I thought how weird it was that Chal's mom was upstairs, that she had no idea we were doing acid in her *home*. I remember thinking, *This isn't normal, nothing about this is normal.*

"She's cool with this." Chal shrugged. His eyes looked white.

This isn't normal, nothing about this is normal. And I'm pretty sure Chal's mom isn't cool with her son disappearing. I stood, suddenly too warm, my clothes glued to my body. Sweat poured out of my armpits as if I were leaking. *Jesus, Chal, turn down the fucking heat.* My mouth tickled with cotton. I needed another beer. I opened the front door. A blast of cold air blew up my shirt and I had the odd sensation that bugs crawled over my flesh. I heard their tiny legs scratch across my bones. My heart beat louder. I needed to leave. I knew the way home. I saw the hospital where I was born. I wanted to start over. I walked. The streets curved in front of me. Thin buildings stretched taller. I walked between them, felt the walls close in on me, crush me until I pushed against the cold bricks. Dragon heads spit fire from the lamppost.

Footsteps pounded behind me. "Wait," Chal's voice thundered in my head.

But I couldn't wait. I was light as a feather. I floated over the rooftops, over the dirty city.

"Are you all right?" Chal's fingers gripped like claws in my shoulder.

My head hurt. I stared down at gray slabs. *How did I get here?* Rain pelted my back.

"You're in the cemetery, man," Chal said. "You passed out on someone's grave."

"Why do we do this, Chal?" I mumbled, and every part of my body hurt.

"Why do we do what?" His voice sounded like an echo.

"Acid?" Slow-motion voice.

"Because it helps us to *think*."

"Right." I nodded. "I do have clarity now."

Large raindrops smacked the pavement around me. My clothes grew heavy, cold. My hands looked pale and slick like wax. I shivered but I was dry. *How'm I dry, Chal?* For what seemed hours I stared into the wet street. Headlights bloomed around me. Water splashed over my ankles. Cars honked at me. I heard their tires rumble like thunder. One swerved to miss me. I stuck out my tongue and the rain tasted salty, like tears, like oceans of sadness.

The next day was New Year's and I was one of ten thousand who watched the traditional Mummers Parade from the bleachers on Broad Street in South Philly. It was one of the few traditions, like Mardi Gras, that joined the whole city. Bright sun speared patches of ice in the street. My head buzzed with anticipation and haze. A string band played, at first a single violin plucked by a clown dressed in red glitter and sequins. A large feather crown bloomed from his head. His white face wore a permanent bloody smile. Painted tears dripped from his eyes. He looked at me, moved his bow across his instrument, and I thought he played exclusively for me. Other clowns joined him, dressed in bright white balloon overalls that sparkled like sun on fresh snow. They had skulls for faces. The saxophonist towered over the others in stilts, his eyes covered by a black, sequined mask. When he blew, it seemed the whole street moved. A smaller clown with garish green robes played the glockenspiel; the sound, like tiny chimes, made my ears vibrate. His black-painted face had a smile like a scar. Glitter dazzled his eye mask. Padlocks draped his shoulders. Chains wrapped his chest.

Dancers somersaulted into the street, their bold red capes smearing the sky like blood spatter. They whirled faster and faster as the audience cheered and clapped. The percussion beat like a heart. A bass violin joined in, bold strokes along the strings. The instrument practically toppled the clown. He wore black like the future. His gold mask glittered in the sun. His band was Just Plain Dead. All around him, colors blurred like streamers, the masquerade bright bold, dazzling against the snowy street. But when he glanced my way, I felt his chill, his darkness, like a haunting.

Animals paraded next; a carnival of costumes formed leopards, jaguars, and zebras. Bright greens mixed with gold spots, striped feathered heads bobbed in the crowd. The violins wailed as they mimicked a chase. Behind them the Captain bloomed in a headdress of white tusks trimmed with gold ribbon. Band Before Time dragged a large fire pit made of bright orange taffeta. The colors snapped in the wind. The figures dressed in animal skins and carried clubs. They draped their kills across their chests. Their wild, bloodshot eyes transfixed me. Wind blew open my coat. I envisioned Mongo, who used to love the Mummers Parade, doing the 2 Street Strut alongside the clowns, his laughter now a ghostly echo. The bleachers that once filled with Pagans now held regular citizens.

Giant floating heads bobbed in the air above me. Cartoon characters that were supposed to be cute, not garish; playful, not frightening. I loved the parade because of whom I could watch. Children beamed at me, stuffed their faces with caramel corn. I munched on a sack of french fries and grinned back. Suddenly it didn't matter where I came from. It didn't matter that no one knew my name. Strangers smiled at me. A whole community smiled at me. And the brightness was stunning.

A woman nudged me. "They sound like professional musicians." She wore a pale blue suit with shiny gold buttons. Her cheeks flushed in the chill. She crossed her lean legs. Sleek leather heels rubbed against my ankles.

"They'd be disqualified if they were," a fat one next to her said, and laughed. She stuffed a plume of cotton candy in her mouth and winked at me. Her short-cropped hair bobbed. Her half-moon breasts draped over her large belly, and I was drawn to her softness, imagined my face smothered in her flesh. She was so unlike the biker women, who had a hard edge to them, more like a drug fix. The Wench Brigades followed. Rows of garish women whirled past us, their striped blue skirts and lace ruffles flapping in the wind. They blew me kisses, winked at me. I wanted to leap off the bleachers and dance with them, put my coarse hands around their tiny waists and whirl into the music and giddy pageantry. Confetti littered the air and it looked like snow, colorful flakes that stuck to my eyelashes.

"They look cold," the woman with the gold buttons remarked, and she bit into a hot dog.

"Very blue," I added, noting the blue-painted faces accented with dark circles beneath their eyes and their banner that read THE BLUE HOPE.

"They worked for months on those costumes," the woman in the suit remarked, as if I related, as if I understood pretense, costumes, masks, and clubs. She chewed thoughtfully. I watched her lips curl around the hot dog.

"I'm sure." I popped another french fry into my mouth.

"We had a clubhouse near my place. I heard them hammering away at sets, moving huge structures in and out of the street."

She had beautiful teeth. I loved the idea of movable scenery. I watched her speak, not hearing her words. The inflection in her voice sounded like music. She had an elegance about her that was almost spooky. Her leather-gloved hands brushed stray strands of hair from her cheek. Sun glinted off her dark sunglasses. She reminded me of a gorgeous spider.

"Do you know who you'll vote for?" She swallowed, crumpled the foil wrapper. That was part of the fun—voting for best in show. Winners scored large cash prizes.

"The prettiest." I squeezed her elbow. I was no longer paying attention to the parade.

"The most grotesque." She crinkled her nose.

"Strange always gets my vote." I laughed and stuffed the rest of my fries into my coat pocket. "Can I take you home with me?"

She laughed, cocked her head sideways, and said, "*How* old are you?"

"How old do you need me to be?" I slipped her gloved hand inside my pants. She didn't pull away. She felt warm next to my cold skin. She parted her lips, started to say something, then closed her mouth. She removed her sunglasses with her free hand and her brown eyes heated.

"This can be quick, right?" She swallowed. "My Bentley's parked a few blocks away."

I left the Mummers Parade around dusk, alone. I hesitated in front of my apartment in Marcus Hook and twirled my keys around my finger. The color of poverty dulled my mood, the muted browns and grays, the little chunks of beer glass sprinkled in the concrete, the bold imperfections in the ice patches. My boots crunched on bits of brick. Not a soul around. The scenery hadn't moved in years. I looked at the empty street, salt-licked and frozen. *Who would choose to live here?* I pulled my coat tighter, my heart heavy with resignation.

"Hey, man, what you in for?" the homeless man in the cardboard box joked with me. He'd pulled the flaps down for warmth. His was a disembodied voice. A stubby blue toe poked from the other side.

"Just doing my time, man, doing my time." I jammed my key in the door.

"Don't be out here at nightfall." He wagged a bony finger at me.

"It's always dark around here."

"I've seen things." He poked his head out slightly. I saw his frightened eyes, his tangled beard. I wondered whom he'd been before. *We all wind up in a box someday.* The Saint's words echoed through my head.

"What have you seen?" I played along.

"Bullet shells in the puddles." He pointed to a pothole slushy with mud.

"I'll be careful." I disappeared inside.

Later that night a blizzard formed a moving curtain outside my window. Wind tunneled through the bullet crack in the glass, a remnant from the last tenant. The front door banged open, the dead bolt busted from the last police raid. The street was empty now and dark. The homeless man's box blew away. He shuffled after it, barefoot in the whiteness. Candles flickered in the window because the storm had busted out the fuse box. Moisture leaked through cracks in the plaster. The wooden baseboards swelled and buckled. Rusty nails jutted from the floor and snagged the mattress. My building had been condemned several months ago. My street circled, dead-ended like a drain.

The walls in my room were painted gunmetal, as if layers of skin had peeled back and left the dead and rotten core. Across the street, a long steel warehouse spanned several blocks. Large wooden *X*'s marked the windows. Whole sections of city just crossed out. In one corner of my room a child's drawing remained, stick figures etched into the wall. One loomed larger than the others, a giant *X* through its head. A bloody handprint shadowed the background. I carried a flickering candle into the hall where the communal bathroom flooded.

The other apartments were vacant. The toilet door lay busted on the floor. The water in the bowl had a foul cream color. A rat bobbed on the surface. Old newspaper articles piled in a corner. I could wipe my ass with the headlines. My eyes watered in the darkness. I listened to the wind howl. *How had I become this?* Depression hit me. I felt like some kind of circus freak who hid in the shadows by night and emerged during the day for nourishing light, for brutal human contact. Back in my room, I lay on my mattress. I blew out the candle. I listened to the wind howl. I dreamed of humping Spider-Woman.

My life had become a series of moments punctuated by boredom, sex, and drug trips. But that afternoon one phone call shattered my routine. Staci, my old flame, invited me unexpectedly to a party at her place. "Just a few friends hanging out," she promised. I hadn't seen Staci in over a year. But it wasn't *her* I missed. She lived half a block away from my mom. Staci, at that time, worked for a well-respected marble company, and she had invited quite a few of her coworkers.

"It'll be fun," she promised. "I want them to meet you."

"Why?"

Chiseled and refined, the marble guys wore pressed slacks and collared shirts and had intelligent-sounding names such as William and James and Bryce.

"They think we're animals." My friend Chal swallowed his beer. "Look how they stare at us."

"They don't even see us," I said. We lingered in the kitchen by the refrigerator. Fluorescent lights flickered over our faces. Cold beers chilled our hands. I concentrated on a brunette by the stove. Large breasts spilled out of her leather corset. She had a tiny waist, like a dropped neck, wrapped too many times with fake gold beads. She had an unfortunate face, sunken and older than her years. But I liked her eyes. They had a smoky, haunting quality, like globes in a spooky painting that moved independently from her head. She caught my gaze, fluttered her lashes at me, and nodded toward the linen closet. I grinned already imagining what I would do with her belts. I tapped Chal's hand with the butt of my beer and said, "I'll be back in a little while."

"Animal." Chal shook his head, downed the last of his beer, and tossed the bottle into the trash.

Staci's house looked plucked from a magazine, rich, tired rooms brushed in chilled heather, eggplant, and orchid. I followed the girl to the linen closet. She pinched my hand.

"Are you excited?" she whispered.

Excited? I had to think about that. Out of the corner of my eye I saw Marble Guy stumble into the guest bathroom. He held his stomach. He left the door open. Multi-layers of wallpaper bulged from the seams. He hurled into the bowl.

"Can't hold it," Staci's little brother mocked, and unzipped his pants. He pretended to piss on the Marble Guy's head.

"Is that all you've got?" The Kid made retching noises, called him weak, called him other names as well. No one paid attention to the Kid.

The toilet flushed. Sounds of swirling water filled the pause. A strange foreboding overcame me. I stopped, pressed a finger to my lips.

The girl frowned. "What's wrong?" she pouted. She looked disappointed. She slipped out of her heels, held them in her hands. She followed my gaze to the hallway, to the Kid with the glasses and short-cropped hair.

Marble Guy lifted his head, wobbled to standing, and spit into the sink. He dragged a hand through his perfect wavy hair. Marble Guy smirked at the Kid and in a flash grabbed him by the throat, squeezed the boy's soft white flesh, and hoisted him high in the air. He shook the Kid until the boy's face mottled bluish white and the blood vessels in his eyes burst. *Christ, he was going to kill the Kid.* Marble Guy laughed, a deep guttural sound like an animal's, and something snapped inside me, a fury I could not contain. Chal's bottle of beer clattered in the sink. Violence hung in the air like a vapor. The room crackled with noise.

I slammed Marble Guy into the wall and he released his grip on the boy. We both fell backward into the coffee table. Shards of glass sprayed across the wooden floor. Sharp pain shot into my arm. Someone pulled the china cabinet down on Marble Guy's head. Dishes shattered. Furniture splintered, glass beads lit up the floor, lamps broke, the walls indented with holes. I saw a blur of movement. Fists knocked my teeth, my temple, then a hard kick hit my lower jaw. Marble Guy's thumbs jammed into my throat. I couldn't breathe, couldn't feel my arms anymore. The room darkened and I felt weightless suddenly. The chaos spun away from me. I was high up in the air looking down on the wreckage, so exhausted that I didn't care anymore about the outcome. In a flash, my head slammed into the floor with such force I thought I had gone *through* the floor. Wood chips cut into my nostrils. I couldn't see. I couldn't feel my lips. I heard my friend Chal's voice: "He's fucked-up." Fear was in his tone, real terror, like I'd never heard before. Someone grabbed my arms. Sirens whirred in the distance. I couldn't see my legs.

The voices again: "Get him to the bathroom." Someone dragged me upstairs. Carpet burned my knees. More pounding. *Please make it stop.* I honestly just wanted to die. I squinted, struggled to open one eye. I saw my friend, tears in his eyes. Now I was really afraid.

"You look dead, man." He choked back a sob. *I felt dead.* I couldn't talk. My throat scratched like cotton. They pushed me into the upstairs bathroom. I fell against the sink, caught myself on the porcelain lip. *Shit.* I didn't recognize my own face. I looked like hell—dragged down, pale, as if all blood had drained from my heart. One eye swelled shut, the other eye bursting with bright red fluid. I crouched beside the toilet and dry-heaved as my body rejected images that seeped like poison into my brain. When the spasms stopped, I sank defeated on the floor, feeling weak and clammy, willing my mind to be logical, to think straight. *Too much stress. Too little sleep.* I heard the sirens closer now. Just outside Staci's house. The ambulance wasn't for me. I had no health insurance. I couldn't afford to get better. It was actually cheaper to die, to be cremated and have my ashes dumped somewhere on the outskirts of Philadelphia.

Part of me was indignant. The other part of me was just embarrassed. I couldn't pass away from a kick to the jaw. Death had to have *some* dignity. I thought of Mongo. He worried that the cat would kill him. I thought of the program I'd seen on *National Geographic* of the teacher who was bit by a red army ant while hiking in the woods. His body swelled to the size of a tent. When his girlfriend found him, he begged her, "Please, don't tell anyone an ant got me." I heard commotion downstairs, raised voices. *Who did this?* the cops snapped. Then the Kid's plaintive voice: "LT. This is his fault." I couldn't believe it. I felt sick. For years that Kid would blame me for trying to save him.

"You can't stay here." Staci stood at the bathroom door. She sounded nervous, upset. I wished I could see her, but my face was numb. I crawled into the tub.

"The cops are going to arrest you," she said simply. "You destroyed my folks' house. They're going to kick me out because of you."

I stumbled out of Staci's wrecked house shortly before dusk. My legs actually creaked, and with each step pain shot up my thigh like a bolt.

My eyes smarted, stung the insides of my lids. I heard sirens wail behind me. A gray film draped the bare branches and gravel. My heart raced. I saw my mom's house jut from the corner, pale and cracked like a tongue. I had imagined our reunion differently; triumphant almost, where I would return as a warrior with a severed head tied to my cane pole. But instead I resembled a circus freak, swollen and bruised and utterly broken. I hesitated outside her front door. The streets were deserted. Blood caked my hands. I could see only slits of light in the window. Half a tree branch tickled my shoulder. I thought I was dying and the world around me had shattered into brilliant mosaics, pieces of colored stone that formed incomplete scenes of my life. The emotional horror of what my presence might do to my mom sent a shiver through me. My mom could not bury me, *would* not bury me. Cold wind bit into me. The temperature dropped. Darkness enveloped me. Headlights hurt my eyes. I knocked on the door and my knuckles burned.

My mom inhaled sharply at the sight of me and hugged me fiercely, like a small fist closing.

"What's happened to you?" She choked back a sob.

He broke me. The son of a bitch broke me.

She pulled me inside, gently lowered me into piles of soft clothing. I wanted to sleep for a hundred years. I wanted something to numb the pain.

"Chuck," she hollered. I heard a man shuffle into the room.

"What's wrong with him?" her boyfriend asked.

"He's fucked-up."

"Should we get him to a hospital?"

But I'm not ready to die.

"Get some ice," my mom instructed, then after a moment added, "And some alcohol."

She stroked my cheek. "I never stopped loving you," she whispered in my ear when she thought I had slipped unconscious. Her runny face was close to mine. Tears formed little rivers near her eyes.

"You let me go." I could barely get the words out. We were silent for several minutes. I closed my slits and my world turned satin black. I never cried. I hadn't cried since I was born. Maybe I *should* have? I was too tired to cry. Too sick and tired of being sick and tired.

"I thought"—my mom's voice shook—"it would be easier on you."

I was aware of time slipping by, of drifting apart, of all the time my mom and I had lost, and I knew it was more complicated than abuse. The feelings, the fears, the pride, and the pain that had wedged between us had all been genuine. It had been easier to just let go . . . and that had been the hardest thing I had ever done in my life.

"I've missed you so much," I whispered. I wanted to tell her so much more. She nodded and seemed far away from me. We stood in the waning darkness, holding hands with our shadows, afraid to exhale, or to let go. I knew the instant I released her, she would return to her lonely world because it was familiar and safe, and I would exist as a beautiful memory.

My heart constricted. Even together we were apart.

When I finally recovered three weeks later, I vowed to curb my drug habit to weed. Marijuana calmed me, fogged my brain. I drifted from my mom's place, lodged in one apartment after another, and bothered the margins of the club. The distance was closeness. The Saint disapproved of my drug habit. Dope, he said, fried a person's brain, made a person completely useless. I couldn't agree more. I just didn't care. The Saint confided that he'd had a bad trip once: "The whole room bled, cast the place in a kind of red glaze. I saw the devil." I was pretty sure I'd seen the devil too but it wasn't on a drug trip.

I gravitated back to the club because I hadn't really *survived* anything. Survivors lived momentarily in hysterical relief—narrowly missing a bullet, walking away from a burning wreck, wriggling free from a kidnapper's grip—only to succumb to their fate weeks or even years later because they couldn't just move on. They couldn't forget or pretend what had happened to them happened to someone else. The thing is, they weren't supposed to survive in the first place. It was all some horrible mistake, the guilt, the pressure to do something decent with the rest of their life, the whole idea of second chances. It was all crap. Really they were missed, simply passed over. That's how I found my way home.

PART III

16

∿ ∿ ∿ ∿ ∿ ∿

Raising Hell

These old guys, they paved the road that we
ride on, but we're fixing the potholes.
—THE SAINT ON THE "OLD ERA"

Change is coming." The Saint chewed thoughtfully one afternoon on his roast beef sandwich at his favorite deli and nodded to a cluster of bikers gathered outside the restaurant. Their T-shirts read SUPPORT YOUR LOCAL '81's. Hells Angels. We were seeing more Hells Angels in West Philly, where they had never before been. They were encroaching on Pagan turf, muscling in on the club's bookmaking, drug-dealing, and prostitution rackets. The whole "war" between the Hells Angels and the Pagans, as one cop plainly described it to the *Philadelphia Daily News,* was over "the oil," the P2P chemical used in the manufacture of methamphetamine. The Hells Angels and the

Pagans were "like dynamite and a match . . . mix the Mafia into the equation and it becomes nitroglycerin."

I followed the Saint's gaze into the street. My stomach felt tight like the inside of a drum. I didn't know how to change things. I knew how to end them. Sometimes they were the same thing.

The Saint paused midchew. "What do you have on you?"

"Nothing." It was the first time I didn't carry my twin guns.

The Saint swallowed, tore another bite of his sandwich, and pushed his butter knife across the table. "It's already starting to stink around here."

But the real war began with the Gorilla, the Pagans' Philadelphia chapter club president. Rumor swirled that Gorilla was a former rogue cop, which made others at once wary of him and inspired. As the Saint liked to remark, "Better to have a cop become a Pagan than a Pagan become a cop." Ironically, Gorilla became a Pagan *because* he was once a cop. He was fired in 1982 after three years on the force, accused of loan-sharking. The charges were later dropped, but Gorilla considered that a "turning point."

He insisted, "My life was ruined for something I never did. I'd never been arrested. Never been in any kind of trouble, and I had to become a police officer to be arrested."

Gorilla understood rank and file. He understood protocol and rules. He understood discretion. Some acts were not discussed with club members, they were just done, and if someone wanted to be a psychopath on his own time, that really wasn't the club's concern.

Gorilla's old lady, who suffered from multiple sclerosis, was his albatross. Pagan mamas were about utility and service. They were property to be used and discarded. Illness was confusing and inconvenient. Unlike Terrible Tony, who could still be propped in a corner at club functions, women lacked that same legacy. They could not survive deterioration. Degradation was another matter entirely. *That* was expected, even anticipated. The women devised coping mechanisms: drugs, suicide, cutting. Men like Gorilla did not *care* for old ladies. When property became a liability, that property was simply discarded or exchanged. Gorilla did the only reasonable thing: he divorced his old lady. And he shuttled his two young daughters to live as "cellar dwellers" in a basement with his parents in South Philly.

I considered it a mercy placement. Gorilla's girls were safe underground, protected. It was the best arrangement for them. After all, his daughters were white and young and beautiful and they could have lived like me. With his defective property safely hidden, Gorilla prowled for successor girlfriends. Finding and keeping an attractive woman impressed drug dealers and Mafia types and brought a touch of class and distraction to Gorilla's operations. Better to be an "adorned" animal than a reviled one. I imagined Gorilla's replacements stayed with him out of fear; they no doubt felt Gorilla's presence like an amputated limb. My mom had confided that sentiment once to me about my own old man: "I felt a sense of loss when I married him, like I was shedding an old skin and stepping into a new life, raw."

My mother had been a mule, useful to the club, to the cause, and to my father. That was her survival. It was also mine. Most of the women in the Pagan culture worked as strippers, turning performance into profit. They were my early teachers. Even at five I peeped through beaded curtains, watching bare-breasted women nurse purple bumps below their eyes and swollen, bloody cracked lips. They became my babysitters. There was no such thing as propriety; children accompanied them like accessories, a boa, a purse, a G-string.

The women applied ointments to their skin to tighten their buttocks and twisted their legs around a rusty pole on center stage, their bodies glistening with sweat. Lipstick containers concealed hidden blades. Dim red pin lights glowed around them in the bar, casting a bloody hue to their complexion as they danced to the rhythm of money and desperate power. I was too young to understand the players or the game, but I saw the wads of cash flash between hands, heard the snap of G-strings and the slap of flesh, and I knew if I stayed quiet, hidden in the backdrop, I would be safe. I imagined myself a train, moving fast through a dark tunnel, my scream a long whistle obliterated by steam and noise, where no one noticed me except as wind rushing past them.

Gorilla's girlfriend marked a turning point for him. Like cause and effect—had Gorilla never divorced his old lady, had he never tucked his children away in a basement, had he never met a girl whose parents owned a deli in South Philly, had she never entered a bar one night frequented by mobsters, had one of them never flirted with her, had she never rejected his advances, had that mobster never retaliated with choice words for Gorilla, maybe Gorilla would not have returned in the dark armed with an automatic weapon and sprayed the bar with bullets. People later reported that Gorilla sat calmly at a table, surrounded by filmy gun residue, and slammed down a beer. He then demanded the phone numbers to all the mob bosses and waited for them to arrive. He waited until dawn surrounded by debris—splintered chairs, broken glass, spilled beer, shattered counters. No one called the police. His business was personal and it wasn't over.

If the mob's bosses wouldn't come to Gorilla, he would go to them. Days later, we learned that one of the mobster's bodyguard's went for a jog in the early dawn. The streets were mostly deserted. Gorilla watched him from his car, pinned him with his binoculars, and let him run a short distance so that he sweat. Then Gorilla calmly gave his own henchmen the signal. Rumor has it that the man was beat up for days, rolled in a carpet, doused in gasoline, and tossed into an alley Dumpster. It was a visible warning, retribution. Not a club-sanctioned event but still a necessary payback. I never confirmed the details, but I know that no one messed with Gorilla's girlfriend again.

But it wasn't that simple. There were always repercussions, cause and effect. Days later, clouds swirled in the afternoon sky and threatened to pour. A pall of apprehension hung in the air at the Saint's tattoo shop. The place was fairly empty. Customers typically teemed in after ten o'clock. I had a keen sense of foreboding; the hair on my neck bristled. The phone shrilled. I put down my rag. The Saint cradled the phone to his ear, his boots propped on his desk in the office. He had shut the door but I could see him through the wide glass windows. The Saint's expression sobered. He suddenly stood, paced the tiny space, and shook his head.

When he opened the door, he announced, "Gorilla's been shot."

17

∿∿∿∿∿

Payback

It was like Philadelphia with La Cosa Nostra
and who's ratting out whom?
—THE SAINT ABOUT THE NEW REGIME

Paramedics rushed Gorilla to Thomas Jefferson University Hospital, where he was treated for multiple gunshot wounds to the hands, face, chest, and stomach. The Saint and I drove to the scene in separate cars because we weren't officially part of the club anymore. We idled in the parking lot like two people at the back of a crowd as other Pagans roared up on their Harleys, dismounted, and headed for the hospital doors grim-faced, sweaty, and defiant. They filed in one after the other. Some lingered outside, passed smokes and beer, and said nothing.

The Saint and I muscled past them, down the long, bright corridor to the emergency room. The hallway bustled with people, frightened mothers with clinging children, street gangsters still dressed in their chains and black-and-white markings, inmates handcuffed to cops, reporters anxious to learn more about the Pagan's "infamous famous man." Eyes followed the Saint and I as we filed past them to the room with cots separated by gauze curtains. Nurses snapped at us, wrestled with an inmate to keep his veins plugged.

Pagans fanned to the side of Gorilla. He lay propped on pillows, his breathing labored, his face swollen and raw. Tubes threaded through his nostrils. Needles punctured his veins. Bags of liquid dangled on a pole. A flicker of recognition skittered across Gorilla's face as he spotted the Saint. He tried to lift his head. Alarms sounded on the monitor. He relented, lay back. Nurses scurried into place, scolded us for being too close, shooed us away. Gorilla protested, tried to speak. "Wait." He grabbed the nurse's wrist. A frown creased her forehead. She pried his fingers loose. Other Pagans filtered in. They lined the perimeter of the room like roughshod soldiers poised for battle.

"You'll have to leave now," the nurse said, seemingly unfazed by their dress, all intimidation and bravado dissolved. They weren't so tough here, in this place where even presidents wore paper half-clothes and expired with or without protocol. I watched the Saint's pale face, his eyes dull pinpricks. *You think you can prepare for death, but it just happens,* he had lectured me time and time again. That was the real terror. In the end, no one had control.

The green mountains on Gorilla's monitor suddenly flattened.

"We're losing him," the nurse hollered. White coats blew open the gauze curtain. The family next to us screamed. Doctors in face masks pushed us aside. We scurried like roaches into the hallway. A pall of apprehension surrounded us. I'm sure I forgot to breathe. Pagans spoke in hushed tones. They shuffled their boots. Fluorescent lights washed their faces in an unnatural white glow. They huddled together, argued. Some paced. Others slumped against the wall, chattered, smoked, nibbled chocolate bars from the vending machine. The Saint stood for what must have been hours, unmoving except for a slight tick in his jaw.

Hunger tore at my insides. I didn't dare voice my own needs. I waited for something to happen, some surprise announcement. Pagans consulted the Saint. They held impromptu church in the hallway. I watched the clock on the wall. Night fell. The shift changed. Fresh faces checked on Gorilla.

"What do you think we should do?" the Pagans asked, and I could tell their nerves were shattered. They had no leader. The Saint was Gorilla's natural replacement.

"We need information," the Saint pacified.

"Can you speak to him?" a Pagan asked.

"How long should we wait here?" another inquired.

"He needs guards," the Saint advised. "As long as he's alive, he'll attract visitors."

I volunteered. No one noticed me. I'd be perfect for the job. Satisfied that someone would stay through the night, some of the bikers drifted home, reluctant to be the first to leave, to acknowledge needs such as sleep and hunger. The Saint lingered in the doorway with me. Patients filled the cots behind the gauze curtains. We moved to Gorilla's bed. His nurses and doctors had filtered out. Gorilla's mom was there, sobbing quietly. She was handsome, small-boned, with chiseled Italian features, wide-set eyes, and a severe chin. She stroked Gorilla's hair, and the skin on her hands resembled crushed velvet. She lifted her head when we entered and pinned the Saint with watery, bloodshot eyes.

"Make sure she makes it home safe." The Saint nodded to me. "Help her clean up the bloodstains on her sidewalk."

Gorilla stirred. He lifted his head off his pillow and winced.

"That's not a good idea," the Saint said softly. He moved closer to

Gorilla. I watched the monitors for any signs of distress. Gorilla's chest heaved beneath a series of bandages.

"You know something," the Saint whispered.

Gorilla mumbled. Sweat moistened his forehead. I watched the monitors. The two men huddled. I couldn't hear their exchange, but judging from the Saint's expression, I knew he learned something strange had happened. The conversation proved to be too much effort for Gorilla. The green peaks on his monitor flatlined. Alarms sounded. A flurry of nurses threw back the curtain and pushed us aside. Doctors with masks followed. They held their gloved hands high over their heads. I knew Gorilla was in trouble. The Saint and I retreated into the hallway, dwarfed by the surrounding commotion. Defiance cut deep grooves in the Saint's face. Nerves chafed in my insides. I glanced at the large clock again, watched the seconds tick by until finally a doctor framed the entrance to the emergency room. She spoke through her mask, her eyes darting from the Saint to me: "I'm sorry. He's slipped into a coma."

I spent the rest of that night spraying down the street outside Gorilla's mother's house where he had been gunned down. She lived in a quiet cul-de-sac. Curious neighbors watched from behind drawn curtains. I saw their silhouettes. Predictably, they saw nothing, heard no car backfire, no gunman flee on foot. As dawn hit the streets, only water stains remained. My bucket was filled with bloody rags. Whoever shot Gorilla was as good as dead.

When I finished mopping, I returned to the hospital. *As long as he's alive, he'll have visitors.* The Saint's words echoed in my head. I stood in the hall of the emergency room. This time I was alone. Occasionally, Pagans would visit, drop in, ask how Gorilla was doing, but he remained in a coma and there was little anyone could do. I watched for tremors, unfamiliar faces, uniforms slightly altered, anything that sounded an alarm. My true gifts shone. I was an unassuming, silent, and deadly mole. I blended with the hospital décor, pale and wan. I had finally found my one purpose.

Speculation swirled that Gorilla's assailants may have been members of an Irish street gang who ruled Tenth Street and Oregon Avenue and were miffed about paying the mob's street taxes. But in truth no one had a clue. The only thing for sure was that it was a cowardly hit, not a Pagan's style. "We don't sneak up and hide and shoot in front of your mother's house," one Pagan member explained to a reporter after the shooting. The member was really referring to the club's code of ethics, and how the rest of the country failed to live up to the Pagans' standards. Gorilla was family, and when someone hurts family, Pagans retaliate; the only thing certain was that somebody else would be shot.

As the days passed, the club's loyalty for their president dwindled to general paranoia. Trust between members dissolved. There were rumblings: "If it could happen to him in broad daylight, it could happen to any one of us." Suddenly, the whole ethic, One-for-All, All-for-One, had some qualifications; no one wanted to stick his neck out for a leader, for a cause, if it involved personal risk and an unknown enemy. Crisis brewed and led to infighting, spats between Pagans and isolation by Gorilla, as players and enemies were divided and sorted. By the time Gorilla sputtered awake several weeks later, he found himself mostly alone.

He sat upright in his hospital cot, sedated still, the holes in his chest plugged, and looked at me. "Why are *you* the only one here, kid?" I didn't overanalyze it. I had no agenda, didn't expect any favors out of it. I stayed out of respect for Gorilla. Someone needed to hold vigil and alert the club of surprise night visitors. I did it because the Saint asked me to, because the Saint sponsored Gorilla, because the Saint was family, because he was *my* family. It didn't matter that I wasn't officially part of the club. I belonged.

The nurse smiled at me. "He's well enough to leave." Maybe she

thought I was his son? No one else had stayed. Gorilla met me in the
lobby. He looked fully recovered except for a slight limp. He had no
bodyguards, no fanfare, no Pagans to greet him. If he was surprised by
that, he didn't show it. He didn't say much of anything as he slipped
into the passenger side of my car. That he trusted me to drive him
home spoke volumes.

"No one's following us, right?" Gorilla's voice halted me.

I glanced in my rearview mirror as I peeled away from the curb and
pulled into the middle lane, noting the Honda behind us, the Beetle
to my right, the elderly woman to my left whose head barely peered
over the steering wheel. I could see the hands of all the drivers. No
weapons.

"Don't see anyone," I assured.

"Lot of guys out there still looking to whack me," Gorilla mumbled
under his breath. He crouched low in the seat. Bright sun shone through
the window and I wished I had a visor to block the light. Questions
swirled in my head. I wanted so much to interrogate Gorilla, to tell him
what I knew. Not much. But who was I. Just a seventeen-year-old kid.
Besides, I didn't need to tell Gorilla his witnesses saw nothing, that they
would never testify, that no one, except his mom, darted screaming into
the street to cradle his bloody head in her arms. Silence stretched between us. After a while, Gorilla remarked, an undercurrent to his tone,
"Anyone visit me in the hospital?" His question was more than idle curiosity. He wanted to know whom he could still trust, who had remained loyal to him.

I debated whether to tell him his own bodyguards were less than
vigilant.

"They had another agenda," Gorilla hinted before I could re-
spond. "Maingy's making up for lost time." Maingy was still Mother
Club and technically still Gorilla's boss. It was a nagging detail.
Chapter presidents reported to Mother Club. Gorilla's decisions could

be vetoed by Maingy. Maingy had taken little interest in Gorilla's recovery, but that was Maingy's character: he cared about Maingy. Gorilla could be replaced.

I changed the subject. "Maingy's been recruiting lames."

"Fillers. Geriatrics, dopers, anyone with a bike." Gorilla paused, "I haven't seen Thinker since I got shot." His words vibrated with the threat of anticipated violence. I didn't miss a beat. A real killer never telegraphed his next move. He executed with precision and purpose. And he disposed of evidence. A real killer would never leave a body writhing in the street in front of his mother's house with too many witnesses. I decided Gorilla's would-be assassin wasn't a real killer.

"My sources tell me two brothers tried to shoot me, gangsters from the Tenth and O. I blasted their deli a while back," Gorilla confided. "It was simple payback. One of them disrespected my girlfriend."

He told me the story. "It was a quiet Saturday morning. I had my .357 with me. I busted the entrance and opened fire. Bullets zinged off the countertops, lodged in the wall behind the burners, and exploded flanks of beef. Glass shattered, screams erupted, bodies dropped under tables. One of them fled into the side kitchen. When my gun clicked empty, I reloaded."

"Did you hit anyone?"

"I shot one of them in the ass."

"You think he shot you as payback?"

The explanation might have made sense but for one misplaced detail: Gorilla wasn't dead. And he *should* have been—six bullets? His execution-style hit was sloppy. Why not one bullet to the back of the head? Gorilla would have been dead before he hit the pavement. But it wasn't my place to disagree with Gorilla or to voice an opinion. Gorilla didn't need a sounding board. He needed a confidant, a trusted loyal source who would listen without judgment. I detected inflection in Gorilla's voice, as if he were considering a scenario, not fact. As if Gorilla was unconvinced.

Had *I* planned the hit, I would have tracked Gorilla for months, noted his habits, his style of dress, his favorite drink, his preferred bar or club, what he ate for breakfast, when he went to sleep. A proper hit required attention, hours and hours of boredom punctuated by moments of terror. I would have parked outside Gorilla's house hours before the scheduled hit just so my car blended with the others and my windshield glistened with frost. Never mind that my fingers froze or turned blue, or my teeth chattered, or I pretended to sleep beneath a worn wool blanket that smelled of mildew. Hits required planning, props. Hell, I would even have borrowed a stranger's dog just so I could walk it by Gorilla's house and stare into his living room. But more than that I would have ensured my hit was clean. I would have casually walked away from the scene of the crime, bullets and gun in tow, and tossed both into the river. I would have made damn sure there were no witnesses. Killing was about balls. Anyone could hold a gun and bullets and react. Hell, even I carried two guns strapped to my side, wrapped in plastic sandwich bags, ready to shoot right through the plastic. No fingerprints, no hair, no threads from my jeans. Nothing to trace me back to the murder. Cold-blooded execution required methodical planning, patience Gorilla lacked.

"I didn't kill him." Gorilla shrugged, drummed his fingers on the dash. "But it doesn't matter." Gorilla's eyes darted to the street. Out of habit I noted the cars parallel-parked, whether any idled, any headlights blinked, taillights out, license plates covered. I checked out the woman too in the street, dressed in a halter and tight sequined skirt. I noticed the two tough guys behind her who looked like feds in their crisp striped suits.

"You packing, kid?" Gorilla asked.

I always carried a gun, but for my own protection, not Gorilla's. I nodded. I understood Gorilla's intentions even if he never articulated them.

"You can't be too careful. Friends"—Gorilla snapped his fingers—"they'll snitch you off in a heartbeat. Some will just lose to win. You know what I mean?"

I wasn't certain which category I fell into. I thought of *my* closest friends, some of whom I'd known since childhood, and wondered whether they would betray me under pressure. Whether any would visit me in the hospital, hold vigil, be there to clean up the mess or to drive me home, and my chest constricted. Paranoia seized me. Too many shadows were in the street, too much noise was in my head. I decided I couldn't live like Gorilla, suspicious, paranoid of sudden movements, knocks on the door, cars backfiring. I had to trust people because the enemy of my enemy might later be my friend.

"The cops surprised me that night," Gorilla continued. "They showed up unannounced at my mother's place, said they had a search warrant. One of them sounded almost apologetic. I answered the door in my crimson bathrobe and invited them inside. 'You won't find a thing,' I told them."

"Did they?"

"The cops searched my mother's living room, mindful of her antique armoire, careful not to displace papers and shit on the kitchen counter. They found no weapon." Gorilla grinned. "I asked them if anyone was pressing charges." He paused. "The cops just stared at me with a blank expression and I said, 'I didn't think so.'"

I pulled up in front of Gorilla's mother's house. He had his hand on the latch. He frowned, glanced over at me. "They had to have known something."

"Who?" I asked.

"My bodyguards." He flipped open his copy of the *Philadelphia Daily News* and scowled at his mug on the front page. The headline blasted, "Who Shot Gorilla?"

> The attempted assassination of Gorilla may rank as one of the city's legendary hits that missed. . . . His would-be killer used a .380 caliber handgun, which gun experts say would never kill a guy like Gorilla, at 2:29 AM Saturday near his home on 12th Street near Bigler. . . . Not too many mobsters or bikers can survive a hail of bullets, except in Philadelphia where hits and misses have become an art form. . . . Some lead missiles fall so wide of the mark that their executioners have been dubbed "The Dumbfellas" and "The Gang That Couldn't Shoot Straight."

Some called it Philadelphia's curse. For a time in the early nineties it seemed mobsters had a hell of a time killing *anyone*. Former mob boss John Stanfa, for example, tried to assassinate his rival multiple times with bombs, cyanide poisoning, and even silencers without success. Then *his* rival mob faction retaliated, tried to snipe him as he drove on the Schuylkill Expressway en route to his pasta warehouse; the mob missed and shot Stanfa's son instead. Both survived. Next Joey Merlino, upset that Ciancaglini's brother, Joseph, was Stanfa's underboss, had Ciancaglini shot five times in the only mob hit ever

Former boss of the South Philly chapter of the Pagans, Steve Montevergine (aka "Gorilla") just released from jail. *Courtesy of the* Philadelphia Daily News, *Kitty Caparella*

videotaped by the FBI. Ciancaglini survived but lost his hearing and eyesight. Then in a debacle one Halloween, Merlino, dressed in a masked costume, reportedly test-fired his MAC-10 submachine gun only to run out of ammunition when it came time to actually kill his target.

Rumors circulated that Gorilla's hit was retaliation by the mob. "He had disagreements with Merlino," one cop speculated. "Apparently, one of Merlino's people may have been kidnapped by the Pagans, roughed up and released." Merlino and Gorilla had a pact to work together based on their childhood friendship. But as mobsters started "flipping" or cooperating with the government, their "marriage of convenience" fizzled. One mob source complained to a local reporter that "[the Pagans] only care[d] about money and sex. When you take that away from them, what do they have? They don't care about respect, honor."

But of course that wasn't true. Some even speculated that Gorilla's shooting signaled a warning to Merlino that the New York mob and *its* muscle, the Hells Angels, were taking over. The truth was the bikers were becoming more influential than the mob.

Retaliation had a certain finesse that was supposed to signal an end to a conflict. The rules of engagement went something like this: The first harmful event triggered payback. That payback induced another payback, and another and another, until the end mirrored the beginning and no one ever really settled the score. Gorilla shot up Michael's Deli.

"This isn't over." Gorilla lowered his voice although we were in a closed car. He pulled a pack of cigarettes from his vest pocket and, with shaking hands, lit one.

"They'll want to finish what they started," I agreed.

Gorilla shook out the flame, cracked the window, and tossed the match into the street. Smoke billowed between us. Gorilla rolled up the window.

"Unless *they* never started anything at all?" Gorilla said thoughtfully. He inhaled slowly. "Pagans retaliate. We don't initiate. And payback never settles the score."

Gorilla's phone shrilled. The voice on the other end accused, "How come I got eight sets of colors in my trash can?"

Gorilla emerged from his coma during mass pandemonium. Pagan defectors, or "sheeples" as I termed them, patched over to the Hells Angels in droves.

"They'll take any swinging dick," Gorilla remarked. The Hells Angels needed raw numbers to start a charter in Delaware County. Their goal was to gut the competition and weaken the Pagans' leadership. During Gorilla's hospitalization, my old man patched over and convinced thirteen lames to join him. The Hells Angels offered him better career advancement and he became a traitor for promotion. It was a business decision.

New York Pagans marched down the streets holding banners like flags, chanting, "Die, die, die," and, "Murder, death, kill." These Pagans would later be denied bail by a federal magistrate for having exercised their freedom of speech. The Pagans had found the perfect venue to exact revenge, the Hells Angels' annual Hellraiser Ball, a two-day motorcycle tattoo expo extravaganza held at the Vanderbilt, a few miles from the waterfront in Long Island.

Media reported that Pagans, anticipating bloodshed, had drafted wills, wore bulletproof vests, and armed themselves with baseball bats, ax handles, and machetes. The scene transformed rapidly from festive to a combat zone as Pagans charged onto the twelve-thousand-square-foot marble floor packed with nearly a thousand bikers, tattoo artists, and Hells Angels and fired randomly. Upstairs the blues band Little Wolf jammed while celebrity Angels such as Chuck Zito of *Oz* signed autographs and Sonny Barger promoted his new book, *Ridin High', Livin' Free*. Pandemonium ensued as one Pagan carved an Angel's face with his ax handle and popped out the biker's eye. Bullets struck several Pagans, and fearing police intervention, Pagans dragged their fallen brothers from the scene bloody and unconscious.

Another legendary miss. Gorilla had nothing to do with Hellraiser Ball, but he had a stake in the outcome. He reviewed the plays with me much like an athlete studies the mistakes of his opposing team. Note #1: The Pagans had no plan; they had a kamikaze mission. Note #2: The only exit/entrance was a revolving door, easy to trap bodies. Note #3: Cameras recorded the slaughter on tape. Note #4: Witnesses survived to testify. Note #5: The Pagans missed their targets. Note #6: With one Pagan dead and 74 arrested, there would be retaliation. Gorilla made sure I understood the pitfalls of that mission. He made sure I understood what he expected me to do about Maingy.

"He took me for a dead man in that hospital. He might as well have tried to kill me himself," Gorilla ranted. I had to admit my old man had an impeccable strategy. If *I* were planning a mutiny, I would wait until my leader took multiple bullets in the chest. But I would probably make sure my target expired first.

"What happens now?" I asked.

"We're going to raise some hell," Gorilla said, his face, red and sweaty, pressed close to mine.

My cell phone chirped. The Saint's voice on the line tensed. He sounded breathless, agitated. "It's about Maingy."

"I hope they killed the motherfucker," I interrupted, the words coming out as mere bravado. There was a pause, a lull in conversation. *Shit. Maybe someone has killed him?*

"Meet me in the tattoo shop in fifteen minutes."

I didn't remember the ride over or the traffic lights I must have blown. But when I arrived, I straddled two spots in the parking lot, slammed my car door shut, and raced through the entrance. The Saint's place was unusually quiet for six o'clock. No machines hummed. Lights were dimmed. Gorilla sat in shadow, lost in an overstuffed chair. His breathing was labored. He rested his chin in his hands. No one spoke.

"What's happened?" I finally broke the tension.

"Sit down." The Saint pulled back a chair but I preferred to stand. He leaned against his desk, piles of paper littered the floor.

"I've been a damn fool." Gorilla's voice was chilly. "All this time wasted chasing ghosts." He struggled to get out of his chair but his legs didn't reach the floor.

"I don't follow you," I said. I shrugged at the Saint. *Should we help him get up?* I mouthed. The Saint shook his head, frowned. Maybe I was being disrespectful. Gorilla's legs wiggled. He reminded me of a roach turned upside down, struggling to right himself so that he could make a point.

"Elusive targets others tip off before anyone has the chance to kill them."

I looked to the Saint for some kind of translation.

"Maingy contracted with the Tenth and Oregon Gang to put a hit on Gorilla."

"He was too much of a fucking coward to do it himself," Gorilla spat, and he was finally out of the chair, pacing around the room, stepping on balls of paper.

The news was not unexpected; it was validation. I slumped against the wall. My knees buckled. I felt suddenly dizzy. I caught Gorilla's hard stare, his black, impenetrable eyes that studied me the way a predator studies prey. Maybe he thought *I* had set him up? That *I* had somehow put Maingy up to this? The Saint propped on the edge of his desk, arms folded across his chest. He clicked his pen on and off like a light switch.

"The HA loaned Maingy five hundred thousand dollars toward the purchase of a clubhouse." The Saint's voice was surprisingly calm. "The fucker bought a fifty-thousand-dollar rental and converted it into the HA headquarters in West Philly." The Saint put down his pen. He gauged my reaction. "He pocketed the rest, used it to fund his recruitment campaign."

"He needed me out of the way," Gorilla growled. He blew around me like a storm.

"But he was Mother Club. He would always be the leader of the Pagans, leader of Gorilla," I insisted. I felt cornered suddenly.

"He couldn't control Gorilla." The Saint's jaw slacked. "He wanted his *own* leadership." *His own puppets,* I thought.

"So he recruited Thinker." Gorilla threw up his hands. His face glistened with sweat. "Made *my* bodyguard the Hells Angels' acting president of the West Philly chapter."

I was in trouble. It was one thing for my old man to screw with me, sell my treasured uncle's motorcycle for crumbs, preserve a house while his family starved and his son became a drug addict, but it was quite another to plan the hit of his own rival. Gorilla bore into me and I actually felt the heat from his stare. I knew what was coming. His was a test. Although Gorilla never said the words directly, instinctively I felt that if I wanted to live, *I* would have to be Gorilla's scapegoat and plot to kill my own father. The wall pressed into my back, tiny popcorn projections pricked my skin. Shadows infused me with a strange kind of courage, adrenaline that made my heart pound. Inside I screamed, *I'll do it,* before I even had a chance to process the thought. It would be worth it. Five years. A hundred years. It was the righteous thing to do. Restore honor to my family, to the Pagans, to the code.

Had I lost my fucking mind?

But before I had a chance to act on my convictions, Gorilla applied his own form of vigilante justice. He arranged to meet his rival gangster, a member of the Tenth and O, at high noon at Eleventh Street and Oregon Avenue. A reporter for the *Philadelphia Daily News* described the gunfight as "like a scene out of the O.K. Corral, South Philly style." The showdown over control of Delaware County, much like the control of Tombstone in the Wild West, climaxed months of threats, rivalries, shootings, and pistol-whippings between the two gangs. Except that unlike the legendary sheriff Wyatt Earp and his deputized brothers, Gorilla worked alone.

"The story goes," one reporter wrote, "that both gangsters showed up but only one brought firepower. And without waiting for a signal, Gorilla shot . . . and missed the gangster."

The butcher on the corner had another version. *He* saw "two thugs" immediately "blast each other." One "twitched on the pavement" afterward, then "stumbled and limped away."

"He still had a cigarette dangling from his mouth," another witness gushed on the evening news. "The fight lasted thirty seconds tops." She whistled and shook her head.

"What color was the gun?" The reporter smiled over her microphone as if that were an important detail.

"Dark bronze." The woman's eyes widened to saucers.

"We may never know *who* shot Gorilla, or whether *Gorilla* shot anyone," the reporter ended her broadcast.

But Gorilla always finished what he started. One week later,

Gorilla's daughter's boyfriend tried to do the honors, but he *too* missed. The gangster then shot into the boyfriend's black Blazer. He was charged with attempted murder.

With the first payback complete, Gorilla next turned his attention to my old man. He planned to kill him one night after church. Gorilla couldn't wait for me to put something together.

I had never seen Gorilla so hyped. He commandeered an abandoned warehouse for "the big event." The place was drafty, smelled of engine exhaust and shaved metal. Flashlights brightened the darkness. The steel door's lock broke and the panels banged open like a grand announcement. When Gorilla spoke, he echoed, sounded as if he used a megaphone. His voice boomed through the dark hollows of the warehouse. His heavy boots hammered across the concrete. I cringed from my position in the street. My breath frosted the shattered windowpanes. The streets were deserted. Wind blew trash over my shoes, a crushed beer can, a styrofoam cup, a straw, reminders that we were not alone.

Members paced inside. Their arms flapped in protest and their flashlights bounced wildly across the walls. From the outside the flickers looked like beacons, distress signals of some kind. They had problems with Gorilla's plan.

"That's it?" one challenged. "You're just going to invite him to church?"

"When he walks through those doors, I'll shoot him," Gorilla said simply. He forgot about his echo. He worked like a director, producing himself. He tucked his revolver in his pants, shuffled tables and chairs, muttered his lines, barked at his bodyguards, and obsessed over time. He synchronized three watches on his wrist. He sent me on errands. I had doubts about Gorilla's plan. Sometimes simplicity wasn't just simple, it was stupid.

Predictably Maingy never showed. Instead federal agents swarmed

Gorilla's warehouse. They booked Gorilla for a parole violation, for "fraternizing with known felons." He served only twenty-three months in the Allenwood federal prison in Lycoming County, Pennsylvania, a place many in Philadelphia referred to as "South Philly South."

The town still smarted from its *last* parolee, a Warlock who had killed a police sergeant in 1995 just three months after his release. There was also Tom Thumb, a former Pagan leader, who served life in prison for killing Upper Darby police officer Dennis McNamara. Rumors swirled that my old man worked as an informant. Gorilla's bust happened too quickly, a little too conveniently. The club worried that Gorilla might switch sides and become a Hells Angel. The temptation was there; the Pagans had disbanded their three Philadelphia chapters and had just lost more than seventy members following the Hellraiser Ball debacle. But the Angels had a policy never to recruit former cops. The Pagans didn't have that standard. I'm not sure it would have made a difference.

News of Cheese's death stalled any further revenge. My mom's longtime friend passed in his sleep from diabetic shock. Pagans rode full throttle to the no-frills Our Lady of Joy funeral home, where Cheese was cremated. A police escort controlled traffic congestion. Cheese didn't own a motorcycle. If he had, I would have ridden it to the funeral home and paid Cheese special tribute by placing a rival club's colors on the ground beneath it so that oil from his bike leaked and soiled the cloth.

A light drizzle fell outside the funeral home. A crowd huddled around me, their voices hushed and low. Women held hands. Some openly wept. Cheese's citizen relatives mingled with the outlaws. They joined together in an uncommon grief. One old lady hugged another, exposing the stinger on her scorpion tattoo. Expectation crackled in the air. There was no priest, no prayers muttered, no final grace. Diabetes claimed parts of Cheese, rotted his fingernails, left holes in his teeth, deformed his foot, and reduced him to a mere husk of his former self. His death hit me especially hard. Inside the pine-paneled funeral home, the crowd shifted and sweated in the stifling, overheated room. There was no music. One biker rose, opened the back door to let the wind rush in. Cheese's wife, Crackers, wailed suddenly, her red hair fanned around her runny face. Her body shook with grief. She lifted her head, exposed her toothless mouth to me, and hollered, "I loved him. I loved him."

I recalled the night she lost her teeth. I was partying with the Saint and Cheese at a fellow Pagan's house. Cheese was bombed, on his fifth beer at least, which he chased with a time-release opiate patch he swallowed whole. His face contorted at once from laughter to dry heaves. His chin disappeared into his shoulders. His glasses slipped from the bridge of his nose. Sweat coated his body from the alcohol consumption. Cheese threw up his hands in despair at me and complained, "I can't control her, man."

I wasn't sure what to do. I was only a kid, and theirs had always been the best example that two people could actually love each other.

Crackers, locked behind a bathroom door, banged on the walls with her fists, and when that proved ineffective, she threw her boots at the ceiling. Glass shattered inside. High on dust and booze, she slurred her scream. "You're a pussy. You're a pussy."

I watched the scene unravel until the Saint said, "Crazy bitch." He squeezed Cheese's shoulder, moved toward the bathroom, and tapped lightly on the door. "You're okay now, right? Come on out."

Slowly, the doorknob turned. A chilly stillness filled the air. Crackers peeked outside. The Saint punched her hard in the face. White chips flew onto the tiles. Blood pocked the Saint's fist. Crackers wailed again and on her hands and knees scooped up her broken teeth.

"She's under control *now*. You shouldn't have any more problems."
My old man had once controlled my mom like that too.

"She had a darkness about her," the Saint explained. "That kind
of rage has to be contained, you understand?"

I understood the darkness. After a while my old man ordered Crackers to be my mom's bodyguard. I envisioned the two women, Crackers,
the she-man, dragging my mom by her ponytail and wielding a club
when my mom whispered too loudly.

Crackers sobbed, and despite her loss of teeth, Cheese meant something to her. Not love exactly, but witness, fierce attachment. I thought
of my own mom. I might have given up trying to rescue her, but I still
cared about her; I was still a part of her. And if *she* passed . . . I wasn't
sure I would survive the terrible silence in her wake. I studied the
crowd gathered around me, their wet, swollen faces, and wondered if
they understood why they were here.

"Few people in this life can say they truly lived." I remember the
speech I gave. My voice hitched. I had never before spoken in public.
But Cheese's life deserved something like a prayer. Few among us could
boast affection, love, or even true intimacy. Cheese was the exception. I
swatted the flies that buzzed around my lips. *Amen*s rumbled through
the mourners.

"Cheese was legally blind, but Crackers was his Seeing Eye dog.
They had each other. Two lives were lost today." I paused, and the
stillness in the air resembled transition. "As fucked-up as we all are,
we all need each other. We're all family. We're *here*."

Applause resounded through the crowd like punctuation. Thunder
rolled through the gray afternoon. Mourners parted for Gorilla, whose
large hands smacked together like mitts. He resembled a cartoon, with
his broad forehead, fringe of dark hair, and wide upper chest that

nearly exploded from a small, cinched waist. He stopped abruptly in front of me and pressed his palms into my shoulders.

"Don't you think it's time you put the coat on?" I learned a long time ago that everything meaningful had a sinister complement. Wind whipped around me, blew debris onto my boots. Gorilla's nails pressed into my shoulder. I didn't answer him right away. Part of me wasn't sure Gorilla's was a question. The other part of me thought the gesture was redundant. After all, I already *lived* as a Pagan. I already belonged without the formal invitation. As far as I was concerned, I had earned my patch. The Saint left his post by the entrance and moved closer to me. The drizzle outside turned to rain.

"What are you doing, Gorilla?" A hint of threat laced the Saint's voice. Rain spit at the windows. Unease itched up my spine. I tucked Cheese's glasses into my jacket pocket, my one tangible memory. Water fogged the windows. Tears streamed down Cracker's cheeks. She blinked at me, resignation in her expression. She had lost more than Cheese. She had lost her identity. She would never recover from his death.

"It's the kid's decision whether to prospect for the Pagans."

No, it wasn't. I either had to join Gorilla or risk being Gorilla's target. I decided then that if I prospected for the Pagans at all, it would be on my own terms, not Gorilla's. I had my own mission after all—revenge against my old man—and if my goal aligned with Gorilla's, even better. Officially becoming a Pagan had its advantages: I had instant reinforcements, easy access to my target, and armed soldiers willing to defend me. Gorilla didn't need to know my reasons for joining. Better to let Gorilla think he controlled me.

Rivers of mud snaked down the pavement outside the funeral home. Mourners scattered. The Saint put a hand on Gorilla's shoulder and the boss released his grip. Gorilla gave me a nod and walked into the rain. I watched him leave feeling as if I'd narrowly missed a bullet.

No one refused Gorilla without consequences. Even the Saint didn't intervene. It wasn't his place. I was old enough to make my own decisions. I wouldn't have taken his advice anyway. The road slicked with rain. Gorilla straddled his bike, revved his engine, and roared away from the curb.

"Did I teach you nothing?" the Saint exploded. He smacked the side of my head with an open hand. My face smarted from the blow, but by this time I was numb to violence. Rain splashed over me. The Saint never flinched. He looked at me with pity in his eyes.

"Everything I know I learned from you," I said quietly, and braced myself for another punch. But the Saint shoved his hands into his coat pockets and said almost under his breath, "You're not like us. You don't have to prove anything to these clowns. You don't have to be a hero."

He needn't have worried. There was nothing "heroic" about surrender.

"I need to do this." Cold wind scratched my cheeks. Neither of us spoke for several minutes. Mud streaked my jeans and face. I was only partly lying.

"Gorilla's using you." Anger swirled around us. A flurry of people sprinted past us to their bikes, sheltered their heads with their hands. Rain soaked through them. I was using Gorilla. I needed access to my old man and an excuse to take care of business.

My teeth chattered partly out of cold and partly out of fear.

I made excuses. "I've *lived* this life."

"All the more reason you shouldn't choose it," the Saint said pointedly.

"It was good enough for you but not for me?"

"I left," the Saint reminded me. "The worst thing I ever did to the club was leave it."

"No one ever leaves this life. I tried. I got tired of living in a red world. The drugs, they fucked up my head. Don't you ever get tired of . . . just existing?"

The Saint said nothing but I knew I'd touched a nerve. He blinked at me and his expression sobered. I think he finally got it; I was no longer a kid, no longer invisible, no longer someone he could control. *I* had passed over, and whether he approved or not, the club *was* my life. I was born into it, born into the madness. I couldn't leave it, couldn't disown my old man and expect to just go on. The difference between the Saint and me was that I didn't want to *be* a legacy. I wanted to leave one.

18

N N N N N

Prospecting

We're going to break up civilization so we can make
something better out of the world.
—CHUCK PALAHNIUK, *FIGHT CLUB*

Prospect," Gorilla barked at me on my first official day of hazing.
"Fetch me a beer." Being Gorilla's bitch slave didn't come easily. As
far as I was concerned, I had already paid my dues. I was *born* a prospect. I had already earned my colors. I required no special training,
though I'll admit I lacked stamina to jog up and down multiple flights
of stairs, stay awake for nights at a time (without crank), and clean
other members' toilets.

Being a prospect meant being prepared to hustle drugs at a moment's notice, sometimes multiple times in one day, at different locations across town. It meant standing guard at a vacant post for hours,
doing nothing, waiting for something to happen, or running to different

shops searching for certain brands of chocolate, beer, or Moon Pie. We understood all else in our life was secondary, family, kids, dogs, God, country. None of it mattered anymore. Our first priority was the club. If we were tasked with a mission, we were expected to perform even if it meant we might go to prison. If we hesitated or refused, there were consequences. We risked a beating, humiliation, or, worse, death. If we wanted to be "outlaws," we had to act like ones.

It was early evening and Gorilla prepared for church. He ordered prospect Chewie and I to guard the street. Mostly we counted empty cars and took turns hustling beer and smokes inside for the members. By the fifth or sixth run, Gorilla hollered at me, "Get me some meth."

"You just *bought* him dope earlier today," Chewie protested under his breath. He had a mass of brown beard, eyes like tacks, and a nervous disposition. He lumbered when he walked, breathed a little too hard, and stuttered when alarmed.

"What are you standing around for?" Go-Fast poked his head outside and handed me his revolver. I stuck it in my waistband. Light faded to dark. Thunder rumbled in the night sky. My feet dragged like rubber. I hit the pavement, heading for the cemetery where I knew I could score. At least the task was some reprieve from the barrage of orders and beer errands. Go-Fast's gun chafed my belly. My heart beat faster. If I was pinched with dope and a weapon, I could do five years. *And that is supposed to prove what?* I thought. *That I am loyal to the Pagans, that I am down for the cause?*

I flipped the collar of my trench coat up and headed into the sparse grounds. Drizzle fell. My nerves were shot. I started to question my sanity. How many times could I do this drug dealing and get away with it? I beeped my contact, padded softly to a crushed mound of leaves near Mr. John Plumb's grave. He had died in World War II. I liked the graphics on his headstone. The words looked Egyptian and ancient. He had been a soldier. He had died for a cause and so that made him some kind of hero. I shivered as the first raindrops hit my face. I wondered what war I fought and if I would die for a cause.

My drug source emerged from the street, a skinny, shadowy figure that resembled one of the dead. He jogged over to me. He had a clear plastic trash bag draped over his head. Rain dampened his black, stringy ponytail. He looked pale in the dark, skittish and old. His coat had no zipper. We never exchanged words. He never looked at me. Instead he looked over his shoulder into the darkness. I flashed him cash. He slipped me a baggie. Simple. Quick. Clean. Off he darted through the graves. I stuffed the dope in my pocket. I didn't feel triumphant. I felt stupid. *What does it prove anyway?* That I could score dope? I kept waiting for the hard-core stuff, the reason I prospected in the first place.

By the time I returned to the clubhouse, I was soaked. A party was already in full swing. Loud percussion pounded the street. I hesitated at the entrance. Chewie did push-ups inside. Punishment for some perceived screwup. A young bouncer blocked the door. Built like a mountain, he leaned forward, his breath reeking of whiskey straight from the bottle. His mouth drooped half-open. His steely blue eyes filmed over like a fish's. A chain snaked through one hand. He shook the chain in my face. Behind him the door opened to a stairwell that spiraled down into the dark. He wore a white T-shirt seared to his chest, brown boots with thick heels. He punched me through. Women emerged from the hole; their pale skin and black cow eyes followed me hungrily as if they could smell the meth on me. They looked runway thin and moved with legs like columns upstairs into the murky light.

"Prospect."

The room, already crowded, reeked of beer. My eyes smarted from the bowl of smoke. I found Gorilla in a back room draped with women. Candlelight flickered along the walls. Strippers straddled his stubby legs. Some licked his grizzled cheeks. Their tongues looked soapy, streaked with white residue. They had stage names like Chastity, Luscious, and Enchantress. I knelt by Gorilla's head, flashed him my score. Gorilla nodded, turned lazily to Go-Fast. "You think it's enough?"

The Pagan pretended to inspect the meth, winked at Gorilla. "Nope."

Gorilla put his fist in my chest. Pain shot through me. I stifled a choke. *What the fuck?*

"We'll need a bucket." Gorilla laughed.

"You've got to be shitting me," Chewie panted when I told him I was off again.

"That's what we signed up for," I said, pulling my wet coat tighter, not at all sure how this furthered the brotherhood or the cause or whatever other bullshit I promised to fulfill.

"I didn't sign up for this," Chewie protested as we heard simultaneous barks of "Prospect."

"Better get moving," I said.

Chewie shot me a distressed look and grunted. With only two of us and me off again scoring dope for Gorilla, Chewie became the members' only bitch slave. By now it was pouring. Sheets of rain fell. Cold bit through me. I trudged into the wet street feeling sick. I didn't return to the cemetery. Instead I walked for what seemed like miles into a maze that formed the projects. Flashes of my former street life hit me. *What the hell am I doing? The same thing I've been doing for years, only now I'm doing it for "family," for Gorilla.* Except that now I didn't even get to keep the score. The streets buckled beneath my feet. I stumbled over potholes. I staked out a familiar crack house, scoped the different cars that pulled in and out of the driveway. Foiled windows blocked my view of the inside. I waited for an opening.

When I returned hours later with more dope, Chewie looked as if he were ready to break. He looked pale, dragged down. Red lines scratched his eyes. He stank of beer. The party was in full swing. As I waded through the limbs in search of Gorilla, I heard the barks again: "Prospect." It was after two in the morning and I knew my day would repeat in a few hours. I couldn't remember my last meal. A dull ringing resounded in my ears. I slammed back beer just to stay awake.

"Is it quitting time yet?" Chewie huffed under his breath. He hustled by me with two cold beers. Pagans partied sometimes for days at a time, fueled by meth. There was no such thing as "quitting time." Technically prospecting wasn't like a job where we had scheduled work hours. If we were lucky, we had white space. At least I *knew* what I was getting into. I should have known better. I worried about Chewie. His sponsor had run him ragged for the worse part of ten hours without reprieve. So far his had all been grunt work, fetching beer, moving furniture, mopping vomit and piss from the floor. I wondered how he'd react the first time a member asked him to shoot someone.

The partying showed no signs of letting up. I found Gorilla snoring. His face was buried in a stripper's lap, his pants pooled at his ankles. I gave the meth to Go-Fast. As I headed out of the room, a parade of strippers stomped in front of me on a makeshift stage made out of two tabletops pressed together. Loud music blared from the speakers. The women writhed seductively to heavy percussion, shaking out of their skimpy, bright middriffs and flinging their bras into the crowd of salivating Pagans. They wriggled out of their jeans. One flung her panties in my face. Thongs wrapped around lamps like slingshots. The strippers stood completely naked except for slim heels. Cheers erupted. Money flashed. Members called out sex acts, such as wild pool, "ball to the corner pocket," and the girls, desperate for cash, spread their legs and rocked to a primitive erotica. The Pagans tore at them like savage wolves. Scratch marks puffed their skin. Soon, they were no longer women, no longer even human. Bodies pressed together, mutating into one lumpy sculpture.

Long arms dragged me to the stage. I felt nauseous and dizzy, vaguely aware of a stripper's hands unzipping my jeans. Another raked her razor nails along my belly, leaving little half-moon cuts above my navel. Suddenly I was part of the show, in my own exhibition. Pagans clapped for me. Sweat stung my eyes. I was on my back staring at the bladed shadows of a ceiling fan. The room spun. Large breasts flopped on my chest like giant Moon Pies. Lights flickered over the women's faces. They bobbed around me like disembodied heads. They whispered my name, flashed their pointy teeth, bit me in places until I went numb. Laughter echoed in my ears, made the hair on my neck bristle. My head throbbed. I groaned into one stripper's crotch. She rocked robotically until I gagged. A member yanked her away from me by her hair and shook her at the crowd like a prized trophy. He pawed at the stripper and aggressively devoured her.

I rolled off the stage. My head hit the ground with a loud thud.

"Lap dance, lap dance," boomed in my ears.

"You're bleeding," a stripper whispered in my ear. She poured beer into my wounds and licked the edges. Her tongue burned like fire. I couldn't move. Boots crushed around me. One pinned my hair to the floor. I needed to leave before a stampede took me into the street.

Chewie shoved a beer in my hand. "Keep drinking. It will help. You won't remember any of this."

The next evening Gorilla wanted me to meet him at the warehouse before church. I hadn't yet recovered from the night before. My head pounded. I was pretty sure I was still drunk. When I rolled up, Gorilla

sat at the head of a metal card table he'd arranged in the middle of
the room. Four members joined him. They spoke in hushed tones.
Prospects typically remained outside, not privy to business negotiations, but Gorilla wanted me present. Beer cooled in the portable refrigerator. Night air whipped through cracks in the windows. Gorilla
snapped his fingers at another prospect, Marshall, who, like a trained
monkey, produced a bottle of beer for him.

"This is how it's done, kid." Gorilla took the beer from Marshall
and calmly let it slip through his fingers. It crashed to the floor. Am-
ber liquid sloshed over chunks of glass.

"Get me another," Gorilla demanded. "And clean up this mess."

Marshall dropped to his knees and mopped the beer with his shirt.
He returned to the refrigerator and brought Gorilla another full
bottle. Gorilla removed the cap with his teeth, took a long pull, and
spit beer in Marshall's face, pouring the rest over Marshall's head.
The prospect never flinched. Acceptance was the first sign of respect.
It was a game I wasn't sure I wanted to play or even could.

"How come your shit doesn't stink?" Marshall asked later as he
joined me outside the entrance to the warehouse. The Pagans had no
interest in testing me. They knew who I was and where I came from.

"You're not from around here, are you?" I lit a blunt and leaned
against the steel doors. The air smelled of chemicals and exhaust. Marshall's skin was baby fresh with a bridge of freckles. Wet pools stained
his armpits. He smelled of beer and piss. Not exactly outlaw material.

"I'm from the same place you are," Marshall deflected, not giving
up his secrets. He glared at me, his ruddy complexion a little too moist
in the frigid air.

"Shitsville?"

"Is that dope?" Marshall's tone sounded more like confirmation
than accusation, and I wasn't sure if he was recording me or taking

notes for Gorilla. Prospects couldn't do drugs; *selling* them was perfectly acceptable. But I didn't take orders from Marshall.

"Do you pay my bills?"

Marshall frowned. Silence stretched between us. I took another hit and dropped the blunt to the ground. I jammed it with my boot toe.

I switched the subject. "How long you plan on doing this?"

"As long as it takes." It was a good answer, a well-rehearsed answer. Prospecting had no particular time frame, though some clubs, such as the Hells Angels and Mongols, insisted prospects pledge for a year or more. The Warlocks prospected for twelve weeks. The length of time had everything to do with security, discovering punk bitch cops who worked undercover in task-force operations. Most clubs understood that law enforcement had limited resources, manpower, and surveillance personnel and couldn't sustain an infiltration for more than a few months. As an additional safeguard, the Pagans conducted background investigations on prospects. The club needed to verify the identity of its applicants. They checked phone records, addresses of relatives, work history, and criminal records. They made surprise visits to the prospects' relatives. Still, I wondered about Marshall.

"Where're you from?" I challenged him.

"Same place you are." Marshall's answers sounded safe, deliberately vague, like a cop's, and it occurred to me that the two organizations, cops and bikers, were really not so different. Both adopted a rank-and-file structure similar to the military's, conducted background investigations of prospective members, and required that each applicant pass a series of tests, psychological, physical, and, in the cop's procedure, written. Both clubs wore uniforms, earned patches, carried weapons, and considered themselves a "brotherhood" of like-minded misfits. Both spoke in code and referred to one another by a moniker. Both had rogues; the cops had their choirboys, the Pagans had their drug addicts. Both posed control problems and compromised the integrity of the club. It wasn't such a leap to think Marshall might be a cop.

"How long have you lived in Shitsville?" I asked.

"Four years."

Turns out all of Marshall's answers were "four years."

"What do you think of Marshall?" Gorilla asked me weeks later. It was an odd question for a full patch to be asking a mere pledge; but Gorilla didn't think of me as just another prospect. I took the bait. We were alone. We could speak freely. Church had ended.

"I don't trust him," I said without elaboration.

"You don't like him?"

"I don't trust him. There's a difference."

"Okay." Gorilla sniffed, drummed his fingers on the card table.

"I think he's too rehearsed," I qualified. "He *sounds* like a cop."

Gorilla scraped his chair from the table and paced to the window. He bent a slat of blind with his thumb and studied the street traffic. Paranoia seized me. *Is he expecting someone?* Sweat creased my hands. *Is he setting me up? Did I say the wrong thing? Am I going to get jacked?* Instinctively I reached for my waistband and regretted not carrying my gun. I didn't wear any cuts at all. I didn't want to be labeled. I convinced Gorilla I was more useful to him anonymous. Utility was important to Gorilla. I realized then that he didn't give a fuck about my opinion. I was a mere fungible. He wanted information. He wanted to test my loyalty, find out whether I would tell him the truth about other prospects, whether he could trust me. Maybe he had commissioned Marshall to do the same and was playing us off one another? I was disappointed. I would have preferred that Gorilla pair me with someone tough and loyal, someone who would kill for me as quickly as he would get me a cigarette. I wanted to add that Marshall wrote letters to his mom, that no one wrote letters anymore, and wasn't that fucked-up?

But Gorilla didn't move, didn't face me. He stared into the street, let the blind snap back, and said simply, "I like him."

The next night, Gorilla ordered me to provide security for him while he barhopped. He brought along his new girlfriend, a shaggy young woman with an oversize head and thin waist who had a perpetual purple eye. Several other full patches brought along their dates, mostly strippers with paper-thin skin and corded veins. They wore short shorts, spiked gold heels, and long, colorful coats. They draped the bikers like costume jewelry. We arrived at the Chip, an overcrowded bar with televisions mounted on every wall. Music blared from a jukebox. Spilled beer soaked the floor. The place reeked of smoke. The bar owner looked more than a little nervous as Gorilla muscled his way inside. He commandeered a stool at the bar; his girlfriend stood next to him and their shoulders touched. He ordered her a beer, massaged her ass.

I lingered behind near the bathrooms where it was dark and I had a good view of the action. A fresh-faced grunt at the end of the bar held his gaze a little too long on Gorilla's date. The grunt looked glazed, held up his beer, and toasted, "To nice asses." Gorilla's face flushed. He snapped to attention. His girlfriend wobbled beside him, her droopy eyes stared blankly at him. Gorilla smacked her with an open hand and she fell backward, hitting her head on the floor. She looked stunned, disoriented. She brushed her hair from her eyes, licked the blood from her lower lip, and crawled on her hands and knees through the maze of legs. Part of me wanted to help her, drag her out of the dark, pull her toward the street, and hail her a taxi. I didn't like to see women abused. But it wasn't my place to help her. She knew what Gorilla demanded. She participated willingly. She blended. Battle wounds were expected.

"What the fuck are you lookin' at?" Gorilla slammed his fist into the drunk's chin. The citizen's beer stein tumbled out of his hand and crashed to the floor. He fell backward, righted himself, and whined like a pig. I leaped to Gorilla's aid like a good prospect, grabbed the man by his hair, and pummeled him with my fists. My first thought was to drag him out of there before Gorilla pulled out his buck knife and carved up the guy's face. But another Pagan joined in and kicked the drunk square in the jaw with his steel-toed boot.

The drunk's head snapped backward. His bottom teeth cracked. Blood splattered onto my hands. He flopped like a rag doll in my arms. Barstools went airborne. Pretty soon everyone was fighting someone. Patrons screamed around me. Gorilla looked crazed, half-animal, half-human. The veins in his neck bulged. He let out a howl. Another drunk pounced on Gorilla's back, encircled his throat with his fingers. Adrenaline rippled through me as I lunged at him, pried him off Gorilla. Out of nowhere a fist caught me in the eye, blinded me momentarily, and knocked my head into the bar. I reeled back, recovered, and responded with a fast shot to the assailant's nose.

Noise faded around me to dull, muffled thuds. Fists, clubs, glass. Gorilla's date huddled in a corner, knees pulled to her chest. Her body shook. Spilled beer dampened her head. She waited obediently for Gorilla, willing to take the fall if necessary. I could smell the citizen's breath full of cigarettes and alcohol and rage. My heart raced. The scene shrank. My legs moved slowly, clumsily, as if I were underwater. I heard only the pounding in my heart.

"Motherfucker," I screamed at my attacker, hoping to draw someone's attention.

The drunk on the floor lay still, curled in a fetal ball, hands clutching his head. Pagans continued to savagely kick him, the sound like a bat to a pillow. Sirens blared. In a flash the blade disappeared. Patrons spilled into the street. The owner and the bouncer tried to control the mêlée. My heart pounding, I dragged Gorilla outside, rolled him onto the curb.

"You need to get out of here," I panted as blue and red wigwags flashed over my face.

"We should have shot the motherfucker," Gorilla said fiercely. He held on to my coat collar, his face splotchy with rage. My hands shook. I knew there would be consequences; no one disrespected a Pagan president and lived.

Gorilla obsessed over the drunk. For the next several nights he ordered me to stake out the bar, find the citizen who disrespected his old lady, and "take care of business." I tucked a revolver in my waistband, watched the bar from across the street, pretended to hunt down the target, and knew I wasn't going to shoot anyone. I made up a story: "Your guy is lost." I shrugged.

"What do you mean *lost*?" Gorilla's nostrils flared. He paced the tiny garage where he had just finished church. He cracked his knuckles, skimmed his hands across a metal tabletop. The door slit open and the air smelled of rain. We stood in shadow. A cold draft blew around us. The member whose house Gorilla borrowed lived with his mother. I heard her shuffle inside. A teakettle whistled. A television blared. Canned laughter filtered through the door.

"He probably got spooked, found out he'd messed with a Pagan president, and took off," I lied.

Gorilla stopped pacing. He fixed me with a hard stare that made my palms sweat.

"Maybe he's not so stupid after all."

◆

Gorilla's focus turned to defectors, "turncoats" he called them. At the time Delaware County only had a handful of 1 percenter biker clubs—the Pagans, Warlocks, and Wheels of Soul. With the encroachment of the Hells Angels into Philadelphia, members of other clubs switched allegiances. Some Pagans "patched over"; Warlocks lost some of their own to the Outlaws. Gorilla panicked. "I need to know who's on the fence." He paced one night at church. "Bring in Upland Garage." Upland Garage was one of several local "duck clubs" in the area, Pagan supporters who were not 1 percenter bikers, but who aspired to be recruited by them.

Gorilla was high as a kite and manic. It was early evening and he held church in Sal Reddy's basement. The place was stifling hot as if the radiator had busted, as if hell itself licked at the walls. Upland Garage's president, wearing denim cuts, thick construction chains, and a large gold cross, towered over Gorilla. My eyes smarted from the cigarette smoke. The wooden stairs squeaked with the Upland Garage's president's weight as he descended into the meeting like an animal into a den. A strange musty smell hung in the air. Prospects and members abruptly scraped back their chairs from the long table where they gathered, their expectant faces flickering in the dim light like bulbs. Gorilla snapped his fingers and Upland Garage's president sat, his leg shaking, on a wooden stool in front of him. Animals responded to weakness. Gorilla paced in front of him growing more and more agitated. His arms dangled to his knees. No one spoke. Not a sound in the room except Gorilla's labored breathing. The Pagans resembled a small army. Like soldiers we lined the perimeter, blocked the only exit to the stairs and to the outside. We displayed our pick handles and guns. Expectation hung in the air. Gorilla wanted the tension to build, wanted the president to squirm. Most of all, he wanted Upland Garage to know where their loyalties belonged.

"Are you on the fence or off the fence?" Spit flew from Gorilla's mouth. The president hesitated, blinked at Gorilla. I could tell he was nervous. Sweat stained his armpits. He stuttered, mumbled something unintelligible, looked around the room for a clue. Gorilla's nostrils flared, and with a swift movement he whipped out his pistol, pressed it to the president's temple, and pulled the trigger. The gun clicked. Gorilla laughed.

Just answer the fucking question, I telegraphed.

Gorilla's bodyguards moved in and took turns slapping Upland Garage's president. They made a game of it, as if the president's head were a tennis ball.

"I don't understand the question," he mewled. Slap.

"Are you on the fence or off the fence?" Gorilla repeated. Another slap.

"Repeat the question." The bodyguard delivered a hard smack with the butt of his pistol. Gorilla's eyes narrowed. I knew some of the prospects in Upland Garage. Some knew my old man. Gorilla not only tested them, he tested me. The game was as much for me as it was for Upland Garage in case I had any thoughts of switching sides. The stool toppled over. The president crawled into fetal position, cupped his hands around his head, and blocked another blow. A wide blood band darkened the president's scalp. I scanned the dimly lit room and saw the panic in the prospects' faces. The scene had an unreal quality. It replayed over and over as if no one, not even Gorilla, knew how to *stop* the play. At some point the violence had to reach a climax, a point. I envisioned the room red. Upland Garage's vice president dropped his cigarette to the floor and smashed the butt with his boot. He looked wired, anxious, as if he was ready to sacrifice. I knew him.

"Are you on the fence or off the fence?" Gorilla's voice resounded in my ears like tin.

"Let *him* answer the question." I pointed to the vice president. It was crazy, talking out of line, interrupting Gorilla's show, even *suggesting* another player answer the question. As a mere prospect, I wasn't allowed to have an opinion. I wasn't allowed to disagree with Gorilla, especially not in public. All eyes turned to me. I held my breath.

"We're on the fence. Of course we're on the fence," the vice president assured.

"Can you get me a gram?" Gorilla ordered. Unwittingly I had become an expert dope dealer. Gorilla preferred to be wired for church meetings, which he held wherever he could, in members' basements, in bars, at clubs, any place Gorilla could find to huddle with a few of his core members and discuss TCB, or "taking care of business." All formality had disappeared with Gorilla's reign, and maybe that, after all, was the club's downfall. Without a central meeting place, the club had a nomadic, scattered feel to it.

I assumed my usual post, guard duty at the top of the stairs, where I could eavesdrop as Gorilla unveiled his grand plan to avenge turncoats. I worked alone that night, which wasn't so unusual. It just meant I worked harder servicing the members, running up and down the stairs armed with beer and cigarettes. Mostly I just stood hours and hours waiting to be useful.

"We'll kill them, take their jackets by force." Gorilla's voice filtered upstairs. He sounded juiced, stoned out of his mind. Adrenaline pumped through me.

"And who's going to head *that* mission?" I recognized Granny's voice. An older Pagan in his fifties, he should have retired his colors long ago. But the club kept him in play. No one had expected him to live as long as he did, and there wasn't really a mandatory retirement plan.

"The kid," Gorilla said. I perked up at that. I liked that he called me "kid" rather than "prospect." It elevated me somehow. Either Gorilla made me his first choice because he thought I was the best for the mission, or he selected me because I was one of his disposable soldiers. Gorilla knew I would do it, not because I wanted so badly to be a full patch but because Maingy was one of the turncoats and Gorilla knew how much I hated my old man. Our agendas aligned.

"The kid?" Granny was incredulous.

"He's no kid," another Pagan seconded Gorilla's motion.

"He needs to put in his time," Granny quipped.

Anger simmered inside me. *Who the fuck does he think he is? I've put in more time than all of them combined. I should have been wearing that jacket by now.* I couldn't help myself. Completely against protocol, I shouted downstairs, "*Granny* shouldn't be in church."

My remarks were met with silence, and I thought I'd really done it. I was out before I even started. I had lost my advantage. I waited for the storm, the clatter of boots on the stairs, the blow to the back of my head, the five-shot revolver pressed into my temple. Someone scraped his chair. Another cleared his throat. Conversation restarted as if I hadn't disturbed the flow. *Come on, you motherfuckers, fight me. Put me in my place. Tell me to shut the fuck up. Do something.* The meeting continued. I lost respect for Granny that night. I imagined Gorilla hushed Granny and the others downstairs, put a finger to his lips, warned them not to mess with me, that I was "good people." Good enough to sacrifice.

Snippets of conversation drifted up to me and I realized I was being volunteered for a crime spree. I tried to rationalize the situation. *Even if I get busted, I won't do more than five years. I'm the lookout, not the triggerman.* But my thoughts quickly soured and I realized

Gorilla wouldn't be that kind: *Accomplice, ringleader. You'll do the most time.*

How hard can it be? I envisioned planning hits, the chaos before *the* pivotal moment when it all went down. Prospects, armed with pistols, baseball bats, ax handles, and machetes would enter the bar where the turncoats drank. They would wait for my signal. If citizens lingered inside near closing, I would postpone the whole mission. I had rules—no hits took place near women or children.

"Kid, get down here," Gorilla interrupted my thoughts. The meeting had ended. Members shuffled upstairs. Most didn't look at me. I didn't take it personally. I was Prospect to them. It was late, nearly four o'clock in the morning. My legs wobbled with fatigue but I jogged downstairs anyway, nearly tripped on a tack in the rug, and landed breathless in front of Gorilla.

"I'm putting you on a mission. You're doing this for me. You accept no other assignments." He kicked out a chair and motioned for me to sit.

"What about mandatory meet and greets?" The club required all new prospects to attend social gatherings so that other members could meet them, assess their merits, and critique their sponsor's choice. But more than pleasantries occurred at these functions. Inevitably brawls erupted, testosterone challenges, head butts and fire spray. Police hovered on street corners. There was risk attached.

"I'm excusing you," Gorilla said, and surprisingly I knew what he meant.

"People will think you're playing favorites."

"What do I give a fuck what other people think?"

"You want surveillance?"

"For starters." Gorilla paused. He stood, adjusted his weapon on his waist, and ordered, "Take Marshall with you."

I tried to tell myself it was just business, but like hell was I going to train a suspected cop about reconnissance missions. Still, I knew better than to protest. Either Gorilla didn't quite trust me to play well with others, or he needed me to keep tabs on his new recruit. Some prospects were forced to roll around inside oak barrels all day down a grassy hill at the Farm, traipse around the city collecting chocolate éclairs for their sponsor, run beer errands, stay up for days, but I had to train Marshall. *How* I did that was up to me.

"What's the plan?" Marshall met me later that night. He parked his black-and-white motorcycle near the curb. We called them Zebras, cop bikes. Maybe they were standard-government-issued rides? Maybe it was just coincidence that Marshall rode one? He slid into the passenger side of my car and shivered. I don't think he liked me much either. I shut the heat off. I planned to park it for a while and I couldn't have a warm car melting the ice from my windshield.

I lay down my ground rules. "Never talk to me in this car. If you want to say something, you use your hands. Okay? I don't know what's bugged and I don't know where you've been."

"Okay. Never talk to you in this car."

"I don't like it when you do that."

"Do what?"

"Repeat everything I say. Are you recording me?"

"I don't know what you're talking about."

"Don't fuck with me, okay," I warned. "I know what you're about."

Marshall threw up his hands in mock surrender. He shook his head incredulously.

"Gorilla—," he began.

"Gorilla may be my sponsor, but I don't work for him, understand? I call the shots. If I don't like the way the plan is going, I'm going to call it off."

Marshall squinted at me. Maybe he was shocked by my irreverence. Maybe he couldn't wait to get out of the car and snitch me off.

"Something you need to know." I lowered my voice. "I don't like
you. And I don't trust you. You're only here sitting in my car because
Gorilla wants you here."

Marshall rubbed his hands together. His breath blew cold. We had
some sort of understanding. I told him the plan, the hours and hours
of surveillance ahead of us. I told him about possible turncoats, the
bars they targeted, the women they fucked, their mothers' addresses.
And then I told him to get out of my car.

"Open your coat," I demanded.

Marshall blanched. He protested weakly. It was cold. His hands
were practically raw.

"Open your fucking coat." I reached for his collar, unzipped his
denim jacket, patted him down, and kicked his legs apart.

"What the hell . . ."

"I have to be sure you're not wired." I had heard back in the day
that undercover cops wired tape recorders and microphones to their
groin and chest.

"You want me to strip right here for you, asshole?" Marshall hollered.

"Yeah, why don't you do that, get fucking naked right here in this
street. You fucking fag."

"I don't like you either," he spit at me, narrowing his eyes. I could
tell he was shaking.

I laughed at that, put a hand to my heart mockingly. "Now you really hurt my feelings. I'm telling."

"Fuck you." Marshall pulled his coat together. The cold made his
face splotchy. He shivered for a few seconds, then asked, "How will
we know when we have enough?"

"Enough what?"

"Intelligence."

"We'll know," I said simply. Surveillance wasn't an exact science. In fact it was a little like zoo tracking. I could arrive at the lion's cage, wait hours, and the beast might never show. Or the animal might greet me with teeth bared and catch me completely off guard. That was part of the excitement; the other part was fucking with Marshall. I arranged for him to meet me places and then just didn't show.

"Why aren't we riding together?" he'd ask.

But I never told him the truth, that I'd really concocted *two* plans each time, the real one and the decoy. If Marshall caught on, he never said anything. He just reported several exasperating "mishaps" to Gorilla. He complained about waiting hours at specified locations only to learn later that the place was wrong, the time was changed, or the plan had been scrapped altogether.

"That's the way surveillance is." I'd shrug unapologetically. "Hit-or-miss. Mostly miss." I wanted so badly to set Marshall up, the punk-bitch cop I thought he was. I had fun with him. But more than that, I wanted to show Gorilla that I didn't need a chaperone.

One night I reminded Marshall, "Be sure to wear your vest. If a fight breaks out, the good guys will need to know you're one of them so they don't take you out as well."

I never wore mine. Gorilla didn't want us prospects to wear any identifying markers. "That's how the clowns at Hellraiser Ball got arrested," he said. "They had the word *prospect* on the bottom of their vests."

I was more effective invisible. I could slip undetected into forbidden circles and eavesdrop on conversations as if I were a regular citizen. My invisibility impressed Gorilla. Marshall nodded, assured me he always did, and straddled his bike, looking worn and dirty. He headed for the decoy. I watched him leave. Guilt churned inside me and I wasn't sure how long *I* could keep up the charade, the double life.

As he rode off prepared to freeze another few lonely hours on a side street staring at drunks as they stumbled out of whatever local shithole I had sent him to, I drove to South Philly, to the real dive. The place was crowded, dimly lit, with large windows near the front. I parked across the street and shut off my engine. I had all night to wait. I pulled out binoculars, fixed them on the entrance and exit, a small wooden door riddled with bullet holes. A large bouncer whose name tag read THE BULL stood to the side. As far as I observed, the Bull was unarmed. Citizens streamed in and out of the place. Rock music made my car vibrate. My teeth chattered inside the cold car. After a while I pissed inside a beer bottle.

Hours passed, and then, just before closing, I spotted a turncoat stumble toward the entrance, flash the Bull his ID, and enter. I followed the turncoat inside with my binoculars, watched him wind his way through a dwindling crowd and sit alone at the bar. Turncoat ordered a beer. A few minutes later, he ordered another. Three in the span of an hour. Those kinds of details were important. Either the Turncoat expected company who never showed or he was a regular, comfortable enough with the bar to drink multiple beers without concern for a brawl.

I studied his colors too. Patches telegraphed a man's deeds, commemorated sex acts, certain crimes. The Pagans, for instance, created a patch for the James Gang Crew, a money pouch that memorialized the members' bank heist. There were red diamond swastikas and memory patches for fallen brothers. Old-timers had patches that boasted PHILADELPHIA MANIACS. Cuts divulged a man's secrets, said a lot about a person's rank and tenure in the club, about a person's habits. The turncoats wore Hells Angels colors; they were awarded instant full-patch status. I focused on women too, noted their hair color, their pumps, the size of their purses. Large ones were more likely to stash guns; smaller ones, dope. I paid attention to the bouncer, whether he flirted with the women, pinched their ass, or waved them through.

I never took the same route twice, ate in the same restaurant, walked down the same street in one afternoon. I don't think it was conscious, just instinct. Muscle typically traveled together. They had hidden bodyguards, dressed-down thugs, women draped on either side, a different broad every night. They couldn't be too careful. They were moving targets. I understood why Gorilla assigned more than one person to the mission; some distracted while others executed.

I checked in daily with Marshall, mostly to make sure he followed protocol. We parked our cars on opposite streets and walked a few paces apart from each other. Cool breeze on our faces. I focused intensely on details, aware of sounds, approaching footsteps, patches of ice, Marshall's freshly shaven face. He asked me, "Are you sure we've got the right bars?" He hadn't seen any turncoats. I assured him everything was going according to plan and that when the time was right, we'd move to Plan B, taking them out. Marshall needed clarification: "Who's going to pull the trigger?" Secretly I hoped Marshall would do the honors. But I recalled Gorilla's warning: "One day they're shaking your hand and telling you they want to be a Pagan, and the next they're putting a bullet to your head."

The Pagans had an expression for overzealous prospects; they called them the Shit. The word described impulsive, impatient, reactionary, badass wannabes. When my two-plot plan ran its course and Marshall and I found ourselves ready at last to take care of business, the turncoat we'd targeted never showed. We waited in sleet, in the cold, unheated car. My heart ticked like a bomb ready to implode. Something didn't fit. I didn't make mistakes. I didn't rush to judgment. I had seen other foiled attempts. Hellraiser Ball came to mind. Rash, impulsive action promised negative exposure. That's why I counseled prospects to be patient, to take out targets in the street, in public places, not in homes or inside bars where cameras recorded faces and confessions. No one was supposed to ever know what went down or why.

19

~ ~ ~ ~ ~ ~

The Shit

The infinitely little have a pride infinitely great.
—VOLTAIRE

What the hell happened?" Gorilla leaned across the table, his voice a tight whisper.

"Nothing." Although I suspected Marshall had tipped off the cops. I sat across from Gorilla in Greasy Tony's and picked at my pastrami sandwich feeling small and insignificant. The place was noisy, crowded with holiday cheer. I strained to hear Gorilla over the cheap piped-in Italian aria. Dim lighting picked up Gorilla's worry. We sat at the front of the restaurant near the entrance. Customers streamed in and out through the one door. A Christmas tree glowed in the corner. Festive window foam blocked my view of the street.

"The guy is still alive." Gorilla's voice was tight. He blew out a disappointed sigh. "When you put in work for the club, I expect results, not a fucking mess. People are starting to talk."

"Because I work for you?"

"Because you work *exclusively* for me." He paused as citizens streamed past him. A woman with a large shopping bag knocked our table, spilling my glass. Fear quivered across her face. She hesitated, shifted her weight, and slung the bag tighter over her shoulder, unsure whether to blot the beer with a paper napkin, offer us another one on her, or simply walk away and pretend she hadn't seen us.

Gorilla shook his head, wriggled into his duster, and motioned for me to follow him outside. No important conversations ever happened inside. The government had zoom lenses, videos, bugs. We went for a walk.

"Maybe you need a little help identifying the players. There's a Christmas party I'd like you to attend," Gorilla said.

"A meet and greet?"

"It's fucking cold out here." He pulled his jacket tighter.

"It's winter." I shrugged and slipped on a patch of ice. I was already on edge. Silence stretched between us. We walked for several blocks in the wrong direction, darted down side streets, and zigzagged back down separate alleys. My teeth chattered. My legs numbed. Gorilla seemed oblivious of the cold. His breath blew around us in a white fog. He glanced behind him every so often looking for the shadow people.

"You can't be too careful," he schooled me.

"Right." I nodded.

"These feds"—he chuckled and shook his head—"they think they're so tricky. With all their fancy technology, television screens inside their vans." Gorilla stopped. He looked right at me. "I'm smarter than they are."

"Yes," I said without conviction.

"I never meet in the same place twice." He held up his fingers and began to count off.

"No," I agreed.

"I leave no footprints in the snow."

I nodded.

"Never walk the same street," he said.

"Right." I felt exposed, raw.

Gorilla held his gaze on me a little too long. "I need to know who my friends are." His breath blew white around us. I could no longer feel my toes. I understood Gorilla's implicit instruction. He was losing patience. He needed to identify more Pagan defectors. Even now, he didn't know who they all were. I had gathered information through surveillance, but it was taking too long. At a Pagan-sponsored party, I would have the perfect opportunity to eavesdrop on conversations, interpret codes, and listen for anything suspicious.

"Am I bringing a date?" I hated to ask the question.

"Marshall's out of this one, too risky." Gorilla paused. More silence. I waited for my exit cue. "You could learn a lot from him."

A chill coursed through me. Gorilla might as well have pressed a knife to my throat. Without another word he walked across the street. Snow sprayed with each heavy boot step. He opened the passenger side of his car and slipped inside. Flakes blew against my cheeks and dusted the street with fresh powder. After a few minutes I shuffled to the car, pulled open the door, and climbed in.

Gorilla held church the next night in the basement of a member's home. The secluded place was on a residential street in a mostly working-class neighborhood. Marshall and I were once again relegated to guard post outside in the cold without coats.

"What the hell happened to *you* last night?" Marshall broke the tension.

"I followed instructions." I barely glanced at him, afraid I might reveal too much in my expression.

Sweat beaded Marshall's temple despite the frigid temperature. The prospect stared straight ahead, gazed into the empty street, his face pale and overbright in the glow from the bald streetlamp. I studied Marshall's profile, his dark tuft of beard, swollen, red sleep-deprived eyes. I wasn't sure what I expected to find; moles never *looked* like moles.

"You were supposed to wait for me." Marshall's teeth chattered. He punched his hands together for warmth. "How come you never showed?"

"Prospect," a bark interrupted our sparring. Marshall happily shuffled inside to prepare cheese sandwiches for one of the members. I watched him from the open living-room window, bobbing up and down the stairs as predictably the bread was too stale, too burnt, too soft. On the tenth pointless delivery Marshall's sponsor stood at the top of the stairs and tripped him. The sponsor was overweight, broad-shouldered, and resembled a retired boxer. Marshall stumbled, fell forward. His plate of crusts flew from his hand and shattered around him in tiny white shards. Blood beaded in the web of his fingers.

"Lick it up, prospect," the sponsor ordered.

Marshall crawled on his hands and knees, flicking his tongue along the tile, while his sponsor grinned. Marshall finished, coughed, gagged on debris, sat back on his haunches, hands on his knees.

"Did I say you could rest?" His sponsor grabbed Marshall's pony-tail, yanked it backward, pressed his face close to Marshall's, then sucker punched him hard in the ribs. Marshall winced, moaned, looked as if he might hurl.

I returned my focus to the street and wondered fleetingly if my suspicions were founded. Had Gorilla paired me with Marshall so that I had a decoy, a bitch slave who distracted while I put in *real* work for the club? Cold bit into my cheeks. Wind rustled the bare tree branches.

The front door cracked open. Gorilla poked his head outside. "Got a little problem, kid."

I gratefully followed Gorilla to the kitchen table, relieved to be out of the cold and to feel my limbs again. The other members, including the homeowner and Marshall, scattered through a back exit. I heard the roar of their engines in the alley. Gorilla scraped a chair back. His hands shook and I knew he needed a fix. This was the part where I forgot about being a prospect and I moved immediately into the role of confidant. Prospects didn't talk to presidents; they didn't speak until spoken to, and if I had rendered an opinion in the company of the other members, I would likely have been subjected to an ass-whipping. But I wasn't always good at remembering protocol, following rules, giving deference to rank. More often than not, I talked out of turn and was taken to task until some old-timer piped up, "Hey, he's Maingy's kid," and all hands suddenly disappeared from my throat.

Gorilla got right to the point. "Bullet got tossed from the Oasis last night. The bouncer claimed Bullet tried to stick him."

"Did he deserve it?" Bullet was a lame Pagan who enjoyed the *idea* of being a Pagan more than the protocol of becoming an outlaw. The Oasis was a stripper club. I knew the bouncer well through various surveillance missions, knew him to be a towering six-foot-something third-degree black belt. Any citizen who strong-armed a Pagan deserved retribution unless . . . the touch was justified.

"What do you know about the bouncer?" Gorilla asked. He was suddenly out of his chair, pacing the kitchen, careful to avoid the cracks in the tiles. He twitched as he walked, rapidly glancing over his shoulder, worried about shadows on the wall.

"He knows better than to mess with a Pagan."

"Does he pack?" Gorilla scratched at his arms.

"Have you seen the surveillance tape?"

That was the first step, verify what actually happened. It would have been foolish to just retaliate without reason. Rogues pulled knives on citizens just because. Pagans reacted for revenge, retribution; there was always a motive. Hellraiser Ball was still fresh in our minds, and the Pagans who'd randomly charged like bulls into a volley of bullets.

"I have to be sure," Gorilla said. He was righteous like that. He held his own court. He was judge and jury and he alone decided whether Bullet was justified in pulling a knife on a citizen. He arranged a meeting the next afternoon with the owner of the Oasis.

The slight Italian led Gorilla and me into a back room to watch the black-and-white film clip *Bullet v. Bouncer*. The cramped office reeked of tobacco and stale sex. The pea green carpet crunched under my boots. The corner trash can overflowed with crushed beer cans and discarded fast food. No one said a word. The owner switched on the camera. Grainy figures flashed onto the television screen. Bullet, dressed in his denim cuts, wagged his finger at the bouncer and spit in his face. Muffled voices changed inflection. Bullet's rose an octave. Bouncer's hands left his chest, flew to Bullet's shoulders. Bullet drew his buck knife and pressed the blade to the bouncer's throat.

"What the fuck is he doing?" Gorilla was incredulous.

"He thinks he's the Shit," I said.

Gorilla shook his head, snapped his fingers at the owner; he'd seen enough.

But before Gorilla could take care of business he received another call as we headed out of the Oasis.

"I want my stuff back." The irate citizen blew up the phone line.

"Who the fuck is this guy?" Gorilla handed me the receiver. We were walking toward my car. Patches of ice caught my boots. The citizen's voice stuttered in my ear, "Bullet stole my plasma TV and dope."

I was impressed with Citizen's courage. It took balls to confront a Pagan boss and accuse one of his prospects of stealing. Few survived the insult. No president happily accepted that his nominee misbehaved. News that Bullet messed with a stripper while he was also married with two kids was not the problem. That he stole from that stripper's citizen boyfriend while the boyfriend was incarcerated was not the problem.

"He abused his position as a Pagan," I said.

"That's a problem," Gorilla agreed.

Restraint and control were important attributes for any prospect. There could only be one dictator, and Gorilla didn't appreciate competition.

"I run this club," he reminded me every chance he got. "What I say goes."

Bullet had to go.

"Handle it." Gorilla tasked me and other prospects with the problem. "And take Marshall with you."

"Why does he like that asshole anyway?" Bullet whispered confidentially to me the next morning as Marshall slipped into the backseat of my Cougar.

"Everyone likes his own reflection," I replied curtly, not at all pleased that I had two lames in the car with me.

"Huh?"

"Marshall loves Gorilla a little too much," I said impatiently.

"Where to?" Marshall asked.

"Ever been to the Plant?"

"First time," Marshall managed.

"You'll like it." I smothered a smile. "It's quiet."

The Plant was a deserted field powdered in snow on the outskirts of Philadelphia surrounded by rows of barbed wire, high-voltage signs, and a power plant. Miles of cracked, white landscape made a decent place to dump a body. Even without regular snowfall, it was unlikely anyone would discover the corpse for weeks, and by then the person would be nothing but decomposed flesh and bone chips.

I glanced in my rearview mirror. "It would take four years at least before anyone would find a body out here, huh, Marshall?" The prospect registered my sarcasm.

"What's the plan anyway?" Bullet asked, practically salivating over the idea of setting up the citizen. But in the end I wasn't sure who really set up whom.

"The citizen is supposed to meet us here, alone," I said.

"He'll bring his goon squad," Bullet said.

"You're not worth it." I shrugged, though part of me hoped the citizen would.

Bullet flipped him off. "I'm practically a Pagan."

"You're a punk bitch," I qualified.

As we rounded the curve in the road, I spotted a dirty white pickup truck parked sideways near a row of barbed wire. The citizen stood outside his vehicle, arms folded, shorter than I expected, stocky and heavily tattooed. He wore ripped jeans, a muscle shirt with a layer of long sleeves underneath, and a baseball cap. The temperature was frigid, but I guessed apprehension was enough to make the guy sweat. I was impressed already by Citizen's courage. The Pagans ought to recruit *him*.

"This is your fight," I remarked to Bullet.

"It shouldn't take long." Bullet grinned, opened the door.

"Hey," I yelled after him, "mind your manners."

Bullet and Citizen were fairly matched. Bullet lumbered toward the guy, arms dragged to his sides, black coat flapping open in the wind. He reminded me of a giant crow swooping in for his prey. I opened the door, stepped outside, and propped against the car.

Marshall followed suit but watched from the other side. "What happens now?" he asked stupidly.

"Bullet makes this right."

"And if he doesn't?"

"*We* make it right."

"I want my stuff back." Citizen pushed himself away from his truck; his tone was firm but not altogether disrespectful.

"Can't do that." Bullet grinned. I knew we were all in trouble. Bullet thought he was the Shit and he'd be damned if he was going to return Citizen's stuff.

"What is this?" Citizen held his ground, shot me a look of disbelief. Apparently he thought he was dealing with rational players.

"Come and get it." Bullet flashed his blade at Citizen.

"What the fuck is he doing?" Marshall's voice quivered.

"Being a lame," I said.

Citizen didn't wait for intervention. He lunged at Bullet, grabbed Bullet's wrist, twisted it backward, and jerked the knife free. The blade dropped into fresh powder. Citizen toppled Bullet, pressed his face into the snow, held him down. Bullet's legs flailed. Citizen yanked Bullet's head back by his hair and Bullet gulped air, his cheeks and lips flaked with snow. Citizen shoved Bullet's face down again into the powder. Bullet struggled, his arms and legs forming a snow angel.

"Should we help him?" Marshall asked.

"This isn't our fight," I said.

"What if he—"

"This isn't our fight."

Citizen stood, stepped on Bullet's back as if he had just plugged a deer in a hunt, and was contemplating how to bind him.

"I want my stuff back," Citizen repeated simply. Bullet wriggled beneath Citizen's boot. It seemed a reasonable request. Citizen kicked Bullet in the face and rolled him over. Blood streamed down Bullet's face. Citizen collected the knife, wiped the snow from the blade with his sleeve, and tossed it into the bed of his pickup truck.

Bullet struggled to sit.

Citizen crouched to Bullet's level, his elbows on his knees. "Are we clear?"

"I fucked up," Bullet said sheepishly as I helped him into my car. He dabbed the blood from his eyes, panted, and looked smashed in. I knew he hurt, but Bullet would rather pretend he took a few punches on purpose. Later, he'd probably nurse his bruises in a dark corner of a bar and numb the pain with a pitcher of beer. He'd be lucky if that was *all* that happened to him.

"It's over," I replied, and slammed the door shut. I wasn't just referring to the fight either.

"It was lame, pulling a knife on an unarmed citizen," Marshall piped in.

"Do you even have his stuff?" I snapped.

"Why would I keep his shit?"

"You set him up?" I smacked my hand against the steering wheel.

"Is that wrong?"

"He did the righteous thing," I began. "He showed up alone. He wanted his stuff back. And you pull a knife on him? What were you planning to do? Stick him?"

Bullet shrugged. He still didn't get it. We weren't a bunch of barbarians. We had rules of engagement. Fair play required sacrifice. But the Philadelphia Pagans' motto—When One Swings, We All Swing—excluded rogues like Bullet. He was on his own.

"Did you really expect me to give him his shit back?" Bullet was incredulous. He pinched the bridge of his nose with his fingers to stem the blood flow.

"You're a lame." I shook my head.

"Are you going to tell Gorilla?"

"Of course I'm going to tell Gorilla."

"So this was all a setup?" Bullet sounded like a wounded child. "Why meet at the Plant then?"

"In case *he* brought a knife," I said simply.

"What are we going to do about Bullet?" I asked Gorilla confidentially later that night in the street, though I really had no business grilling Gorilla about punishment scenarios. We lingered outside the Bravi Restaurant. The place was festive, bright, and Christmassy. A plastic Santa Claus rotated in the window. Patrons hustled inside, and as the glass doors swung open, the whiff of cinnamon and freshly baked bread hit my nostrils.

Gorilla lowered his voice. "He's out."

"How do you want to handle him?" I wasn't foolish enough to think Gorilla would task me exclusively with the mission, but I knew I'd be involved. I knew Bullet would at least lose his bike, assuming he *had* one. Bike repossessions were the ultimate punishment for disrespect. It helped that I already had some experience in the area: in middle school I stole brand-new BMX bikes from customers who shopped at a popular racing store called the Bike Line. I pretended to be a customer; I could have been. After all, I raced BMX bikes. But I was more interested in the bikes the customers purchased and their home addresses so that later that night, while they slept soundly, I could steal the goods.

My goal was simple: I needed money. Stealing for me was never about thrill, it was about survival. I tried to minimize the harm I caused to people by reselling the same bike over and over, so that I could double and triple my profits. But it was never enough money. I was still hungry. So I masterminded the heist of a commercial business when I was only twelve, busted out the alarm, manned the perimeter with five of my closest friends, and gave them each a walkie-talkie. I even commissioned one of them to walk his dog along the main street so that he could alert me to approaching cops.

We removed several trash bags of merchandise and stored the items in my friend's attic for a year, too afraid to even *look* at the goods for fear we might give ourselves away. But then what was the point? I still had no money. I had to traffic the merchandise in order to eat. That's what happened with crime after a while, it lost its utility. Sort of like fights that fizzled because no one remembered why they started punching each other in the first place. I suppose I could have just kept the stolen goods in my friend's attic indefinitely. It's not that I didn't trust him to keep our secret. He had no choice. He was an accomplice. It was that I wanted the *value* from my risk. I sold the items the following year on school grounds, even filled orders, item by item until the trash bags disappeared.

Bike repossessions happened when someone failed to prepay for a meth delivery, disrespected another Pagan's old lady, stumbled down a flight of stairs and knocked a Pagan's beer on the way down, or made a fool out of someone else.

"What about Bullet's brother, Ghost?" I asked, knowing Ghost aspired to become a Pagan too, knowing Ghost now had no chance. He was part of the rotten family tree and the club couldn't risk the association. Rogues were unpredictable, attracted heat, attracted scrutiny by the cops.

"He's out too," Gorilla said simply.

"What about the citizen?" I asked, thinking Citizen's actions resembled the bouncer's at the Oasis.

"Maybe he'd like to become a Pagan?" Gorilla said with all sincerity.

"He'll want his stuff back first."

Later that night Gorilla ordered several Pagans and prospects, including me, to take care of business. We arrived unannounced at Bullet's duplex, a run-down building in a bad part of town. Dirty ice filled the cracks in the concrete pavement. The place was quiet, dark, and cavelike. I glanced across the street, always aware of my surroundings, and noticed the neighbor's spider window, the flickering television screen inside the living room that featured a nature channel, a black bear swatting at salmon in a raging river. In the next room, a curtain fluttered in the night wind and exposed a thin woman on the edge of her bed, looking old, looking twenty. Her hand curled around a needle. Boredom etched into their expressions.

The Pagan Club's enforcer, Tiny, pounded on the door. He was a giant of a Pagan, with a thick neck that looked more like a tire than a body part. He was an improvement from the club's last enforcer, Tough Luck, who only had one leg.

"Open up," Tiny hollered. I heard movement inside, furniture scraping against concrete, curses. Bullet must have expected trouble.

"I'm busy." Bullet didn't slide the chain back.

Tiny shoved his boot into the wood and warned, "Don't make me break this down."

Bullet opened the door. His eyes widened at the sight of all of us. He waved us inside. The smell of filth assaulted my senses. Papers buried the kitchen table. Cardboard pizza boxes littered the floor near the plasma television set I was sure belonged to Citizen. On the screen, a pretty anchorwoman warned about approaching blizzards. On the stove a pot simmered. A spoon filled with brown, metallic liquid rested on the lip. *The fucker is cooking meth.* A small child poked his head around the corner. Food stained his T-shirt. He wore cartoon pajama bottoms. Large, brown eyes were sunk into pale flesh. All surprise and curiosity had flickered out of them.

"Lana, get the kid out of here," Bullet hollered.

The boy reminded me of me at four years old. The ruckus probably woke the kid. He'd stumbled into the living room to investigate, ignorant of the violent current that threatened to suck him under. Like me, the kid probably never slept worried that he might lose himself in the darkness. He blinked at me with his large brown lashes. I wished I could reassure him. I wished I could tell him everything would be okay, that he could make it despite his old man. I wished I could lie.

Bullet's motorcycle filled the living room where a Christmas tree should have been. Nothing special about the bike except that it worked. Bullet had left the keys in the ignition. Draped over the handlebars were his denim cuts, the bottom rocker prominently displayed. He'd scattered patches on the kitchen counter. Pagan patches, insignia no prospect would have earned. I could only conclude the fucker had stolen them. Bullet stood shirtless in his boxers. The apartment was drafty. Wind whistled through a bullet hole in the window. Bullet padded to the burners, put on an oversize cooking mitt, and grabbed the pot handle.

"We came to take your bike," Tiny said calmly, displaying his Colt for Bullet's benefit in case Bullet decided to be stupid.

"I fucked up," he began, though no hint of apology was in his tone. He had his back to Tiny.

"Gorilla's decided," Tiny said without explanation. An eerie calm fell over the room. Bullet removed his oven mitt slowly. I expected resistance, a fight of some sort, a tense and messy ending. It hardly mattered that Bullet was unarmed, barely clothed, and sorely outnumbered. He would act instinctively, charge without warning like a cornered buck, as with the bouncer, the citizen. Bullet's hands shook. He turned slowly. Nerves colored his neck. He threw up his hands in mock surrender and said plaintively, "Just one more chance?"

But people like Bullet didn't deserve second shots. They were lucky to leave with their teeth intact. Tiny snapped his fingers at Marshall and ordered, "Take his bike."

"What about the citizen's stuff?" I moved across the room, unplugged Bullet's television set from the wall, and tucked it beneath my armpit.

"It's not like the asshole was going to miss it," Bullet whined.

Tiny ignored him. He gathered the patches from the counter and said, "Give me the money in your wallet."

"I don't have any," Bullet protested at first, but then relented. "You're stealing from me too?"

Tiny took the cash. "This is for the drugs you owe the citizen."

"You respect a citizen over a brother?"

"*Gorilla* respects fair play," Tiny replied as he counted the cash and pocketed it in his coat.

Bullet's exit could have been a lot worse. Images of Fast Tank's torture and mutilation swirled in my head. The scene might have ended differently had Bullet resisted, had he pulled a knife on *us,* had he been predictable. But Bullet's real punishment was that like Fast Tank he slipped effortlessly back into his former life—drug dealing and getting high. He lost his one chance to be a part of something greater. Bullet embodied my worst fear, regret.

20

~ ~ ~ ~ ~

Mission Impossible

We don't see much of you around here," one prospect accused during a rare moment of downtime. A group of us clustered in a member's kitchen in dim candlelight waiting like soldiers for church to begin, for our orders. Nerves carved a hollow pit in my gut. The prospect shuffled a deck of cards and said pointedly, "You don't dress like us. You don't work like us."

I leaned against the counter, spun a dirty fork absently between my fingers. I wore recycled jeans, a double-layered T-shirt, and a black trench coat I tossed over the back of a chair. My guns glinted on my waist.

"He's Gorilla's boy," another prospect chimed in, joining the other one at the table. One by one they emerged from the shadows, mere spectators to a strange rehearsal. The prospect was shorter than the others, stumpy and pasty white. He slicked his hair back and smelled of cheap aerosol. He looked too fresh, easy bait, and when he grinned, he flashed a clean row of teeth.

"Is that right?" The other dealt the cards and I resisted the urge to dislocate his jaw.

"What are we playing?" Marshall suddenly emerged from the outside, shrugged out of his coat. Snow flaked off his boots, left slick wet tracks from the entrance.

"War."

As if on cue, Gorilla shuffled into the gold glow. He scratched at the sores on his arms, opened the dark refrigerator in the kitchen, and stared at the rows of empty shelves. The member's electricity had been shut off. Gorilla's red eyes glazed over. He shut the refrigerator. His hands shook. By now I was used to his paranoia.

"Are you on the fence or off the fence, kid?" he said, and the other prospects scraped back their chairs and scattered like roaches.

"You know where I'm at," I replied calmly. I chewed the inside of my cheek. The president could barely keep it together, a fact I used to my advantage. Gorilla stumbled over to me, stood inches from my face, and said, "You like to party?"

"You know I do." I didn't move from the counter. The fork dropped, clattered to the floor.

"I like a bit of noise myself." Gorilla grinned. "A grand entrance, if you know what I mean." Candlelight washed over his face, giving him a yellowish tinge.

"Grenades?" I clarified.

"There's a party in another county." Gorilla's eyes darted around him. Shadows elongated on the walls. A door slammed in another room. Gorilla jumped. He dropped into a chair, rested his head in his hands. I held my breath, knowing I would get no further instruction. It was up to me to learn which party, where, and when. I never questioned the why because there was only ever one purpose, to identify turncoats.

"That's why I like you, kid," Gorilla said, his head still bowed on the table. "I don't need to explain things to you. You just get it." He paused, lifted his head, and said thoughtfully, "You get *me*."

Maybe I did. The less information Gorilla knew about the party and the turncoats, the better for Gorilla. He had his scapegoat. He delegated and I jumped. I slipped into my cold car, left the engine off, windows closed. Ice glazed the hood. I rationalized with myself, assured myself that whatever risks I took I did for me, not Gorilla, not the club. But my conscience warned, *You'll do life for this . . . if you get caught.* All that talk about catching cases, being prepared, didn't translate to real time, hard time in a prison cell for life. Doubt gripped me and suddenly I wasn't so sure anymore that I wanted to risk *that* much for the club, for Gorilla.

Prison wouldn't make me heroic, just forgotten. Did *thinking* about murder qualify as conspiracy? My heart raced. I couldn't breathe. I wasn't sure anymore. I wasn't sure anymore I could do it. But there I was, in thick, and I couldn't just walk away. I had committed. I chose to prospect, to take orders from Gorilla. My hands shook. Stress made me dizzy. But I couldn't show fear. Animals sensed fear. I had no choice, either I did this for Gorilla or I risked being his target or, worse, being set up. Gorilla, as payback, could commission another prospect and promise that guy instant promotion if he would just execute my plan *for* me. Or just execute me.

"The frame is worse than the deal," prospect Big Beard said to me. "You never know *what* he might pinch you for."

"You think he's going to set me up?" I lit a blunt, inhaled deeply, hoping to calm my nerves. My head throbbed. Thoughts swirled to Dagger, whose murder was mere reflex. He never plotted, never thought about it, never put in work for the club with the Greek. And *he* was serving life. No one would know Gorilla commissioned me. I was fungible.

If I got caught, Gorilla would pretend he didn't know me, that I was a rogue, and that the club had never sanctioned my hit.

"You said it yourself, Gorilla can't *make* you do anything you don't want to do."

"He can just make sure I go down for it," I said.

What the hell am I doing? I had no cell phone, no signal, just Gorilla's voice in my head. I inhaled again. My uncle Russell committed suicide, *died* for the club, because he thought it was the honorable exit. But martyrs weren't heroes. They were examples. Other Pagans framed their lives around that concept: righteousness, integrity, sacrifice. I wasn't that selfless. I didn't put in work for the good of the cause. I plotted because I hated my father and I owed it to the club to make my existence right. Did that make my mission less righteous?

I jammed my blunt into the ashtray and turned on the engine. Wipers scraped across the windshield. The defroster cleared enough vision for me to peel from the curb. It was Christmas Eve. The streets were fairly deserted. Red-painted figurines spun in display windows. Dirty snow piled on the sidewalks. Old couples ate wordlessly across from each other in wide vinyl booths; spittle formed in the corners of their mouths as they chewed. Quiet buzzed inside my car. The solitude was peaceful, dreamlike. I glided past the festive people in the restaurants, holding hands with their shadows. Some glanced up, registered my black car, and looked away, pretended not to notice me at all. *That's right. I don't exist in your world.* Eventually their red coats, fuzzy hair, and holiday cheeks blurred from my vision.

It had been years since I even thought about Christmas as a holiday at all. The day blended with other days, only colder. Sometimes it snowed and the softness wrapped around me like a blanket. I liked working alone. Others respected that, respected me. Maybe they thought I knew something they didn't? I recalled the night I bolted awake to pounding at my door. I reached for the gun beside my pillow, my hand on the trigger. My heart raced at the intrusion. Sweat dampened my sheets. I had replayed scenarios like that a hundred times in my head. "It doesn't matter that you didn't do it. They'll think you did," the Saint had warned me about perception.

I recalled the night I heard a frantic voice behind my apartment door shout, "Open up."

At the time I raised my gun and thought if whoever it was wanted to kill me, he would shoot through the door, not knock and announce. Satisfied with my own explanation, I slid back the dead bolt but left the chain in place. Through the slit I saw two prospects I recognized, their clothes wet and crusted with mud. They looked weathered, whipped, the way prospects should.

"We didn't know who else to turn to," one of them stuttered. He looked scared, as if he didn't know what to do with his hands, as if he wanted to bolt, as if he couldn't believe what he'd done. I had developed sort of a reputation for fixing problems. People called it street smarts, sixth sense. I just called it common sense.

"Yeah, sure, get in here," I undid the chain and ushered them inside. Sweat moistened the prospect's eyes. His breathing was labored. He smelled of wet stone. He was short and tough-looking with skin so white it looked bleached. The second prospect towered over his partner. He had a square jaw and wide-set eyes like a wolf's. He glanced behind him, skittish, as if they worried someone had followed them. That's when it clicked. They had fucked up. They had deviated from the grand plan, a little too impatient to make their bones, to be promoted to full patch. Gorilla could not care less *who* carried out his orders. Gorilla stressed about Gorilla. He made sure he never had firsthand knowledge of anything, just "versions" of what happened. No one spoke about details. We understood we were just "average" Pagans, and killings and beatings were just a lifestyle.

"Did you get rid of the piece?" I started with simple questions though I didn't want to be a part of the heat at all. Gorilla couldn't have prospects running wild doing work he never authorized or deviating from his plan. "What kind of a club would we have then?" he'd lecture. Maybe he'd even remove them?

The larger prospect with no neck looked sheepish, shrugged, reached into his waistband. His prints were all over the gun. I grabbed a shirt, took the gun from the prospect's hands, and wiped it clean.

"What's the matter with you? Are you *trying* to get caught?"

"We were in a hurry."

"Yeah, and meanwhile, the tugboats are moving," I said sarcastically. "Take off your clothes."

"What the—"

"They're evidence."

The prospects stripped. They handed their dirty jeans smeared with blood and grass stains over to me. They watched in silence as I shoved the clothing into a trash bag. I worked quickly, adeptly, as if this stuff came naturally to me.

"We'll burn them later," I said simply. "What about your ride? Is it clean?"

So it went, detail after detail, until I covered up the mess, erased the trail.

I parked in an alley two blocks from the apartment where the Pagans celebrated Christmas. I shut off my engine, sat several minutes in silence before I opened the door and stepped into thin-dusted snow. I'd dressed down for the occasion, no cuts, no exposed tattoos, just plain dark jeans and trench coat. Blend. That was the trick, my gift. If I could stay invisible, I had a better shot at avoiding stares. If I was lucky, everyone inside would be high already, easily distracted, paranoid, and likely to perceive me as a shadow or a bloodred sound.

Rock music thundered from the open windows. Clusters of Pagans gathered around a bare Christmas tree. Snow fell softly at first, then more insistently. I jammed my hands in my pockets, pulled my coat collar tight around my face. I moved slowly to the entrance, where two enforcers checked IDs. They waved me inside the milky haze of marijuana, tobacco, and dust.

"He's Gorilla's boy," they mumbled.

My eyes smarted. I heard sucking sounds, forced laughter, and cheers. I moved to the back of the room, where I had a better view of the scene. The mood reminded me of childhood. Pagans lounged on the checkered couches; some sprawled on the floor. A naked woman straddled a particularly burly one near the Christmas tree, pressed her chest into his face while others leered. One screwed the neck of his bottle between her legs.

I saw Marshall. Dark circles stained his armpits. He looked spent, high; maybe someone had made him ingest crank. I recognized other prospects lined against the wall, arms at their sides, waiting for orders. I studied the partiers' faces, memorized their features, the patches on their cuts, their rank, their voice inflections. One vomited spewing yellow spittle into his beard. Another whistled the sound of a locomotive, "choo choo," and slapped the ass of his stripper before he dry-humped her backside and took her to the floor. Some members were armed and openly displayed their guns. Others wore bulletproof vests. A bowl of red liquid sloshed on the coffee table. Wine stained the carpet.

"You look lost." A thin stripper ran her finger along the back of my neck. She wore a G-string and brass tassels on her nipples. She was probably no more than nineteen, but she looked middle-aged. Stretched flesh, track marks, hollowed-out cheeks. She cupped my elbow in her wrinkled hands and pushed me gently to the couch.

"Want to fuck?" her voice scratched.

"Beat it," I barked, my tone harsher than I meant. She pulled away abruptly, glared at me with shiny, confused eyes. I watched her shuffle across the room, drape her arms around another biker, whip her blond, stringy hair across his neck, and nibble on his ear.

The noise and flash of the partying made my head itch. I slipped out of my coat, draped it over a chair, and headed to a back room to decompress. The bedroom was dark. No movement. No fucking. I shut the door, stood against the frame for several seconds until my hands stopped shaking. I hadn't realized how tense I'd been driving around, conducting surveillance, watching with heightened awareness every shape, sudden movement, shadow flicker, and assigning each a new and sinister meaning. I needed to debrief, alone.

I dropped onto the bed; the wool spread scratched through my jeans. A computer hummed in the corner. Curious, I moved to the keyboard, jiggled the mouse until the screen brightened. I glanced behind me. No one noticed me. I didn't own a computer, partly due to limited funds but mostly because technology left tracks. I preferred old-fashioned research . . . surveillance. But I couldn't resist the temptation. I typed in *Hells Angels, Philadelphia chapter,* expecting to see familiar faces. But instead I saw snapshots inside bars, clusters of Hells Angels guzzling beer, displaying their death's head tattoos, draped in the arms of strippers. I was about to exit the site when my eyes rested on a photo in the center, shaped in the form of a diamond 1 percenter patch. I recognized the Pagans in the photo, some high-ranking, dressed in Angel cuts.

"Fucking turncoats," Gorilla spat later that night after I debriefed him. He paced in the alley behind his house. He worried that his appliances might be bugged. Fine-powdered snow blew around us. At three o'clock in the morning, exhaustion buckled my knees. I knew I wouldn't sleep. I was bone-cold and starving. And my day was just beginning.

"This is mutiny." Gorilla punched the lid off a Dumpster. I knew what happened to turncoats. "We kill them."

Murder was not a prerequisite for induction into the Pagans. I'm sure some prospects wanted to make their bones through killing because they hoped to fast-track to instant full patch, but that wasn't part of my agenda, at least not wittingly. Gorilla pressured me with veiled threats of retribution if I veered too far off course, if I exhibited too much independence. I wasn't naïve about it. I deflected Gorilla's demands and convinced him I was more useful as a mastermind. At least plotting hits bought me time. Gorilla may have been smart, but I was smarter. I knew how to survive, how to stall, how to play a dead man's game.

Through various sources I learned the Hells Angels planned to throw another party in a different county in two weeks. More than time and location, I had to learn the layout of the building. I had to prepare. That meant taking a road trip, alone. It was the only chance I had to truly think, to relax . . . as much as I could relax. I drove without music. Sound distracted me. Even in the dark I registered curves in the road, dips, and patches of black ice that made my wheels spin. I wondered if what I felt was normal, if all potential hit men felt this nervous? I played my own mind games, reviewed scenarios in my head, over and over until I couldn't think of another possible way something could happen.

Just after midnight I approached the site, threw my car into neutral, shut off the headlights, and coasted down the deserted street. The place resembled a vault, sealed with no windows. Metal flakes peeled from a large steel door. Harleys lined the perimeter like headless horses. Gold eyes glinted in the darkness. Dogs, or wolves, were chained to a chrome rod in the ground. They salivated, agitated by the wire cords around their necks. High barbed-wire fencing surrounded the building.

I searched for cutouts, indentations in the ground beneath the wire large enough to wiggle through military-style. Nothing but packed snow glittered in the moonlight. I snapped pictures, my heart in my throat. Empty road stretched ahead of me, to my left whiteness, to my right the impenetrable fortress. I had limited exit points. If I was spotted, ambushed, sprayed with bullets, I would have few, if any, escape routes.

"It's not happening," I reported to Gorilla once I had safely returned to the city. Irritation flickered in Gorilla's eyes. He paced like an agitated general.

"The place is sealed," I continued. "They know we're out there. They're prepared for us this time."

"Can't we use grenades?"

"Not when there's only one exit and entry." *And I could explode like a fireball.* "The fence is too high. Even if I got in there with wire clippers and snipped a hole, there's no way I'd make it through without detection."

"Yeah, okay," Gorilla mumbled. "Maybe it's too hard with all those people around. Maybe it's time to pick them off one by one?"

Gorilla was fast becoming a celebrity. He was the Sonny Barger of the Pagans. Almost daily the newspapers reported something about Gorilla, his strange and close alliance with the mobster Merlino, his several botched payback attempts, his recovery from his own mob-style shooting, his feud with my old man, and the looming threat of a biker war with the Hells Angels. Gorilla loved the attention, loved that the national focus was all about *him*. He abandoned the old-school tradition that promoted secrecy, avoidance of the media, and silence. Gorilla catapulted the Pagans into a new and very public regime.

He spoke often and openly about himself and the club to an organized crime-reporter of the *Daily News*. Gorilla's ego swelled to maniac proportions. He staged photo opportunities, even ordered other Pagans to participate. He'd call the ones who had no jobs. They'd oblige him, meet him at locations and pose, then find themselves front-page news. The photo caption disclosed their real names and monikers. It was crazy. We were making it too easy for the feds. They knew who we were, what we were about. At one point I cautioned Gorilla, warned him that maybe going public wasn't such a great idea, but he dismissed my concerns, assured me that the exposure was great promotion for the Pagans. Everyone would know we were the "new" gangsters.

A lot of the old-school Pagans hated him. It wasn't just jealousy either. Gorilla was all about Gorilla, and that's not what the club was about. It was hard to promote a brotherhood, a *family*, when Gorilla was in love with himself. He thought he was royalty, one of the good "bad guys." It was ridiculous. There was nothing "good" about us. We all knew what we were and where we had come from. We weren't supposed to give a fuck about "public image."

Gorilla was still Gorilla, and protecting his "good" "badass" image was a little like containing a bonfire. My job was to make sure his acts didn't blow up in his face. Gorilla held weekly church meetings to discuss official club business. Most of us respectfully listened to him, then promptly formed our *own* secret meetings to discuss Gorilla's orders. He never knew some of us held secret court. If he had ever discovered our insubordination, we might have become victims of random gunfire.

We had to be careful. We considered Gorilla's objective—usually to eliminate a problem—and reworked the details of the assault. We assured him we would take care of business. He could rely on us. We were his servants, his prospects, and we knew how to follow orders. Gorilla didn't need to know *how* we did his deeds, only *that* we did them.

"He wants us to bust this guy up," I repeated to the others after church one night. A group of us, prospects and full patches, clustered in a stifling studio apartment half a block away from Gorilla's place. The radiator hummed loudly so we didn't have to worry about curious neighbors. I dimmed the lights, propped against the window and drew the curtains. The place was muted in browns, like different shades of excrement. Checkered vinyl covered the kitchen table. The refrigerator was empty. The place belonged to a prospect, Nomad. We used it for emergencies.

"Gorilla ordered us to kill him." CS paced the length of the room. His steel-toed boots clunked along the wooden floor. He looked like a mountain. His shaggy, dark hair crawled the length of his back. His vest exposed his belly.

"We *can't* kill him," I said simply.

"Why can't we kill him?" CS stopped pacing. He narrowed his eyes, looked at me curiously as if I'd lost my mind. He had been with the club for almost ten years. He was probably no more than thirty, but he looked grizzled, at least middle-aged. He had a wife and kids at home. He didn't need this life. He *had* a family.

"We'll *pretend* to kill him," I qualified. Nausea pooled in my throat. Mine was a risky proposition. I didn't have any idea what I was doing really, but I hoped the others would follow my lead. I wasn't trying to be a hero, and I certainly had no delusions that I was the "good guy" in all of this or that I had any intention of protecting Gorilla. I did it for my own selfish reasons: I didn't want to go to prison.

"Huh?"

"Gorilla wants us to blast him," I rationalized as if that were the problem. "It'll leave too much mess. Besides, what if the guy has kids?"

"What if this, what if that," another member huffed. His face pinched. He looked bloodshot and tired. "We have orders."

"Fuck Gorilla's orders," I snapped. The room grew still. The pacing stopped. I waited a beat, feeling my heart in my throat. "What if Gorilla got it wrong?" I said slowly.

"Got what wrong?" One of the members pulled out a cigarette, put it between his lips, and cupped his hands around the match flare. He seemed mildly interested.

"The story." I invoked the Saint's lesson.

"What are you talking about? What story?"

"What if Gorilla never checked out the *other* guy's story?" I threw up my hands. I stared at blank faces. No one else got it.

"He ordered us to take care of business." The member paced again. He panted. I could tell this really bothered him, this killing business.

"I'm not going down for something I don't know for sure," I said. "Gorilla can't make any of us do something we don't want to do."

"What did you mean we'd *pretend* to kill him?"

The next night we staked out the bar where we knew Gorilla's target drank regularly. My mind raced a hundred miles an hour. I didn't know the guy's story, didn't know why Gorilla wanted him "handled." I only knew that we had to deliver or *we* might all wind up with a bullet between our eyes. I drove. Nomad rode in the backseat. Prospect CS took the passenger side. None of us spoke. CS twitched, drummed his fingers on the dash, and cleared his throat. Nomad blew his nose over and over. I thought I might throw up. I double-parked across the street, left the engine running, the headlights bright, just in case we had to pull away quickly.

," I said. The citizen approached an older-model stale looked like an oak barrel, older than us, maybe in his
ruddy face had the look of an alcoholic, puffy and swol-
wound that never healed. His bushy beard hid most of his
face b. he wore a rope drawing on his neck. He fumbled with his
keys and I could see tattoo nails drilled into the backs of his palms,
as if he thought he were Jesus or something. CS clicked open his
passenger-side door. Nomad followed and hitched his gun to his belt.
His nose was red and chaffed from blowing. I didn't have a plan exactly but I gave the signal anyway. The guy saw us approach out of the
corner of his eye.

"Fuck," he said, and tried to bolt.

CS tackled him first, jumped on the citizen's back and rolled with
him into the curb. He jammed the guy's face into the street grate until
deep lines were seared in the citizen's cheeks. Nomad pounced next,
straddled the guy's back, and pummeled him with his fists. I marveled
that Nomad could snap like that, go from zero to warp speed in less
than sixty seconds. He moved with robotic precision, clocking the
man over and over with his fists until finally he pulled out his pistol.

"Easy," I said. "We're not trying to kill him."

"I was just going to whip him," Nomad protested, and shrugged.
He stood and with the gun in his hand kicked the citizen hard in the
back of his neck. Blood caked the front of Nomad's jeans. The violence
had lost its point. The man twitched like a mechanical toy. Nomad
shrugged, wiped the sweat from his forehead. He was about finished.
He waited for me to step in like a flag and announce the end. I tapped
the citizen's coat with my boot, flipped him over, and winced. The
man's face was raw from road burn. He gurgled at me but didn't open
his eyes.

"You think he knows who we are?" CS asked me.

"You know who we are?" I stood over the man, blocked the light from the lamppost. It was the first time I realized that we had just beaten up this guy framed in a spotlight. My heart thundered in my chest. Cars flickered past us but didn't stop. Patrons filtered into the street. They ignored us. I relaxed a bit. They didn't know the players. They didn't know the match. They could change the channel anytime they wanted. The blood and mess didn't concern them.

The citizen grunted.

I knelt close to the citizen's ear and whispered, "Gorilla says to get the fuck out of town. I'd suggest you do it because next time you won't be breathing," I promised. The man nodded slightly. He struggled to sit upright, coughed up blood. I handed him his car keys and closed my fist around his.

"You think he got the message?" CS asked as we drove off.

"If he didn't, he's a dead man," I said, *and so am I.* The last thing I needed was a witness, someone Gorilla might encounter later and use against me. But a dead body, even a weapon with blood prints, would prove worse, and while being Gorilla's dutiful slave might have earned me his *respect,* it would not have guaranteed me escape from prosecution. I wasn't prepared to catch a case, not for Gorilla, not for anyone. I knew I'd taken a risk by letting the man live, by being independent, but it was the better of two options, and I was pretty sure the man would take my advice and disappear.

So it went as we continued to take care of Gorilla's business. I *still* had no delusions we were the "good guys." But Gorilla did some tasks "off the chain." Such as the time he dated a pretty nurse. She had once tangled with a young doctor who was less than pleased that his ex-girlfriend had dumped him for a *biker.* The doctor plotted his revenge. Late one night, during his rounds, he stalked the hallway, stapled on the hospital's bulletin board nude photographs of the nurse in compromising pornographic positions. He captioned the pictures in bloody red marker, DIRTY, HORNY, TRASHY. He baited Gorilla, and I'm sure he had no idea *whom* he had challenged nor the lengths to which Gorilla would go to exact his revenge.

Gorilla bristled at the insult, the disrespect. But he knew better than to commission me to punish the doctor, not only because he probably sensed I wouldn't have done it, but because he considered this a "domestic" problem. He had other fungibles for the detail, fresh faces who wouldn't have known the difference between putting in work for the club and putting in work for Gorilla. He summoned his sergeant at arms and several new recruits to accompany him to the doctor's house. One of the recruits, Big Beard, was among them. He described to me how the group of them waited until dark. Snow dusted the cars parked along the street in the classy, upscale neighborhood. Gorilla rapped his brass knuckles on the doctor's door.

"Who is it?"

Gorilla, without responding, kicked it open with his steel-toed boots.

The doctor stood stunned on the other side. Cold blew into his house. But before the doctor could protest, the enforcer's hands circled his throat and pinned him to the wall. The doctor's young daughter watched from the stairs.

"She was tiny, porcelain white, delicate, and refined," Big Beard told me later. "Next to her, I looked like a dirty smudge."

"We're just taking care of some business," Big Beard assured the little girl as he led her down the skinny hallway with the plush maroon carpets and clean white walls into a cramped room where a television set flashed cartoons. He turned up the volume.

Downstairs, Gorilla smashed the lamps. The living room faded to black. Gorilla paced, snapped his fingers at his enforcer, and ordered him to hog-tie the doctor's hands and feet. When the doctor's mewling became high-pitched, Gorilla ordered his enforcer to stuff the doctor's mouth with his own dirty sock.

"He vomited and gagged," Big Beard said and his face contorted. "We punched and kicked him. I'm pretty sure we busted his nose." Gorilla had no intention of killing the doctor. If he had wanted to do that, Gorilla would have simply blown the doctor's head off. Gorilla wanted to communicate a message—that he *was* terror, that no one disrespected him.

"He ordered us to shred the doctor's pants," Big Beard continued in a monotone. "We looked like fucking animals. We sliced off his boxers. You should have seen the way that doctor looked at us, like we had lost our minds, like we were butchers or something." A long silence stretched between us. Big Beard coughed, shifted his weight from one leg to the other. He folded his arms across his chest, fixated on a tuft of grass in the pavement, and whispered, "Someone said, 'let's shove pipes up the doctor's ass.'" Big Beard looked bewildered. His eyes watered. "I couldn't do it." He started to shake. "I thought we were just going to bust him up."

Gorilla snapped photographs of the doctor, for insurance. Big Beard said Gorilla then threatened to post the nude images of the doctor on the hospital wall if he called the police. I never asked Gorilla about any of this but I understood payback. I understood cruelty. Still Gorilla's darkness chilled me, left me raw and searching for answers.

And I remembered something Gorilla had once said to me as he smacked me on the shoulder: "Someday this will all come naturally to you."

21

N N N N N

Taking Care of Business

A coward dies many deaths. A man only dies once.
—SAMMY "THE BULL" GRAVANO

I smoked three blunts in succession, shoved my hands in my coat pockets. I stood at the train tracks near my Happy Spot. Wind rustled the trees. Bare branches clicked together like bones. The tracks stretched for miles into whiteness. Cold bit into my face. My teeth chattered. *Are you up for this? Killing your father?* I processed Gorilla's orders. I was going to pick off the turncoats one by one. Maingy included.

"This is your old man's fault," Gorilla said. "If it hadn't been for him, the others would still be Pagans. *He* ordered their execution." The gestapo speech worked at first. Gorilla had me convinced that I *had* to finish off my old man. *He* was the root of the problem. He was a Pagan enemy and he had to be destroyed. I'm sure Gorilla wanted me to think of my old man as subhuman because it was easier to murder an inferior. *You knew this was coming. You signed up for this.* I tossed the blunt.

If you do this, Gorilla won't protect you. He'll blame you. Wind snapped my collar against my cheeks. *If you refuse, Gorilla will hunt you. You will be the turncoat. And you will have every fucking Hells Angel **and** Pagan after you whether you hit your target or miss. There is no middle ground. You have no choice. You have to participate. . . . But you don't have to get caught.*

"We do this my way or we don't do this at all," I advised Gorilla later that night. I was stoned half out of my mind, but I thought I sounded impressive. In truth I had always been afraid of self-exposure: that Gorilla might guess I wasn't as brave as I portrayed, that I imploded inside almost nightly, that, after all, I didn't really *like* violence. That was the difference between Gorilla and me, between me and all of them.

An assassin accepted his indifference to the job he contracted to do. I liked to believe I had standards, some kind of moral compass. Women and children, for instance, were out. But truthfully, I wasn't sure I *could* really kill indiscriminately or even on command if Gorilla demanded. I had a conscience. I cared about people. They weren't just temporary nuisances. I had attachments—my mom, the Saint—what would happen to them if something happened to me? Emotions consumed me, anger and fear. Doubt crept into my head. Could I really do this?

"I don't care how you do it. Just get the job done," Gorilla dismissed me. We were seated in my car again, the only safe place to have a conversation. Winter buried most things, bikes included. The saying was that real outlaws rode in the snow. But in truth most spent the white months high or behind bars, their bikes sitting idle in the garage leaking oil. By the time spring rolled around, most of the bikes needed serious repair.

"I'm not doing this alone," I warned. *Who am I kidding? Of course I am doing this alone.*

Gorilla glared at me. "I don't want to know the details."

"It might take a while. . . ." I ignored Gorilla but he wasn't listening. He had already opened the passenger door, stepped one foot into slush, discussion over.

I didn't sleep for the rest of the week. I tossed and turned, practiced loading and unloading my pistol in the dark, not really sure yet how I planned to execute the hit or who, if anyone, I would drag with me. I felt a bit like a chameleon, assuming different personas as the job demanded; before long, I *became* the hard-ass I portrayed, tough and steely. The part of me that *wasn't* tough cracked and died inside a little each day as fear gave way to violence. I felt most alive in the moments I thought I might die. There was great relief in terror.

A cold rain spit against my window. My heart raced. I tossed back the sheets. Pain shot up my neck. Out of habit, I dozed fully dressed in my jeans and boots, in case I had night visitors. I padded to the bathroom, splashed cold water on my face. Dark circles framed my eyes. Dirty, wild hair clumped together. Grizzle sprinkled my chin. I looked as if someone had run me over with a truck and left tire tracks across my face. *Get a hold of yourself. You haven't even killed anyone and you're a mess.* I suddenly understood why people pissed their pants.

I imagined various killing scenarios: Maingy lit up like a Roman candle, engulfed in gasoline and sticky Styrofoam chips to make the accelerant form a gel. But fire was messy and lacked precision. I might burn more than my target. Citizens could get hurt. Innocents. Not cool. An ax to the temple? But what if I missed? Blood left tracks, spatter, and evidence. A gunshot? The sound telegraphed too much. What about a silencer? I needed to leave no trace. I stood, shivered, and grabbed a shirt.

I formed a plan. I decided to go to bars where Hells Angels partied, enter as an ordinary citizen, sit at a table in the back, in a smoke-filled, dimly lit corner, order a beer, and sip it slowly. I'd absorb the scene as if I were in slow motion, as if every sound were amplified, the suction of the front door, the blast of the radiator, deep guttural laughter. I'd watch the bikers, some of them enforcers, swagger into the bar. They'd have women with them. I'd watch them closely. They usually carried weapons. If I was lucky, I'd spot some Pagans, now Hells Angel prospects. A commercial would drone in the background. Hits required patience and a certain monotony. I had time. I had no competing priorities, no distractions. *That's why Gorilla likes you.* It had never occurred to me before . . . that I was the perfect hit man.

"You're charming," the Saint once remarked playfully.

"Maybe to women," I joked.

"No. There's a certain quality about you."

"You forget about me as soon as you meet me?" But I knew what the Saint meant. It wasn't the first time I'd heard it. Some called it focus. Others said it was intensity. Whatever it was, I had a gift, I could walk into a room and sense darkness.

"Maybe that's it." The Saint nodded.

"No," Gorilla had piped in. "You know people."

"Yeah, that's why I keep him around too," the Saint said, trying to lighten the mood.

"No. I mean you *know* people. If I'm walking into a bar, you can tell me within minutes that we need to leave."

"That's because he doesn't want to be seen with you," the Saint said.

"Laugh all you want." Gorilla kept his focus on me. "But he's useful, that one. He's good people."

The truth was, and I'm not bragging here, I was the best person for the job, and the reason Gorilla put me on missions, mostly alone, was because he knew at any given time I probably had company, potential witnesses, cops, feds, lurking in the shadows, parked down the street, bugging my apartment, my phone, my car. He must have known I might be forced to testify, but unlike others, I wouldn't rat.

I turned on the television. An anchorwoman with a helmet of blond hair and pretty white teeth spoke about Stealth, the former Pagan turned acting Hells Angel president, who was gunned down suddenly on the Schuylkill Expressway in a volley of bullets. "One slug struck him in the head as his pickup truck veered out of control on the Vare Avenue exit near New Hope Street."

I stood transfixed at the screen, my heart pounding. This wasn't happening. My mind filled with white noise. I struggled to breathe. My knees buckled beneath me. I slid back against the wall. Realization hit me full force. Even if I had nothing to do with Thinker's hit, Gorilla would blame me. He'd need a scapegoat. The Pagans would need a scapegoat. My phone shrilled. I snatched it up on the first ring.

"Are you seeing this shit?" Gorilla barked over the line. "They have no suspects . . . yet."

I ran my hands through my hair with such force I thought I might pull out clumps. I didn't appreciate Gorilla's accusatory tone. I paced my small apartment. I had few possessions, some clothes, weapons. The room was spare; it would be easy to leave quickly, wipe down my counters, strip my sheets, and leave nothing but a bald mattress. I replayed the newscast in my head, the bold, reckless hit that was more similar to a mob-style execution than any Pagan plot. My heart raced.

I had no curtains. I was utterly exposed to the street, to anyone out there who wanted to silence me.

The phone shrilled again.

"What happened?" Big Beard whispered.

"I don't know," I said, keeping my voice tight.

"Tell me you didn't do this."

I hung up the phone. I knew better than to have a conversation over an unsecured line. *It doesn't matter, they'll think you did.* The Saint's warning buzzed in my head. The frame was worse than the act. I had no control over the frame. I had only fantasized Maingy's murder. I hadn't plotted anything . . . yet. My thoughts grew dark. I was paranoid. My mind turned to the week before Stealth was murdered when I loaned my gun to a prospect. I had done it against my better judgment. I had agreed to meet the prospect at a Wendy's fast-food restaurant to do the return.

"Sorry, man, I don't have your gun." The prospect balanced a chocolate Frosty and double-stack cheeseburger on his tray and headed to a booth.

"Where is it?" A rivulet of ice cream dribbled down the side of my cone. I licked it with my tongue as I stared at the back of the prospect's head. The restaurant had a few stragglers: one woman spilled over her seat at a corner table, a gaggle of teenagers clustered near the front door. The smell of french fries lingered in the air. At the tone of my voice, their conversations hushed. The woman in the corner pushed out of her bench, shuffled her tray to the trash, and wheezed through the doors. I shoved the rest of the cone down my throat and wiped my hands on my jeans. I walked to the booth.

"I don't know." The prospect shrugged, smoothing ketchup into his bun with his thumb. His voice had an edge, an acknowledgment that he'd fucked up.

I pushed aside the tray. The burger plopped to the floor. The milk shake toppled, spilled over the prospect's hand. The prospect did not flinch. Instead his face reddened. I knew I would lose in a fistfight with the guy, but that thought didn't stop me. Even prospects had rank and protocol; I was his senior. More than that, I reported to Gorilla.

"What the fuck is wrong with you?" I was within inches of the prospect's face, oblivious of the eyes watching me.

"Take it easy." The prospect lowered his voice, his gaze on the teenagers still in the place.

But an audience didn't deter me. In my anger I slammed the prospect's head into the table, and still holding a clump of the prospect's hair, I whispered, "I've got a hot gun out there?"

I snapped back to the present. The television replayed the newscast over and over until hours passed and nothing but grainy black-and-white crackle filled the space. I decided hell was a state of mind. I could change the scenery—my apartment, my car—but in the end I still had my thoughts. Better to *act* than to wait around for retaliation by the Hells Angels. The Pagans, as a club, were guilty until proven innocent, and whether they planned Thinker's murder or not, the two clubs hated each other and the Hells Angels would dispense with a formal police investigation. The Pagans were the Angels' perfect scapegoat, Gorilla their usual suspect, and me *Gorilla's* example.

It was an overcast morning. The streets were deserted. The air smelled of boiled eggs, burn-off from the power plant billowing smoke near my apartment. I was used to the quiet, to the desolate expectation. My plan, when I agreed to prospect, had always been to kill my old man. My thoughts turned dark. What if it had been *Maingy* gunned down on the Schuylkill Expressway? Even if I hadn't done it, I would be the Hells Angels' first target. I would be Gorilla's first target.

The risk was too great. I couldn't control the outcome, and for the first time I realized that I wasn't ready to do twenty years for someone else's fuckup.

I had thought about just leaving, throwing my possessions in a sack and heading across state lines, living out of a bag each night, always moving. I thought of Dagger, who nearly lost his mind in his cabin in the snow. I understood surrender, complete release. Betrayal nipped at my heels like a flame. I suddenly wasn't sure anymore why I risked at all. What was the point? I couldn't murder my father on the heels of Thinker's death. I couldn't kill anyone now, at least not on purpose. And I didn't *want* to kill for Gorilla, for the club, for a patch.

If I stayed, I would either spend most of my life in hiding or in a cell, both equally dark, equally lonely. *And who will be there for you? The club?* No one had been there for my mom after my old man went to prison.

News of Stealth's death spread through the Pagan community like a foul wind. At first blush it generated paranoia among members as mental walls shot up and no one knew anymore whom to trust. My phone didn't ring for three weeks. Gorilla agitated over the festering Stealth problem. He held church meetings, ordered his soldiers to collect intelligence, conduct surveillance, and find a suspect. Not for the police, but for the Pagans, for Gorilla. The club needed cohesion, a common enemy, a *known* enemy to solidify their loyalty and lessen their vulnerability to outsiders. Distrust bred distraction and contempt.

"Someone should go to Stealth's funeral," Gorilla announced one night at church. He fixed his gaze on me. His wasn't a question. It was an order. A group of us had squeezed into a member's apartment. The place was standing room only. Someone passed around a whiskey bottle. Chatter buzzed around me. I didn't like Gorilla's tone. *Does he think I had something to do with the murder? Does he think I free-lanced this one?*

"It doesn't matter what he thinks," Chewie reminded me later. "He needs a scapegoat. It's a sacrifice he's willing to make."

But was it a sacrifice *I* was willing to make? I was going to Thinker's funeral.

Gorilla's reasoning wasn't entirely crazy. Killers often returned to the scene of their crimes whether compelled by curiosity, arrogance, or sheer paranoia. If Stealth's murderer was a Hells Angel, the biker would *have* to attend the services. The Hells Angels had a policy, all prospects and full patches, whether official or turncoat, had to pay their respects to a fallen brother. Even my old man had to attend a Hells Angel funeral while he was still a Pagan. He simply boarded an airplane wearing a mask. But the services were never about respect, they were about faith, belief in the club's strength. Survivors glimpsed their own mortality. Even the toughest bikers among them must have sensed that one day they too would succumb to broken teeth, organ failure, and diabetes.

At least two hundred Hells Angels joined another one hundred and fifty mourners for services at St. Joseph Roman Catholic Church in Downingtown. Stealth's family had money. He wasn't cremated. Security was high. Police dressed in camouflage and armed with rifles patrolled the parking lot. More lined the processional route, and at the burial several Pennsylvania State Police troopers guarded the perimeter with their backs facing the grave, scanning for potential trouble. The Hells Angels came from California, Arizona, Maine, North Carolina, Maryland, New Jersey, New York, and even a handful arrived from Germany, Italy, Amsterdam, and British Columbia, Canada. They were dressed in full club regalia, leather vests with the Hells Angel insignia and a patch identifying their chapter. Swastikas and grinning death's heads flapped in the wind. Stealth's parents and son and daughter were present. Police directed traffic on foot. News crews parked in the street. Some reporters waited outside their vans, microphones in hand, poised for interviews about Thinker, the "clipped Angel." Rumors swirled that Stealth's death might spark the beginning of a gang war between the Pagans and the Hells Angels.

Through my binoculars, I saw bikers outside the church, clustered in hushed groups, straddling their motorcycles, sharing a bottle of red wine. Mentally I recorded their faces, their distinctive tattoos, the set of their jaws, details Gorilla appreciated. I looked for anything out of place, a loner, a rival club member, a brewing fight. Later, I'd read that the Reverend William Lynn gave a homily that acknowledged Stealth as a person "who spent his life trying to find himself" and decried, "Why so young?" "Why so violently?" "Some will still answer the question with violence." As far as I could tell, no one listened. Angels tossed cigarettes into Stealth's grave, lay stray ribbons on his coffin as token gestures of regret.

Just when I thought it was a bust, I detected sudden movement to the left of me. A Hells Angel shoved off his Harley, lumbered like a tank through the crowd, his expression mean and hard. He opened his mouth and a siren howl spewed out as he marched toward my car. His hand flew to his waist, to his gun. I jammed my keys into the ignition and switched on the engine. It caught, sputtered, and stalled. A small swarm formed across the street. With shaking hands I tried again. He'd seen my face. *He knows who you are.* I panicked.

I flew down the Schuylkill Expressway. My heart stuttered wildly as my car slid around curves. A debilitating sense of helplessness gripped me. Time froze as flashes of my life clicked by me like a slide show. The road swam in front of me. Quiet sealed me inside my car, a tomb already. The road corkscrewed on me. I hit the brakes, the back tires skidded. If the road didn't claim me, Gorilla would. I knew it, sensed it like a cold hand on my neck. But letting go was almost a relief, feeling the road bend beneath me, my foot on the accelerator, not knowing or even caring where I drove, only that I still had a heartbeat. In the end there would be no easy exit. I swallowed, my throat dry and parched with fear. Paralysis gripped me. Words spilled out of me as I drove. I felt a little crazy, a little out of control. I thought of my uncle Russell and suddenly understood why Dead committed suicide, why ending his life might have been a preferable alternative to his breathless existence. I thought of my mother too, locked inside a dark bathroom most nights, comforted by the sound of dripping water, mesmerized by the bright ribbons of blood. It was all about surrender.

My phone shrilled. I hesitated as I recognized Gorilla's number.

"Get me a gram on your way over here," Gorilla's voice scratched over the line. I cradled the phone between my ear and shoulder. Unease settled over me. I had done multiple drug deals for Gorilla, hand-to-hand sales, drops at Soft Tail's, but somehow Gorilla's demand that night struck a nerve. Maybe I was already too wired, too stressed, but suddenly the club's antidrug policy seemed like bullshit. In the end no one controlled the drug. Drug dealing generated too much profit, too much greed. People like Gorilla ordered people like me to do the street work. If *I* got pinched by the cops in possession of weapons and dope, *I* would do the five years, not Gorilla. I'd spare the club the bad reputation, the heat. Gorilla would dismiss me to the media as a rogue, a low-life drug addict who went berserk, who knew too much about the club, too much about Gorilla, who needed to be handled, maybe even killed.

"My source works on the other side of town," I stalled, and in retrospect my refusal was probably foolish. Pagans had broken limbs and busted teeth for failure to pay or execute deals. Besides, the drive alone required at least an hour through congested traffic. But it was more than that. Heat burned my face. My stomach lurched. I listened to Gorilla's breathing as I slowed. Cars stacked next to me. Windows fogged.

"I need it," Gorilla barked through the line, his command laced with threat. I hung up. Dial tone buzzed in my ear. A chill zipped up my spine. I glanced through my rearview mirror. The car behind me crammed into the space. I remember thinking Gorilla was setting me up, deliberately ambushing me.

The phone shrilled again.

"Are you going to get it?"

"After church." My voice wavered and the urgency in Gorilla's voice made my heart race. It *was* a setup. I knew this would be my last delivery. Gorilla would make me the scapegoat for Stealth's murder.

"I need the buzz *before* the meeting," Gorilla insisted, and hung up the phone again.

Fuck you. I slammed my fist on the steering wheel, dropped my phone. *I'm not going to do it.* Adrenaline rushed through me. I had thought family and club membership was about brotherhood and oath and righteousness. Being a made member was all about thrill and living a cause prospects believed in, sacrificed for, and even died for. But it was all a lie. The club, the cause, was all about greed and power.

My phone buzzed again.

I didn't want to spend the rest of my life ducking shadows, looking over my shoulder, startled each time a car backfired. I used to think it took some kind of courage to become a Pagan; I realized now it took balls to *leave*, to reject the lifestyle from the start. I had clarity for the first time. Tough guys, such as Gorilla, were only tough because they carried loaded guns and pickaxes, summoned muscle to fight their fights and do their prison time. They kept pissants like me stoned and scared so that we would never leave. It was all about control. It was all bullshit. The club didn't do anything positive for anyone, didn't make any money for anyone but Gorilla.

In the end there were no easy exits, just hard choices. No blood money. I didn't want out of the club because I hated Gorilla. I wanted out because I hated who I was becoming. There was no honor in being a criminal, a drug dealer, or a hired killer for a cause I no longer understood or supported. Even soldiers needed a reason to serve. They needed to know in the end that their acts resulted in something important, that their life was worth the sacrifice. I was no soldier but I shared something in common with them: courage.

I weaved through congested traffic, gunned my engine, and nearly clipped a white station wagon. I drove with newfound determination and purpose to the place Gorilla shared with his girlfriend. I pulled into the driveway and left the engine running.

"What do you mean you're done?" Gorilla's girlfriend was incredulous. She blinked at me as I handed her my jean jacket with the bottom rocker. She was small-boned, blond, clad in tight jeans and a skimpy midriff top despite the cold. She filled the open door. Wind blew up her shirt and she shivered. She reminded me of a younger version of my mom, the way she must have looked back in the days when she danced at Turk's, before Maingy, before the club, before my mom disappeared into a dangerously thin shell.

My heart raced. My hands shook. I knew what I was doing. "I'm finished," I said, and backed away toward my car.

"What do you want me to tell Gorilla?" she yelled after me.

"Tell him . . . Tell him he can get his own fucking gram."

I thought I could leave the way the Saint had left, quietly and without confrontation. I thought it would be that easy, that Gorilla would leave me alone too. But in the weeks that followed, nerves chafed at my insides, not fear exactly but uncertainty, a foglike apprehension. I had no hiding place, no safe house, no assurance that Gorilla wouldn't track me down, put a contract hit on my life or finish me off in a dark alley and toss my body in a Dumpster. In some respects nothing had changed. I still lived on the edge, rattled, gun displayed openly at my side, fully loaded. I avoided shadows, ate in public, never put my back to the front door. I lived my life waiting, for change, for freedom, for relief, and when none of that came, I lived as one of the hunted and haunted. I had a choice, to hibernate like a creature who believes his world is perpetually winter, or to risk being seen.

I chose the latter. A raw, deathlike chill bit into my hands as I attended the Daytona Lucky Charms Poker Run as a spectator and supporter. Crowds of Pagans spilled from the bar the Chamber. Several drenched one another in beer, shared whiskey, passed opiates. People shuffled around me in slow motion. Some barely registered my presence. Sounds amplified. The scene had the surreal quality of a dreamscape. A small crowd formed outside. Some tinkered with their carburetors, making last-minute adjustments. Rock music pounded the street, rattled the windows of the bar. Members of other clubs roared up—from Wheels of Soul, Warlocks, the Outlaws. Old ladies straddled bikes, posed for snapshots, stripped to their property T-shirts, and proudly flashed their rotten toothy grins.

I expected retaliation; it was the natural order of things. Gorilla settled his scores. *No one ever really leaves this club.* The Saint's words haunted me even as I deflected invitations from the Pagan Jersey chapter, Chubs and Rooster, who found my invisible qualities impressive. But I wasn't like them. I could afford the luxury of change. I spotted Gorilla and a chill coursed through me. Marshall flanked Gorilla as his new bodyguard. *Son of a bitch isn't a cop after all.* The former prospect was now a full patch and carried a knife and a gun strapped to his waist. Marshall's oily gaze rested on me and his fingers grazed the hilt of his blade.

"Gorilla wants harm on you," a Pagan whispered under his breath

262 ～ Anthony "LT" Menginie and Kerrie Droban

to me. His voice was scratchy, almost muffled. He leaned against his motorcycle, wiped his hands with a chamois cloth. He had a full red beard and a long braid down his back. I recognized Nail. His warning slid like ice down my back. I knew he was right. I knew I would never escape the vibration. Marshall's knife glinted in its sheath. He stared at me with the cold, empty gaze of someone broken. Not a killer exactly. Not even someone who *wanted* to kill. But almost robotic; he would do it because he was told. Because if he *didn't,* he would be killed. I'd seen that look before in biker women, hazy and half-drugged. The look of a soul snuffed out. It was easier to kill, to take orders, to abuse, when something no longer *looked* human.

Marshall waited for a signal, his back to Gorilla. *Come on, you son of a bitch*. I waited for it, was ready for it. I envisioned my own arm pulling back and striking Marshall in the lower jaw, snapping his neck in a clean, lethal break. No bone chips. No mess.

"I see what you're thinking." Nail shook his head. He knelt next to his bike and wiped the chrome until it shone. "Better think again." He squinted at me and his face cracked.

"It'd be worth it," I lied. I didn't really want to die yet. I shuffled closer to Nail, folded my arms across my chest, and kept my gaze on my target.

"You'd be the one in the hospital." Nail paused, handed me his chamois.

It was true I'd lost more fights than I'd won. "The motherfucker has it coming." I rubbed the tires down.

"He's just a kiss ass," Nail said dismissively. But I could tell from the arch in his brow, the slight tremor in his hand, that he worried.

"That's what makes him dangerous." I paused, bunched the chamois in my hands. "He'll blindly follow orders." *What the hell am I doing?*

"He's Gorilla's boy," Nail agreed. A small crowd buzzed around us. I wasn't armed and I should have been.

"He's a cop." I clenched my jaw.

"He's a toad." Nail laughed.

"A cop toad."

"He'll never be Prince Charming."

"He'll still try to kill me." I handed Nail back his cloth. I felt suddenly chilled.

"Yes." Nail sighed. He stood, towered over me, looked bemused. "What are you going to do, kid?"

"What he least expects." I had no idea what that meant. Except that Gorilla probably thought I'd go underground, disappear, live the way a terrorist makes people live.

Nail cocked his head sideways at me. He bunched his face and grinned. "Are you *sure* you won't come back?"

"And leave all *this*?" I said sarcastically. I threw up my hands.

"You're not afraid?" Nail frowned.

"Of what?"

"*Living?*"

"I'm just getting started."

The words sounded braver than I felt. The truth was I didn't have a clue how to "start" living with the specter of death always around me. I thought I could walk away from the club because I was *born* into the madness and living as a Pagan child meant something different to me than voluntary service. But what I didn't realize was that the club would never be my history; the *lifestyle* would forever remain my present, my burden, my blood bond.

"You're like the rest of us," the Saint warned me one quiet summer evening, "a sleeper cell, inactive until challenged to defend what you once revered."

Gorilla's threat loomed large. He could strike at random, when I least expected it, years later, when I thought it was safe to venture "inside." His contract on my life still had no specific performance. His obsession for vengeance had transferred from Maingy to me, and suddenly *I* had become his ultimate "turncoat." Maybe that was the real terror after all, living as prey.

EPILOGUE

~ ~ ~ ~ ~

And so it was over. Just like that. There was no lure, no sweetly rotten intimacy. None of the bullshit the others warned me about. Fire didn't smolder in my veins, only embers. I didn't want the club. I carved out a new identity and with that a simple kind of freedom without protocol or rules or codes of silence. I work out at a gym religiously. I lift weights. I sculpt my new image. I change my outside and pretend my inside will one day catch up. I watch boxing matches on the television set. The boxers' mitts resemble cartoon hands. The players wear protective teeth and pads. They slug each other when the little bell dings. A few minutes later they stop. At least they have some direction. At least they know why they're fighting.

I jog, sometimes several miles a day through the city streets. My lungs burn with exhaust. My heart pounds in my chest until I think it might burst. Sweat pours out of my face, soaks my shirt, and pickles my skin red just behind my knees. Rage is my shadow. It moves with me, darkens in the sunlight, disappears in the clouds. I run in the thunder. Good to feel my head rush. I have no wife, no children, no dog. I will most likely never marry.

I visit my Happy Spot, this time sober, haunted by shadows in the trees. I light a blunt, listen to the rustle of the leaves, the whoosh of a crow's wings. Twigs and debris poke from the rusty nails. My shadow spreads wide like a demon. My breath swirls cold and raw in front of me. I accept the tightness in my chest, the tingling in my fists, the dizzy banging in my head. *The stress. The stress.* My knees buckle. I nick my shin on a protruding nail. A trickle of blood snakes down my skin. I don't wipe it away. I lie back. I remain still for several minutes, close my eyes, afraid to stir, afraid to leave, afraid to leave my imprint. Afraid. When my eyes flutter open, I see the crow again, swirling above me, blue-black and majestic. Crows are attracted to dead things. Sometimes they take the form of the dead. My uncle Russell.

I sit upright, squint at the bright sun. I toss my blunt into the tracks and my hand shakes. Grass spears the air. Wind blows the brown, dead husks and they make a whispering sound. I shiver, scared suddenly of the most ordinary things, telephones redialing, the suction of a door, the roar of a motorcycle, white, white space without definition, without noise. I am scared of living ordinary, of living at all. Mostly because I fear losing what I haven't yet found. I live with heightened awareness, a sensation others compare to shell shock or post-traumatic stress. A bee buzzes near my wrist. If it doesn't spin away, I will shoot it.

"What's it like to have a contract on your life?" a friend asks me later.

I want to tell her, "I sleep with a gun on my pillow. I drink coffee and my gun rests on the tabletop. I jog and my gun creases my navel. I wash dishes and my gun props near the faucet. I cook and my gun warms on the oven rack. I think and my gun is my first thought. I am not powerful because I carry a gun. I am powerful because I know I will never use one."

You're a brave man.

I am scared as hell. It's okay to admit that. *That* takes courage.

"You should write a book about your life," my friend Chal says. "You know, share all the fucked-up shit you've lived through."

"I don't want to write a book," I tell him. "I don't want to remember."

"But people need to know. They need to know they have choices."

"They need to know they're not alone."

Sometimes I visit my mom. She invites me inside her home for noodles when she has electricity. Deep grooves cut across her face. Her voice hitches slightly when she sees me. We don't discuss the past or the future. When she laughs, her whole body rattles. Husky sounds full of cigarettes and alcohol rumble in her throat. She looks small-boned and skeletal. She musses my hair, and in that weak gesture I know she cares. In the end that's *all* I know, all that *really* matters, all I have. I am lucky.